AF531298

HORMONAL DISEASES

ENCYCLOPAEDIA OF ANIMAL DISEASES-II

HORMONAL DISEASES

By

Ashok Kumar

Dept. of Zoology
Bundelkhand University
Campus Department
Jhansi

DISCOVERY PUBLISHING HOUSE PVT. LTD.
NEW DELHI-110 002

First Published-2008
Reprinted - 2014
ISBN 978-81-8356-283-6

Published by

DISCOVERY PUBLISHING HOUSE PVT. LTD.
4831/24, Ansari Road, Prahlad Street,
Darya Ganj, New Delhi-110002 (India)
Phone: 23279245 • Fax: 91-11-23253475
E-mail: dphbooks@rediffmail.com
dphtemp@indiatimes.com

Printed at:
Infinity Imaging Systems
Delhi

PREFACE

The **Hormonal Diseases** has been carefully compiled and edited to meet the long felt needs of increasingly large number of those who have to deal with the different aspects of human diseases in colleges, universities and research institutes. It provides a stimulating and important new view of interaction between animals and pathogens causing diseases. The objective is to introduce to students the essential principles for understanding various aspects of diseases. Most of diseases constitute the largest part of human pathology and are the primary cause of death. Hence, special importance is given to the study of such diseases.

The book is intended to acquaint students of various fields involved directly or indirectly with the major principles of human diseases. The book may be helpful as well to practitioners and those engaged in medical research.

In the preparation of this book large number of books and research papers have been consulted. So no authenticity is claimed.

The author wishes to express his deepest appreciation to the many people who have contributed in one way or the other to the preparation of this title.

The author expresses his gratitude to Mr. Wasan and staff of M/s Discovery Publishing House for their whole hearted co-operation in the publication of this book.

The author tried hard to be accurate and upto date in statement and realises the impossibility of completely avoiding errors therefore, the author will greatly appreciate having his attention called to any questionable statement.

Author

Contents

Diseases Due to Pituitary Hormones

ACROMEGALY

Acromegaly is a condition due to a hypersecretion of the growth hormone and is characterized by enlargement of the hands and feet, and of the bones and cutaneous tissues of the face, and by splanchnomegaly, etc.

History Background

In 1886 Pierre Marie, of the Salpetriere, described two cases, using the term 'acromegalie and quoting five cases, with similar features, from the literature. In 1888 he collected further cases, bringing the number up to seventeen. However, Sternberg recognized acromegaly in Wier's account of a giantess as far back as 1567. In 1932 Atkinson tabulated and analysed 1,319 cases with 265 autopsies.

In his original paper Marie did not ascribe any cause to the disorder, but in 1887 Minkowski connected the disease with the pituitary gland. Benda was the first to detect an increase in the number of eosinophil cells in the anterior lobe of the pituitary; this was confirmed by Lewis in a case in which there was no enlargement of the pituitary. Brissaud and Meige correctly postulated that giantism in childhood and adolescence corresponds to acromegaly in adults. Evans and Long produced giantism in rats by injection of anterior pituitary, and Putnam and others produced acromegalic changes in the head, skeleton, and viscera of English bulldogs.

Pathology

The pituitary gland is usually, although not necessarily, enlarged, and on section an eosinophil adenoma, which may be microscopic in size or very extensive, is found in the anterior lobe. When the pituitary appears to be normal, a differential cell count may nevertheless reveal a relative excess of eosinophil cells; or there may be a local hyperplasia of acidophilic elements. Occasionally a developmental pituitary nest of eosinophil cells is found at necropsy in the sphenoidal air sinuses (Erdheim) or, as in one of Cushing's cases, an enormous eosinophil adenoma may project outwards from the sella turcica, leaving within an apparently normal pituitary gland. Where there is a central eosmophil adenoma within the sella turcica, the rest of the anterior lobe may be greatly shrunken and degenerate. The pituitary gland may press on the optic chiasma, eroding or invading the floor or roof of the sella turcica, the cavernous sinus, and the brain. Cushing recorded a case of acromegaly in a man of 33, with two years history, in which a large cerebellar cyst was the primary lesion; this produced a secondary hydrocephalus, which apparently resulted in an enlarged pituitary anterior lobe, with hyperplasia of the eosinophil cells. The changes in other endocrine glands are dependent on variations in the secretion of their trophic hormones. Pressure of the acidophil tumour may induce a failure of gonadotrophin secretion, but hypersecretion of trophic hormones can occur, usually involving adrenocorticotrophin. However, growth hormone itself influences the size but not the development, or function of endocrine glands, and it is probably directly responsible for the frequent occurrence of adenomata in the endocrine glands of the acromegalic.

The cortex of both adrenals is usually hyperplastic and multiple adenomas are frequently present. The thyroid is enlarged in some 50 per cent. of cases, the usual change being an increase in vesicular colloid. A colloid goitre may be found in acromegaly even when complicated by thyrotoxicosis severe enough to call for thyroidectomy. The parathyroids may be enlarged, and adenomas have been recorded. Enlargement of the thymus and diffuse lymphoid hyperplasia, which also occurs both with Addison's disease and with adrenal cortical adenoma or hyperplasia, are common. The pancreas may be normal or atrophic, or may show hyperplasia, with, perhaps, adenomas of the islets of Langerhans. The ovaries and testes are usually atrophic.

There is not much evidence on the histology of the ovaries, although amenorrhoea is common, but they may be cystic and degenerate, or fibrous, with only a few normal follicles. Cushing states that the mulberry ovaries (corpora lutea) of Evans' rats are not found in humans. The testes are often soft and flabby, the seminal vesicles disorganized, and the interstitial cells degenerate. The heart, lungs, liver, spleen, and kidneys are considerably enlarged, the stomach is often double its normal capacity and both the small and large intestine are considerably increased in length and circumference. Bony changes are considered in the clinical section.

Physiology

The essential feature is the continued over-secretion of growth hormone, producing skeletal and visceral changes comparable to those of experimental acromegaly. Excessive amounts of growth hormone have been detected in the blood of acromegalics.

Insidence

Acromegaly occurs in all parts of the world and in all races. Males and females are affected in equal proportions, the incidence among Jews and Swedes being relatively high. The maximum incidence is in the third decade of life. It may, however, begin at puberty, and Atkinson recorded one case at the age of 8.

Childhood acromegaly is a great rari and is inevitably associated with giantism. If one includes relatively mild manifestations of the disorder, acromegaly, as most other endocrine disorders, shows a family incidence: in one series in 30 per cent. of the cases. Acromegaly is more likely to, develop in tall people. Thus Davidoff found in one series that the average height of men in whom the disease began before 20 was 6 ft. 2 in., and of women 5 ft. 6 in. This may well be due to an increased secretion growth hormone during the phase of growth preceding the excessive secretion which gives, rise to acromegaly.

Aetiology

The cause of the development of an eosinophil hyperplasia, or adenoma, is rarely obvious. Occasionally pregnancy, or bilateral ovariectomy may precipitate the disorder. Although the highest incidence is in the third decade, many patients have had some manifestations at puberty, or in adolescence, and it is probable that the physiological endocrine changes of this period may fail to be autonomously controlled, or limited, in those patients developing acromegaly. The familial incidence in some 30 per cent of acromegalics suggests that this may be the case, and apart from the occasional onset of the major disorder at puberty and in pregnancy, transient fugitive acromegaly may occur at these periods. It is not generally recognized that mild acromegaly is not infrequently found at the climacteric, in certain types of women and men, but it is a slow insidious process. The onset in earlier life is also usually insidious and the disorder may progress for a decade or more before the patient realizes that he is suffering from a serious endocrine disturbance. Occasionally, general infection appears to be a precursor of the disorder, e.g. measles, typhoid.

Clinical Changes

General

As in many endocrine types, there is a considerable resemblance among all acromegalics. The large extremities, awkward movements, thickened features, and drooping shoulders with hands falling near the knees in advanced cases, give the picture of Simian man, and where giantism has preceded the acromegalic changes, of a primitve ape-like giant. Great strength, however, may give place to exhaustion and weakness in the later stages, and in order to understand the symptomatology, one must appreciate that over-activity of the pituitary and related glands, e.g. adrenals, can be followed by exhaustion and under-activity; and further, that phases of activity may alternate with phases of inactivity before the terminal phase is reached.

Skeletal Changes

As indicated by the name of the disease, the more obvious changes occur in the hands and feet, especially in the carpal and tarsal bones. which are enlarged and may fuse. The metacarpal and metatarsal bones are also thickened, and the heads of the phalanges may show outgrowths or 'tufting' on radiological examination. The considerable and progessive increase in the size of the hands and feet, which is due to the thickening of the soft tissues, as well as to skeletal changes, results in the characteristic need for an outsize in shoes and gloves. The fingers are thickened, and somewhat square in their termination, giving the appearance of podgy, spad-like hand, but where skeletal overgrowth has occurred before epiphyseal fusion the fingers may be very long. The long bones of the upper and lower limbs may show considerable periosteal thickening and deformity, or may appear normal.

The skull is considerably thickened, the ridges becoming very prominent, and the external occipital protuberance enlarged. The cranial sutures may be obliterated. Even more marked are the changes in the facial bones; thickening and enlargement of the zygomatic arches, of the malar bones, and especially of the lower jaw, which becomes prognathic through overgrowth and also through changes in the temporo-mandibular joint. The teeth become spaced wide apart as the jaw increases in width. The clavicles are thickened, and the antero-posterior diameter of the chest is greatly increased. The vertebrae undergo atrophy, hypertrophy, and partial fusion, with resulting kyphosis, lordosis, and scoliosis A thickening of the ridge, or bony prominence, occurs where muscles or tendons are attached to bones, and exostoses may appear near joints. Arthritis may follow changes at the articular surfaces of bones, and bony exostoses in the neighbourhood of the joints may severely limit movement. Occasionally a portion of the skeleton, such as one big toe, appears to be more susceptible to the growth hormone and enlarges quite out of proportion to the rest of the skeleton. This illustrates the principle that responsiveness of tissues, as well as the concentration of the hormone stimulus. determine the final result in endocrinopathies.

Muscular System

Hypertrophy of the muscular system associated with abnormal muscular strength, may occur in the initial stages. But though gigantic acromegalics may excel as wrestlers, boxers, or weight-lifters, their early prowess may be succeeded by muscular atrophy and atony. At any stage of the disease the increase of muscle bulk is seldom matched by a comparable increase in muscle power. Weight for weight, voluntary muscle in acromegaly is less efficient than the normal.

Soft Tissues

The tongue is greatly enlarged and the papillae prominent; and in spite of the increased buccal cavity, the tongue may be unable to find room within it, and may interfere with articulation and tend to obstruct the air passages in the recumbent position. The lips become thickened, protuberant, and negroid in appearance. These changes in the lips, and also in the nose, may occasionally precede the skeletal changes. The skin and the subcutaneous tissue are thick, the pores enlarged, and the sebaceous and sudoriferous glands hypertrophied. Fibromata mollusca may be an expression of local hypertrophy of subcutaneous fibrous tissue. Excessive sweating (hyperidrosis) of the whole body may be troublesome and intractable and, together with the greasiness of the skin, results in persistent malodour. The hair on the trunk in both sexes may become abundant, and coarse and wiry in character, the thick, greasy, hairy skin contrasting with the fine, dry, hair-free (or covered with delicate hair) skin of the hypopituitary state. The enlargement of the hands and feet is partly that of soft tissue, and the presence of associated tissue oedema is suggested by the diminution in size within a few hours, following removal of a pituitary tumour.

Respiratory System

In both sexes the voice becomes deep and resonant, owing to the enlargement of the larynx and the increased width and resonance of the air sinuses, though the mucous membrane may be so thickened that respiratory obstruction may call for tracheotomy. Lungs are enlarged proportinately with the thorax. In the late asthenic stage of the disorder, death may follow phthisis or bronchopneumonia.

Cardiovascular System

The heart may be enormously enlarged and all coats of the peripheral blood vessels hypertrophied. Myocardial hypertrophy can occur with a normal blood pressure, but hypertension is common and poorly tolerated by the patient. Indeed hypertensive heart failure or cerebrovascular accidents not infrequently terminate the disease. However, the occurrence of hypopituitarism will diminish the blood pressure and hypotension may be found.

The electrocardiogram may reveal evidence of left ventricular hypertrophy, hypertension or myocardial ischaemia. The latter may be due to an abnormal myocardium rather than coronary artery disease.

Nervous System

Smell may be imparied owing to hypertrophy of the nasal turbinal bones. Pressure on the optic chiasma leads to optic atrophy, bitemporal hemianopia, and later to complete blindness of one or both eyes. Ocular palsies may result from pressure on the third, fourth, or sixth nerves; and involvement of the fifth nerve may produce pain and hyperaesthesia over one or more of its divisions. Deafness may be due to involvement of the auditory nerve or middle ear.

Headache may be very severe and bursting in character. It is occasionally migrainous in type, and associated with vomiting. Severe headaches are often quite intractable to medical therapy. Paraesthesias of the hands and legs may be early symptoms, though these disappear dramatically after operation or irradiation. But true neuritis follows when somatic nerves are caught in obliterated intervertebral foramina.

Various types of chronic inflammation of the meninges of the skull and spinal cord, as well as of bony plates in the spinal dura, have been described. Areas of sclerosis may arise in the spinal cord with resulting ataxia and pseudotabes. True acromegaly may also be associated with syringomyelia, but this should not be confused with syringomyelitic bony deformities. Speech may be sluggish and slow, memory often being impaired, and the general behaviour characterized by apathy and lack of initiative. Depression, irritability, negativism, melancholia, mania, and delusional insanity may be additional symptoms. In the early stages, or in relatively mild cases, however, there may be great alertness, energy, and drive.

The cerebrospinal pressure may be considerable, headaches being temporarily relieved by withdrawing some *30* ml. of cerebrospinal fluid. In one case, Ellinger and Simpson demonstrated an antidiuretic hormone in the cerebrospinal fluid. This was associated with oliguria, positive water balance, and profuse sweating Radiation of the pituitary gland produced a gradual disappearance of the antidiuretic hormone from the cerebrospinal fluid, a concomitant disappearance of sweating, and a normal water balance. This case suggests that pressure, or a nervous mechanism, may produce over-activity of the pars nervosa; but, in other phases of the disorder, diabetes insipidus may be a complication through destruction of the nervosa by the encroaching eosinophil tumour.

Sexual System

Rarely an initial increase in libido may occur in both sexes, especially when acromegaly begins in adolescence. More commonly amenorrhoea and impotence are early features, and are almost invariably present in the later stages. Nevertheless interference with sex function may not be obvious for ten or more years, though skeletal and other manifestations are progessive. Normal menstruation, pregnancy, and parturition occasonally take place when the acromegalic process is well advanced. In adolescent acromegalics, the external genitals may be enlarged and puberty may be premature. In older acromegalics, however, impotence and amenorrhoea are often associated with atrophy of the genitals. The cause of initial sex stimulation in acromegalic adolescents may be ascribed to irritation of the basophil cells by the eosinophil tumour, whereas in the later stages the basophil cells are encroached upon and destroyed.

Carbohydrate Metabolism

The demonstration of the diabetogenicity of growth hormone

provides a clear explanation for the frequent occurrence of diabetes mellitus in the course of acromegaly. Indeed, it is more pertinent to comment on the fact that only about 30 per cent of acromegalics develop diabetes. During the active phase of acromegaly the only method by which the body could avoid diabetes in the presence of excessive growth hormone is the secretion of increased amounts of insulin: Such a mechanism has now been demonstrated by the constant finding of elevated plasma insulin levels in acromegaly.

The occurrence of diabetes mellitus during active acromegaly indicates that the effect of the growth hormone on carbohydrate metabolism has overcome even the increased level of insulin production. It is therefore not surprising that this type of diabetes is insensitive to injected insulin. Treatment of the acromegaly, with a fall in growth-hormone production, may result in a cure of the diabetes or, at least, its amelioration. This variability of carbohydrate tolerance with the phases of pituitary activity is of considerable practical importance as therapy for the diabetes requires constant supervision and adjustment. If hypopituitarism supervenes the patient will become unduly sensitive to the action of insulin and is unlikely to have diabetes.

Diabetes arising in the inactive phase of acromegaly or becoming permanent after an onset coincident with excess growth-hormone secretion is due to 'exhaustion' of the pancreas and a failure of insulin production. The course and treatment of this is essentially similar to that of idiopathic diabetes mellitus.

Manifestations of Adrenal Cortex Hyperfunction

In both sexes there may be extensive growth of coarse oily hair over the trunk. In the female, abnormal hairiness sometimes develops on the face and extremities and the hair of the head falls on as in primary adrenal virilism. Although adrenal cortex over-activity itself produces amenorrhoea, probably by inhibition of pituitary activity through excessive androgen secretion, it is unlikely to be the initial cause of amenorrhoea in acromegaly, since amenorrhoea occurs early and often without any manifestations of virilsim. Similar argument would also apply to impotence in the male.

A clear example of Cushing's syndrome has been observed as a concomitant of active acromegaly.

Thyroid Disturbances

Excessive growth is accompanied by an increased metabolic rate;

the basal metabolic rate of active acromegaly is above the range of normality in 50 per cent of cases.

A palpable enlargement of the thyroid, usually lobulated and with a tendency to the formation of adenomata, is present in about 20 per cent of acromegalics, but should not be confused with thyrotoxicosis merely because the metabolic rate is raised. Radioactive iodine studies reveal no alteration of function in the enlarged thyroid. However, true thyrotoxicosis with frank clinical signs, arises in about 5 per cent of acromegalics. Hypothyroidism may arise in the later phase of the disease, usually in association with other evidence of hypopituiturism. However, we have seen a colloid goitre become atrophic, leading to primary myxoedema. In this instance the thyroid was unresponsive to injected thyrotrophin and there was no evidence of hypopituitarism. Exophthalmos, in the absence of thyrotoxicosis, can occur. suggesting an increased secretion of thyrotrophic hormone.

Course and Prognosis

Acromegaly is usually a chronic progressive disease, taking many years to develop. The changes may be sufficiently slow to last a life-time without grave disability, though a patient can be completely incapacitated within a few years of the onset. Waves of remission and exacerbation occur in the more chronic types, and a stationary phase may last some years. The more active phase of the disease may ultimately be followed by an asthenic hypoactive phase in the same way as thyrotoxicosis may, after a variable course, be ultimately followed by myxoedema, even without surgical intervention.

Despite arrest of the disease by treatment some disability often remains. Personality changes commonly reduce the patient's capacity for work; headache may persist or osteoarthritis develop over the years to restrict movement.

Treatment

Surgical removal of the acidophil tumour is indicated if vision is severely threatened by pressure on the optic chiasm. It is wise to limit the operation to freeing the optic chiasm from surrounding tumour tissue rather than to make an all-out attempt to remove the whole adenoma.

Deep X-ray therapy is often effective in suppressing excessive growth-hormone production, without causing hypopituitarism. This is the treatment of choice for active acromegaly but there is no indication for its use in the inactive phase of the disease. The assessement of activity is mainly a matter of clinical observation over a period of time. Unfortunately no simple method of assay is at present suitable for the determination of the amount of circulating growth hormones Hoever, Reifenstein, Kinsell, and Albright have pointed out the importance of a raised serum phosphorus in active acromegaly; and a raised concentration of plasma insulin confirms a clinical diagnosis of acromegaly.

Oestrogens and androgens have been recommended for their inhibiting effect on , the pituitary. Ethinyloestradiol, 0.1-0.3 mg daily, may be used in the female but its use should be restricted to the mild case as deep X-ray therapy is definitely indicated for all cases in which the disease shows considerable activity. Testosterone propiorite, 25 mg. daily, has been used in males, but we would prefer to restrict the use of androgens to the treatment 0f hypogonadism associated with acromegaly; for this, methyltestosterone, 10-25 mg. daily, by mouth would suffice.

GIANTISM

Definition

Giantism is a Condition of Excessive Height

Aetiology and Pathology

Giantism may be due to: (1) an excessive secretion of the growth hormone before the epiphyses unite; (2) a delayed union of the epiphyses (eunuchoidism), a normal amount of growth hormone thus being permitted to act over an abnormally long period; and (3) a combination of (1) and (2). An additional factor, consisting of an inherent capacity of the bones to respond to the stimulus of the growth hormone, is probable. Giantism tends to run in families and to be common among certain races, e.g. the Swedish. Macroscopically the pituitary gland may be normal or enlarged. Microscopically it may not be possible to detect any abnormality, or there may be a relative preponderance of, or adenoma of, eosinophil cells.

Clinical Picuture

Rapidity of growth is generally noted in childhood, but may be most conspicuous during adolescence. Acromegalic manifestations occur in some 40 per cent of giants, and may be observed at puberty, in adolescence, or later in life.

Sexual development and libido sexualis may be normal or even supernorm at first, but after some years impotence may develop. In the primary eunchoid type, hypogonadism is an initial and persistent feature, the external genitals are small and the seconedary sexual characteristics absent or deficient, and there is delayed union of the epiphyses. For this latter reason growth continues for some years longer than normal. Further, since castration results in over-activity of the pituitary there may be, with hypogonadism, an excessive secrtao, = of the growth hormone. Excessive height is found among those Skopecs (a religious sect) who have been castrated before puberty. The fundi are usually normal, bit in the presence of a pituitary eosinophil tumour, optic atrophy may be observed, with limitation of temporal fields of vision, as in acromegaly. In one patient a girl aged 14, brought to Out-Patients because of rapid growth (5 ft. 11½ in.) and lack of energy (following on previous robust health), bilateral *papilloedema* was a surprising finding and a subsequent ventriculogram showed symmetrical dilatation cf the third ventricle. Later, autopsy revealed a huge *hydrocephalus* resulting from complete stenosis of the aqueduct of Sylvius, the lumen of which was completely obliterated by a subependymal gliosis. Although the pituitary gland showed no obvious abnormality on histological section, one must postulate excessive secretion of pituitary growth hormone. Other clinical features were plethoric countenance; big hands and feet (men's size 9 shoes); slight adiposity, but red lineae distensae of the abdomen and axillae; no hirsutism; and menstruation had not yet commenced. The blood count and carbohydrate tolerance were normal.

Occasionally, in additon to the *general giantism*, one part of the body-for example, a leg or a toe-may grow to a greater extent than the rest. Since the concentration of growth hormone is probably the same at all sites of the body, one must postulate a localized tissue hypersensitivity, the reason for which is as yet obscure. Giants may show supernormal muscular power, but after some years this may be followed by asthenia.

Abnormal growth before puberty may occur, with tumours of the adrenal cortex, the testis, and the ovary, and with other forms of sexual precocity, but premature union of the epiphyses results in a final height below normal. In the physiological section it has been noted that testosterone and oestradiol may produce excessive skeletal growth as long as the *epiphyses* remain ununited.

Pituitary giantism is recognized by the acceleration of a previously normal growth-rate and the appearance of *acromegalic stigmata*; radiological demonstration of an enlarged sella turcica confirms the diagnosis. The growth spurt of the child suffering from sexual precocity is of course inevitably associated with the premature development of secondary sexual characters. On the other hand, eunuchoidal giantism does not appear until adult life as its development depends on a continued stimulus from growth hormone in the absence of epiphyseal closure by the action of sex hormones. Apart from the diagnostic signs of hypogonadism, thes keletal growth is disproportionate; the limbs being of an excessive length compared to the trunk.

Treatment

The disability of pituitary giantism arises from the distortion of the body with the attendant mental stress of becoming a freak. In children, scoliosis and kyphosis add to the troubles of a large frame. The aim of treatment is to prevent deformity without suppressing other aspects of pituitary function; indeed a nicely balanced programme which is difficult to carry out and requires great patience from physician and relatives. Deep X-ray therapy to the pituitary is the method of choice, using the lowest dose compatible with slowing the rate of growth. In consequence, before treatment is instituted, the patient must be observed until the rate of growth is established, and a further course, or courses, of X-ray treatment may be necessary if the initial therapy does not alter the growth curve within six to nine months.

In severe cases, where pituitary radiation has failed, surgical exploration of the pituitary gland should not be unduly delayed, even in the complete absence of optic atrophy. In relatively mild cases, oestrogens-and to a less extent androgens-have been used to slow or arrest, skeletal growth as they depress pituitary function and accelerate epiphyseal union.

Dwarfism

There can be no absolute definition of dwarfism, but if the height is obviously below the arbitrarily accepted lower level of normal limits, dwarfism may be diagnosed. If the condition is to be diagnosed before adult life, the above definition must be qualified by the phrase 'as compared with individuals of the same age'.

Clinical Changes

Some of the causes of dwarfism are as follows:

Genetic (Uncomplicated)

In this group the ony abnormality is a failure of skeletal growth, presumably due to a congenital deficiency in the number of eosinophil cells (compare congenitally dwarf mice). This recessive gene may alternate with the contrasting one determining excessive height, since it is not infrequent to meet exceptionally tall members of the same family.

Chronic illness in childhood

Syphilis, tuberculosis, malaria, pancreatic disease including diabetes mellitus, diabetes insipidus, coeliac disease, chronic diarrhoea (e.g. Crohn's disease), renal rickets, and von Gierke's disease, are all causes of deficient growth, with or without some failure of sexual development. Malnutrition, qualitative or qunatitative, is also a factor which operates in civilized communities, and supplementary dietetic experiments in poor schools have confirmed this Even in the absence of poverty and ignorance the maladjusted child who refuses food or indulges in fads becomes undernourished and fails to grow. In our opinion this type of anorexia is an important cause of short stature. We would also stress that the clinical presentation of steatorrhoea may be dwarfism, in the absence of any disturbance of bowel function.

Achondroplasia

This is a congenital abnormality of cartilage bone formation arising in foetal life, and characterized by short legs and arms, a relatively long body, good intelligence, a big head and face, a square nose with a depressed bridge, and spade-like hands. Underlying endocrine defects have not been discovered. These people breed families of achondroplasiacs. They are active, strong, and acrobatic, with normal intelligence and rather vain, and are to be found on the stage and in circuses.

Prococious sexual maturity

This leads to a preliminary rapid skeletal growth but ultimate dwarfism, because of premature union of the epiphyses. This is well known in connexion with obvious pathological sexual precocity, but it is less well recognized that many girls and some boys have premature union of the epiphyses of the long bones at the age of 14 or 15 instead of 17 to 18.

Diagnosis

In uncomplicated cases this is merely dependent upon the height of the individuals. It is obvious that many short people are otherwise perfectly formed and some occupy very prominent positions. In many cases short stature is merely an accompaniment of some generalized disease and is inessential to diagnosis or treatment. It is very likely that the failure of growth in such cases is due to secondary depression of pituitary function. However, primary failure of growth hormone secretion is extremely rare; a diagnosis of primary pituitary dwarfism in the absence of other endocrine dysfunction can only be made by excluding other disease processes that affect growth. Unfortunately there is no simple assay method available for the detection of normal or subnormal cocentrations of growth hormone in plasma.

Treatment

Any underlying disease or causative lesion calls for its appropriate treatment. No treatment is of avail if the epiphyses are united, or if the patient's chronological age is much above that of adolescence. Pituitary growth hormone is theoretically specific, provided the nutritional status is adequate; but available preparations, although potent in laboratory animals, have proved most disappointing in clinical practice. However, the recent discovery that growth hormone prepared from rhesus monkeys, or from human pituitaries is potent in the human gives great hope for the future. It appears that there is a species difference in growth hormones and that only material prepared from primate pituitaries will elicit a response in the human being. Thyroid by mouth is sometimes helpful, quite apart from cretinism. The treatment of the various endocrinopathies of which dwarfism is a feature, is discussed under separate headings. In boys, androgens will produce a rapid increase in height but at the same time induce sex development and accelerate epiphyseal closure. Such treatment is of value over a short period, provided the dose is kept at such a level that gross development of secondary sex characters does not occur; methyltestosterone, 10-15 mg daily by mouth, will suffice. However, long-term treatment merely closes the epiphyses and prevents further growth. The same problem is inherent in the use of protein anabolic steroids with minimal androgenic potency. Such substances as norethandrolone, 15-30 mg daily, can be used intermittently in girls without causing virilization.

INFANTILISM

Infantilism is a condition of somatic growth and sexual development corresponding to a normal individual several years younger than the patient, and never attaining adult physique or sexual maturity. The term Levi-Loraine syndrome is used synonymously with infantilism. Actually, Loraine wrote a preface to a paper by one of his pupils, Faneau de la Cour, who submitted his thesis in Paris in 1871 under the title 'Du Feminisme et de l'infantilisme chez les tuberculeux'. Failure of somatic and sexual development was thus observed as a result of chronic tuberculosis of various types commencing in childhood. Ettirore *Levi described several cases of infantilism, and in* parti its occurrence in two sisters, aged 15 and 20, in the elder of whom there was enlarge of the pituitary fossa and optic atrophy. He thus drew attention to a pituitary type infantilism, although his account appears to envisage a polyglandular disturbance. also described infantilism as secondary to rheumatic carditis in childhood. One of important diagnostic features stressed by Levi was the ununited epiphyses, which now know as a manifestation of any type of hypogonadism.

Brissaud described a thyroid type of 'infantilism' which is more correctly spoken as 'cretinism' or, if commencing in childhood, as 'juvenile myxoedema'. However, occasionally meets with a type of pituitary infantilism complicated by clinical signs hypothyroidism, and then the term Brissaud's infantilism might be applicable.

Frohlich's syndrome, is by our definition, a form of infantilism, but since infantilis is usually applied only to those patients who are not fat, and who are usually thin, an since Frohlich's syndrome is said to have connotation of fatness as an essential feature this disorder is described separately. Another atypical type of infantilism, associat with a primary gonadal defect, will be considered under a separate heading.

Dwarfism is a failure of one function only, namely, skeletal growth, and may be present with normal sexual development. The term is therefore not synonymous with infantilism.

Pathology

Unfortunately there is little or no evidence of the pathology or morbid anatomy of uncomplicated infantilism. Craniopharyngioma may produce infantilism, but complicated by other secondary endocrine disturbances.

Clinical Changes

Apart from retarded skeletal growth and sex development, patients with infantilism usually present a delicate and gracious appearance. They are pleasing to the eye, and in no sense whatsoever grotesque. Their childlike and often attractive appearance compels friendship and sympathy, and a desire to help and protect them. Their physique is on slender and graceful lines, with narrow shoulders and narrow hips, slender tapering fingers, and somewhat surprisingly-often relatively long, slender, well-shaped legs

The skin is of smooth and delicate texture and the complexion good. In males the penis and testes remain infantile, and there is an absence of sexual hair on the face and body. Rarely there is a small growth of pubic and axillary hair, but the pubic hair never extends onto the abdomen in male triangular fashion. The voice does not break. In females there is amenorrhoea, the uterus is infantile, the breasts do not develop, and the pelvis does not become wide at puberty.

Intellect is in no sense impaired, although the emotional and behaviour pattern often retains childish characteristics. Some people with infantilism, especially incomplete forms, attain intellectual brilliance and high scientific and cultural distinction.

As in nearly all endocrine disorders an incomplete form of infantilism must be recognized, especially as it is probably much more common than the classical complete type. With partial infantilism the general and somatic descriptions given above are usually applicable, but hypogonadism is not complete, and, contrary to our definition, may be inconspicuous. In the male the penis and testes tend to be subnormal in size and the upper margin pubic hair horizontal; the voice is rather high-pitched, the skin of delicate, feminine texture, and facial hair slight in amount, so that shaving every other day may be sufficient. However, such patients may be fertile. In the female the pelvis remains narrow and the breasts small; menstruation is often scanty, but conception may occur. These varieties of incomplete infantilism have their parallel in strains of dwarf mice, in which failure of somatic growth and incomplete sexual development are genetic disturbances associated with pituitary defects.

Clinical Types

Pituitary infantilism

Clinical or radiological evidence of a pituitary defect is a rarity; however, some cases of the syndrome are due to suprasellar cysts. The patients bear a striking resemblance to each other with their childlike features, delicate textured skin, and graceful fragile appearance. If Peter Pan is a fanciful name for them, there is certainly something Barriesque about their sweet temper and delicate air.

Idiopathic Infantilism

This is the largest group. Comparison with known cases of pituitary origin, together with our physiological knowledge, justifies-by inference-a pituitary aetiology. It is confirmed by the response of the gonads, more especially in males, to pituitary, or chorionic, gonadotrophic hormone.

Chronic Infection

This includes the tuberculous group of de la Cour and Loraine. The tuberculosis can be of bone, glandular, abdominal, or pulmonary, but must have continued in a chronic form during several years of childhood. The French writers also postulate congenital syphilis as a cause. Chronic malaria in childhood and, in fact, any chronic infection may be aetiological. The mechanism is obscure. By some ill-understood alteration of the hypothalamic-pituitary relationship secretion of both growth hormone and gonadotrophins is impaired. From the teleological point of view, growth and sex development are sacrificed to concentrate all pituitary function on survival of the organism in terms of maintaining adrenal and thyroid function.

Chronic diarrhoea

Any cause of chronic diarrhoea in childhood, e.g. steatorrhoea, coeliac disease, pancreatic disease. ulcerative colitis and Crohn's disease, may result in infantilism. Poor absorption of food appears to be the most important factor, and chronic inanition may also result in failure of development. It must be stressed that malabsorption from disorders of the small intestine may be severe in the absence of any disturbance of bowel function.

Hypothalamic infantilism

We have met with several cases of arrested development following severe shock, or concussion, or a severe virus disease such as measles complicated by encephalitic symptoms. It would appear that in all these cases a hypothalamic-pituitary mechanism is inhibited, or brought into play.

Metabolic disorders

Severe diabetes mellitus, diabetes insipidus, von Gierke's disease, and renal rickets in childhood may also produce infantilism. Diabetes mellitus, however, may develop some years after infantilism has been diagnosed.

Cardiac disease

Congenital cyanotic heart disease and severe rheumatic carditis in childhood may result in infantilism.

Diagnosis

This depends upon the essential features of subnormal growth, infantile genitals, absence of secondary sex characters, and delayed union of epiphyses. The diagnosis cannot be made with certainty before the age of normal puberty, when maturation of sex characters is not a physiological event. Primary gonadal agenesis, which is associated genetically with short stature, is differentiated by the presence of various deformities, such as a webbed neck, cubitus valgus and congenital cardiac lesions, and the growth of sparse pubic hair. The excessive gonadotrophin excretion of these cases indicates active pituitary sex function. Acquired atrophy of the gonads prior to puberty is difficult to differentiate in that the normal puberty growth spurt does not occur, but growth continues slowly until the patient shows the typical tall thin eunuchoid habitus, with abnormally long limbs. Failure to respond to injected gonadotrophins makes it clear that the primary lesion is of the gonads.

Infantilism -secondary to some generalized disease process provides no diagnostic difficulty; nor does the rare case of craniopharyngioma, with attendant localizing signs of a space-filling lesion in the region of the pituitary. However, delay in the onset of normal puberty mimics infantilism, until sexual development occurs spontaneously. For this reason infantilism cannot be diagnosed with confidence under the age of 18 years.

Treatment

The endocrine treatment of infantilism is often disappointing. The result so far obtained with the available preparations of growth hormone are not satisfactory but should not prejudice the future use of new potent preparations obtained from monkey or human pituitaries.

The use of sex hormones will produce satisfactory development of secondary sex characteristics, and increase in somatic growth and a deepening of the emotions. Such treatment, although limited in its results because neither fertility nor normal menstruation will be induced, is of the greatest importance in transforming the awkward, shy, childlike person into a normal citizen, adjusted to society and capable of normal sexual relationships.

FROHLICH'S SYNDROME

History

In June 1900 Joseph Babinski, the famous French neurologist and pupil of Charcot, presented to the *Societe de Neurologie de Paris* a paper with illustrations of a girl aged 17 years, with failure of sexual development and obesity, apparently due to a craniopharyngioma. The title of this paper was 'Tumour of the Pituitary body without Acromegaly, and with arrest of Development of the Genital Organs'.

In the following year, Alfred Frohlich, of Vienna, described a similar case due to a craniopharyngioma in a boy of 14 years, under the heading, "A Case of Tumour of the Hypophysis without Acromegaly, and owing to historical researches into probable cases described in the preceding fifty years, and fuller description, the disorder is usually called after him. His account was translated into English by Bruch. The French give precedence to Babinski's name, and the Germans call it Frohlich-Babinski's syndrome. The descriptive label adiposogenital dystrophy was introduced by Bartels in 1906.

Both he and Erdheim pointed out that the obesity should not be considered as directly related to the pituitary but rather to a lesion of the hypothalamus.

Definition

Owing to a number of conditions allied to and confused with this syndrome, it is important to lay down a definition which is quite clear, based upon the original descriptions and on clinical studies. The following definition is suggested: A syndrome characterized by a failure of normal maturation of the gonads, subnormal height, and adiposity, the usual cause being a pituitary or parapituitary destructive lesion (craniopharyngioma) involving also the hypothalamus. Primary lesions of the hypothalamus as described below may also cause the syndrome. Diabetes insipidus may or may not be present, and cannot be considered as essential for the diagnosis.

Pathology

According to Kraus the followng lesions have been known to cause the adiposogenital syndrome; craniopharygioma (intrasellar or suprasellar); chromophobe adenoma; third ventricle tumours; chronic hydrocephalus; chronic tuberculous, or syphilitic, meningoencephalitis; epidemic encephalitis, and meningoencephalitis; bullet wounds; fracture of the skull. He further states that 'in cases of severe and long-standing hydrocephalus, the hypophysis shows depletion of the chromophilic cells and finally atrophy of the whole organ'. However, the hypothalamic-pituitary cause of the syndrome is more often a matter of inference based on experimental knowledge rather than one of histological demonsration. Unfortunately the knwon pathology of the allied Laurence-Moon-Biedl syndrome does not add appreciaMIe to our knowledge of the pathology of Frohlich's syndrome.

Incidence

The adiposogenital syndrome, as defined here, must be regarded as one of the rarest syndromes in endocrinology; the label is usually applied erroneously. Conditions which may be confused with it are common, and will be discussed.

Clinical Changes

Failure of sexual maturation is an essential feature. As proper maturity in normal subjects does not occur before puberty, the sexual factor can only have a relative significance before puberty in the male and even less in the female. In the body it may be possible to state from appearance that the penis and gonads are retarded in their development and subnormal in size. At the time of normal puberty, and with greater certainty in adolescence, it will become clear that the penis and testes retain infantile or childish proportions, and no secondary sexual characteristics develop. Pubic and axillary hair does not develop, and the face is free from any sign of male hair. In the female menstruation does not occur.

Frohlich's description included the following paragraph:

The penis, which is otherwise [ubrigens] normally developed, appears to be embedded in accumulations of fat to such an extent that the genitals approach the female type. The testes are palpable in the depth of the fatty tissue, and show infantile conditions [Verhaltnissel. In the neighbourhood of the breasts, there are also considerable accumulations of fat. In the mammary glands several nodules are palpable, but fluid cannot be expressed. Hairs in the axillae are lacking, and only occasional small hairs are present in the genital region. There is at least a suspicion of a myxoedematous condition.

The cause of hypogonadism is failure of the pituitary gonadotrophic secretion, even when the initial lesion is hypothalamic, because apart from morbid anatomy, (1) patients (at least males) respond to a gonadotrophic stimulus, and (2) biological assays show an absence of gonadotrophic hormone in the urine. The cause of the adiposity in Frbhlich's syndrome is probably hypothalamic in origin, as is indicated by the work of Bailey and Brewer (1921). Especially is this likely to be the case when diabetes insipidus is a complication. Contrary to general opinion, the adiposity in the original cases of Babinski and Frohlich was only moderate in amount, and it is doubtful if adiposity of marked degree is a feature of the syndrome. However, the distribution is characteristic, namely, face and neck, breasts, abdomen, pubis, and thighs. The face is not plethoric, and may be pale as in destructive pituitary lesions. The general appearance of the male patients is feminine, and the pelvis is gynaecoid. Drowsiness, polyuria, and polydipsia, when present are regarded as hypothalamic symptoms. Very little is known of the metabolism and biochemistry of the adiposogenital syndrome, and the significance of such studies as have been made depends upon the criteria of diagnosis. A craving for sweet things may be present and associated with a tendency to hypoglycaemia.

Dwarfism, or subnormal height, constitutes the triad of the adiposogenital syndrome, and always permits a diagnosis with greater confidence. In our opinion a height above normal rules out this condition. Ununited epiphyses are a manifestation of hypogonadism. The muscles tend to be hypotonic and hyperextensibility of joints may be noted.

In one of our cases, now 32 years old, the obesity has remained static for the past ten years but some pubic hair has grown. This is probably due to adrenal androgens as the testes remain atrophic. The causative lesion in this case was a craniopharyngioma.

Diagnosis

This depends essentially upon definition, and should not be made with any dogmatism before puberty. Hypogonadism, adiposity, and dwarfism are the triad of syndromes upon which a firm diagnosis can be made. The following conditions should be differentiated:

Constitutional Familial Adiposity

In this condition the genital development is normal or slightly retarded. In boys the penis is often embedded in the pubic fat and therefore appears smaller than it is. This condition is frequently diagnosed as Frohlich's syndrome. In the absence of pathological knowledge one can only theorize as to conditions intermediate between this and Frohlich's syndrome. Frohlich himself referred to the masking effect of the suprapubic fat on the size of the penis is his own patient, so that this in itself obviously does not exclude the diagnosis.

Cushing's Syndrome

If this occurs at or before puberty, sexual development may be delayed. The facies is congested, or plethoric, and the lineae distensae are red or violet rather than white. The obesity spares the limbs, whose muscles are often wasted, and involves face and trunk. Stunting of growth and hypertension also occur.

Adipose Gynandrism

This is a condition with which Frohlich's syndrome has been most frequently confused. It is described in the adrenal section and is essentially different in the following respects:

(a) the height is usually above normal;

(b) plethora, cyanosis and red lineae distensae are usually present; (c) there are no gross intracranial lesions; (d) sexual maturation is delayed but occurs spontaneously.

Infantilism

This should not be confused with Frohlich's syndrome if it is appreciated that by definition infantilism cannot be associated with adiposity.

Laurence-Moon-Biedl Syndrome. This disorder is characterized by adiposity, hypogonadism, polydactylism, mental deficiency, and retinitis pigmentosa. It tends to occur in families.

Prognosis

Babinski's and Frohlich's patients with cranipharyngiomas both died in the second decade. The prognosis in regard to life depends upon the nature of the cranial lesion. The genitals will not mature spontaneously, but respond to gonadotrophic hormone.

Treatment

Any local intracerebral condition calls for appropriate surgical treatment. Adiposit3 receives the general treatment of the condition, namely a low calorie diet and appetitf depressors such as dexamphet amine. Chorionic gonadotrophin, 500 units injectec intramuscularly, thrice weekly, will promote sexual maturation in the male but is no effective in the female. Methyltestosterone, 15-30 mg daily, will develop male secondar sex characters but leave the testes atrophic.

LAURENCE-MOON-BIEDL SYNDROME

A syndrome occurring sporadically and, in families, as an autosomal recessive characterized by *polydactyly*, mental retardation, *retinitis pigmentosa*, with *hypogonadisn* and *adiposity*; and relative dwarfism in some, if not all, members of the family affected.

History

Laurence and Moon first described the condition in the *London Ophthalmic Review of* 1866. Four of ten children of non-consanguineous parents were affected. It is recordec that one of the adults affected measured only 54 inches. Sievert and von Jaksch note(optic atrophy associated with the condition, and realized the possible relationship witl *Frohlich's syndrome*, but it was Bardet and Biedi who postulated thi; connexion more clearly. Professor Sorsby, to whom we owe a great deal fo: modern knowledge of the disorder, although his original approach was as ar ophthalmologist, suggests that Bardet's name should be linked with Laurence and Moon's Cockayne, Krestin, and Sorsby record that during the period 1925-35 thirty isolated cases had been reported in addition to fifteen familial groups.

Pathology

No autopsy had been recorded until 1936, and since that time four fairly complete anc two incomplete autopsies have been described, and are summarized by Anderson In the first autopsy the pituitary was apparently normal; in the second, the sella turcici was enlarged and occupied by a large cyst, only a small portion of the glandular tissuw remaining; in the third there was a strikingly high proportion of basophil cells, and relative paucity of eosinophil cells in the pituitary; in the fourth and fifth cases (Riggs) two males aged 19 and 24 years, infantile testes were present, and certain changes wer(noted in the brain, but not in the hypothalamus or pituitary. Anderson's case was a 15 year-old body with hypertension secondary to polycystic kidneys and fatal uraemia. The adrenals, thyroid, parathyroids, and pancreas were grossly normal and the thymus wa: atrophic. The pituitary and pineal bodies and the brain were, macroscopically, normal In the testes there was no evidence of maturation of spermatozoa, and the interstitia cells were decreased in number. Microscopically the adrenals, parathyroids, and pancreas were apparently normal. The thyroid contained many dilated acini filled with colloid and lined with cuboidal epithelium, and was considered to be a typical colloid goitre'. The pituitary was histologically remarkable. The anterior lobe was composed chefly of basophil and eosinophilic cells. The marked predominance of the basophil cells coloured the sections blue to the naked eye. In serial sections no adenomata were seen. Differential cell counts showed 42 per cent basophil, 36 per cent eosinophil, and 22 per cent chromophobe as compared with the normal 11, 37 and 52 per cent respectively. There was no evidence of any hyaline change in the basophil cells. In the pars intermedia no colloid was seen; however, there was moderate invasion of the posterior lobe by basophilic cells. No definite changes were found in the hypothalamus or brain microscopically, except for diminution of *Purkinje cells* and loss of nerve cells in the granular layer of the cerebellum. Anderson believes the singificance of a preponderance of basophil cells in his and Griffiths' cases may be significant; In both, however, there was chronic kidney disease, and in one, severe hypertension. Autopsies have not really given decisive evidence about the exact pathology or whether the primary lesion is hypothalamic or pituitary.

Clinical Changes

A characteristic case suffers from mental defectiveness, polydactyly, pigmentary degeneration of the retina (retinitis pigmentosa), adiposity, and hypogenitalism. Adiposity is nearly always constant, but of two brothers with the disorder one was fat and the other thin; and one adult became very thin after a fat childhood. Adiposity is often of moderate amount but may be extreme. Hypogonadism is usual, but not constant. Mental retardation is present in the great majority of cases, ranging from mental deficiency to idiocy. Polydactyly is nearly always present, but may be absent in otherwise typical cases. Retinal degeneration (retinitis pigmentosa) is reported by all observers. Generally visual defect is noted in early childhood, but in quite a number of cases it does not become apparent till later. Optic atrophy is occasionally found. Dwarfism is usual, but normal height may be found. Other rare complications are congenital heart disease, microcephaly, head-nodding, choreiform movements, and muscular weakness. One member of the family may have the complete syndorme,_ and another perhaps one or two stigmata of it. Symptoms are usually present from birth.

Diagnosis

This is easy, as defined above. The condition is generally thought of as a special variation of the Frohlich syndrome but in so far as patients may be plethoric rather than pallid it should be considered also in relation to adipose gynism and gynandrism.

Prognosis

This is poor, and intercurrent infection not infrequent. Congenital renal abnormalities may cause an early death in uraemia.

Treatment

No fundamental treatment is possible.

SIMMONDS' DISEASE

Simmonds' disease is a condition of anterior pituitary deficiency and secondary involution and hypofunction of the thyroid, adrenal, and sex glands, manifested in typical examples by asthenia, apathy, amenorrhoea or impotence, hypersensitivity to cold and to insulin, a low basal metabolism, and a very low level of 17-ketosteroids in the urine. Morris Simmonds, a Hamburg pathologist, constructed a clinical picture in retrospect, after observing at autopsy, examples of inchaemic necrosis of large areas of the anterior pituitary gland in patients who died after parturition. However, the subsequent clinical features and obstetric background of severe parturition haemorrhage were illuminatingly discussed by Simpson as long ago as 1883.

Pathology and Aetiology

The essential lesion is destruction of the anterior lobe of the pituitary gland, and the commonest cause is thrombosis of the pituitary vessels following parturition associated with severe haemorrhage and, not infrequently, retained placenta. Infection may be present, but is not regarded by Sheehan as a fundamental factor in producing the thrombosis.

Simmonds pointed out that the arteries to the anterior pituitary are end arteries, and that emboli would therefore lead to infection and necrosis. Reye thought the vascular process was thrombosis, which he contended, was especially liable to happen in an organ like the pituitary, which underwent involution at parturition after being hypertrophied during pregnancy. The penetrating and painstaking researches of H.L. Sheehan have resulted in a valuable pathological and clinical elucidation. He pointed out that 'the illustrations of Simmonds show what appear to be thrombi *in situ* in the capillary sinuses' and suggests that 'it seems probable that in these reports the word "embolus" is used in the sense of a few organsims being carried in the circulation to the pituitary and there forming the nucleus of thrombus formation. No satisfactory description has been given to suggest that the actual thrombus found obstructing the anterior pituitary vessel had been carried thereby the arterial stream.' In fact, in the absence of infective endocarditis, or a patent foramen ovale, it is difficult to see how an embolus could be carried to the pituitary blood vessels.

In the majority of cases Sheehan states that the thrombi are not infective, and predisposing factors are a peculiar distribution of the blood supply to the anterior lobe during pregnancy, the rapid involution of the anterior lobe after delivery, the increased coagulability of the blood during the puerperium, and especially a sudden large haemorrhage during delivery. Puerperal sepsis may be a complication. The thrombosed sinuses, as found by Sheehan, were small, and it was not possible to say whether they were functionally arterial or venous. 'In the absence of any other cause for the necrosis, it would appear that the thrombosis is the primary lesion.' In all cases, even in those dying some time afterwards, the necroses all appear to date from the time of delivery. Characteristic necrotic findings are rarely discernible however, if death takes place earlier than fourteen hours after parturition. The necrosis may be small, large or almost complete, but it usually spares the pars tuberalis, the part just in front of the attachment of the stalk, the region of the pars intermedia, and a thin layer, or small scattered islets just beneath the capsule. Sheehan writes: 'adopting arbitrary figures, there will probably be no symptoms with a loss of less than 50 per cent of the gland, the symptoms will be slight with a 60 per cent loss, moderate with a 75 per cent loss, and severe with a 95 per cent loss'. Judging from the histology of the pituitary in patients who died several years later from other causes it seems remarkable how small a portion of gland need remain undestroyed in order to carry on normal, adequate function, but this is quite comparable with our knowledge of other endocrine glands, e.g. thyroid and pancreas.

Although ischaemic necrosis accounts for the majority of female cases of Simmonds' disease, many other pathological processes have been described. Sheehan and Summers, reviewing the literalure, accepted the following lesions as causing anterior pituitary failure:

1. Ischaemic necrosis
2. Chronic fibroid lesions-aetiology unknown.
3. Tuberculosis, syphilis, and giant-cell granulomata.
4. Trauma to base of skull.
5. Trauma of pituitary or of the suprasellar region.

It is obvious from the varied pathology that recognition of the disorder of function is not enough in itself, for the causal lesion may dominate the ultimate prognosis. Tumours arising from suprasellar lesions may be associated with diabetes insipidus or narcolepsy. As the lesion progresses to destroy the anterior pituitary, polyuria will diminish.

Other Endocrine Glands

Thyroid

Partial or complete atrophy of the thyroid is found, and its weight is less than half of the normal, 25 g. The alveoli are scanty and atrophic, with little or no colloid therein, and there is gross fibrosis, round-celled infiltration, and numerous lymphoid follicles.

Suprarenals

The cortex is atrophied, and the zona glomerulosa and reticularis are very thin and sometimes absent. There is rarely any fibrosis, although the capsule may be thickened. Lipoid is usually present in the cortex, and sometimes in normal amounts, but there may be none. The medulla is normal.

Gonads

The ovaries and uterus may be completely atrophic and fibrotic, or incomplete maturation of Graafian follicles may be found. The testes may be minute and atrophic, with complete disorganization of the normal structure, and no evidence of the presence of spermatozoa or spermatogonia.

Parathyroids

Sheehan found the parathyroids 'rather small', or *very* fatty, or fibrous.

Pancreas

The islets of Langerhans might be very small, or apparently normal.

Effect on Viscera

In contrast to acromegaly the stomach, intestines, lungs, heart, liver, and spleen are smaller than average without necessarily showing any pathological changes. The heart may show brown atrophy. There is a striking absence of fat.

Incidence

In view of the importance of parturition haemorrhage as an aetiological factor, the disease is much more frequent in women than in men. The most common aetiology in the male is a neoplasm in the pituitary region. The disease has always been regarded as rare, but more accurate diagnosis shows that the disturbance is one of the more common major disorders of the pituitary. Not all cases exhibit total pituitary failure; partial failure usually affects growth hormone and gonadotrophins rather than thyrotrophin or adrenocorticotrophin.

Clinical Changes

The condition is usually one of adult life but rarely-when, for example, it is due to slow-growing craniopharyngioma, as in a case under observation-the initial symptoms are seen in childhood as a failure of normal, somatic, and sexual development but even so, the characteristic picture of Simmonds' disease is not fully developed until adult life.

In the majority of patients the disease starts from a parturition which is associated with severe haemorrhage and collapse, frequently with a retained placenta and sometimes with puerperal sepsis. These serious concomitants overshadow any specific manifestations of a sudden destruction of pituitary function, but it is soon observed that the recovery of the patient does not take a normal course.

More specifically, there is a complete absence of mammary activity and of lactation in many patients, and Levy-Solal has described hypoglycaemic shock after delivery, when the blood sugar may be as low as 50 mg per 100 ml. Failure of the pubic hair to regrow after its removal prior to labour is an other indication of pituitary insufficiency. However, in the majority of patients there may be no specific diagnostic features, and the condition may or may not be suspect until the more chronic picture evolves.

General Symptoms and Signs

Behaviour is often characterized by apathy and inertia, and sometimes by phases of irritability or of somnolence associated with hypoglycaemia. The patient appears indifferent to her surroundings and normal social activities. She lacks initiative and spontaneity, and may become careless in her dress, sluggish in thought, and slow in speech. Questions may not be answered until after a long latent period. She sometimes appears stupid or absent-minded, and may stare into space for long periods or lie in bed. Sheehan states that 'more marked mental symptoms are rather frequent in the last few months, ranging from oddness, or alternating attacks of excitement or depression, up to definite insanity'. In moderate cases the patient complains of excessive weariness on slight exertion. Muscular atrophy and atony are concomitant features. Sensitivity to cold may be very marked even when warmly dressed. The patient tends to get completely under the bedclothes. The face takes on a pallid appearance, even with absence of anaemia- a pallor which may be regarded as in striking contrast to the plethora of Cushing's syndrome. The skin may be delicate and fine in texture, with an involution of sweat and sebaceous glands. Delicate wrinkling around the eyes and mouth contrasts with the soft hairless skin to give a curious mixture of youth and age. In others there is a tendency to mucoid infiltration of the skin as in myxoedema. The hair of the head loses its lustre and becomes dry, thin, and brittle. Its colour may also change, e.g. from a dark brown to a light brown. The eye-brows become thin, especially in the outer half. The pubic and axillary hair is usually completely lost. It may be partially retained but thinned in the earlier stages of the disease.

Contrary to the initial concepts of the syndrome, cachexia is not essential to the diagnosis. The early stages of the disease are very rarely associated with rapid loss of weight; indeed obesity may be present if hypothyroidism is the predominant disorder of function. In the later stages, when apathy and anorexia are marked, the patient may become cachectic. This is in contrast to the initial loss of appetite with rapid loss of weight in anorexia nervosa, which is followed by a secondary depression of pituitary function.

Constipation is common and achlorhydria occurs in *50* per cent of patients. A raised sedimentation rate is not uncommon in the absence of infection. Some degree of anaemia is the rule, usually normochromic in nature, but the, pallor of the skin is commonly in contrast to the pink mucous membranes.

Summers found that the anaemia was either of a normocytic hypochromic or a macrocytic hypochromic type; in both the marrow was normoblastic. Glossitis and perleche are rare accompaniments. The normoblastic marrow indicates that there is neither folic acid nor vitamin B_{12} deficiency; the administration of iron, orally or parenterally, is ineffective. Thyroid extract has surprisingly little effect on the blood picture, indicating that the anaemia of hypopituitarism is not the same as the anaemia of myxoedema. However both cortisone and ACTH improve the blood picture considerably; the best results require thyroid and probably testosterone in addition to cortisone.

Gonadal Function

In the female, amenorrhoea is the commonest manifestation of gonadal failure and menstruation may never return after parturition. In other patients menstruation is scanty, and at long, irregular intervals. Very rarely it may be normal, and another spontaneous pregnancy occur. In the male, libido and potency disappear; the testes become atrophic. Atrophy of the uterus and lower genital tract is usually marked in the female; dyspareunia is the rule and libido is absent.

Cardiovascular

Bradycardia is almost invariable, and the blood pressure is characteristically low but occasionally normal. The electrocardiogram shows a low voltage.

Pulmonary

There are no abnormal pulmonary changes in uncomplicated cases, but tuberculosis sometimes supervenes. It may then be insidious and silent, and is often unsuspected, especially as the pulse rate tends to remain slow and the temperature subnormal. Bronchopneumonia may also supervene in the later stages and prove fatal.

Skeletal

Children, when affected with a craniopharyngioma, fail to grow, and a type of dwarfism results. X-rays show a delay, or complete absence, of union of the epiphyses of the long bones. In contradistinction to acromegaly, the hands and feet are diminutive, and the fingers delicate and tapering. Bony absorption and retraction of the lower jaw may occur in adults, so that the opposite condition to prognathism results, the teeth decaying and falling out.

Metabolism

The basal metabolism is almost invariably low. Sheehan states that it lies between minus 25 and minus 33 per cent. in the first 15 years after onset, and later may be minus 40 per cent. In our experience the degree of depression of metabolism does not depend upon such duration. Further, it is important to realize that in some patients showing a definite but incomplete syndrome after parturition, the basal metabolism may be only slightly lowered, e.g. minus 12 per cent. The temperature is usually subnormal, and may be very low, 96°F. Blood cholesterol values are sometimes raised but not, in our experience, raised to the same extent as in myxoedema, even when the basal metabolism is comparably lowered.

Thyroid function

Thyroid hypofunction is partly responsible for the lowered metabolism. Radioactive iodine studies show a slow accumulation of iodine by the thyroid to a maximum of about 10-15 per cent of the dose. Often even less iodine is retained in the thyroid, and the urinary excretion of the iodine is high, particularly for 24-72 hours after the dose, in contrast to the minimal secretion at that time by the normal subject. Administration of thyrotrophic hormone over 2-5 days results in an increase in the rate of thyroidal iodine uptake and retention of a larger percentage of the dose. By this means hypothyroidism of pituitary origin may be differentiated from true myxoedema of primary thyroid atrophy. The exact calibration of the degree of stimulus and response is still lacking; moreover Simmonds' disease of many years standing may show no thyroidal response to the test because of the atrophic state of the thyroid.

Carbohydrate metabolism

Carbohydrate tolerance curves are not constant in Simmonds' disease. The fasting blood sugar is usually low, and the most characteristic curve is a flat one, showing a prolonged plateau at values only slightly above normal, and not returning to subnormal values until after two hours.

The characteristic abnormality of carbohydrate metabolism is elicited best by the intravenous injection of insulin. As Fraser and Smith pointed out, the speed and degree of fall in blood sugar after the injection of insulin is not the important point. The true abnormality, due to deficient adrenocortical function and lack of the diabetogenic effect of growth hormone, is the failure of the blood sugar to regain normal levels within 2 hours. This tardiness in the recovery from hypoglycaemia is termed 'hypoglycaemic unresponsiveness'.

The patient should be well fed (as far as is possible) for three days before the test. Then after taking a fasting blood sugar specimen, insulin is injected intravenously. For normal people 0.1 Units of insulin per kilogram body-weight is the dosage, but for suspected Simmonds' disease a characteristic curve will be given with half this dosage (or even a third). The reduction of the standard insulin dosage is advisable to avoid too severe a hypoglycaemic response, endangering life. It may be necessary to interrupt the test to give glucose or inject adrenaline. Capillary blood is taken at intervals of 20, 30, 45, 60, 90 and 120 minutes after the insulin injection. Typical values (mg per 100 ml) are

Normal control	100 (fasting):	45,	52,	60,	82,	95,	105
Simmonds' disease	70 (fasting):	36,	38,	42,	52,	54,	58.

The initial fall of blood sugar is normal, allowing for the lower fasting basis by calculating as a percentage of the initial blood sugar value; but there is a marked delay in returning to the initial blood sugar values, and in severe cases, especially if the standard test dose of insulin is not drastically reduced, the patient's own resources may be quite unable to maintain, let along increase, the low blood sugar glycaemic crisis may develop. Since, however, these patients usually respond to adrenaline, hepatic glycogen stores are apparently present and mobilizable by an exogenous stimulus.

With anorexia nervosa the insulin sensitivity test is usually normal, but in severe cases it may closely resemble that of Simmonds' disease.

In myxoedema there may be some retardation of the subsequent rise of blood sugar (relative hypoglycaemic responsiveness), but there is also a delayed initial fall of blood sugar concentration.

The above observations on the disturbance of carbohydrate metabolism in Simmonds' disease are of great clinical importance, since spontaneous attacks of hypoglycaemic crisis may occur at any time and may prove fatal. Some peculiarities of behaviour and attacks of somnolence are also ascribable to hypoglycaemia, and in the course of conducting insulin sensitivity tests we have observed their production. In one case the patient had amnesia for the whole period of the test although she had answered questions during it and had not lost consciousness.

Adrenal cortex insufficiency

The assay of urinary 17-ketosteroids measures in blunderbuss fashion a variety of androgens derived from gonads and adrenal cortex. Normal values vary to some extent with the technique employed, but may be taken as being 5 to 18 mg per day.

In Simmonds' disease Fraser and Smith found extremely low values, under 0.5 mg per day; but in mild cases values are below 2 mg. In their four cases of anorexia nervosa assays ranged between 2.7 and 14.7 mg per twenty-four hours.

Very low levels of 17-ketosteroid excretion have been observed by us in patients with anorexia nervosa who are grossly malnourished. However, values of 2 mg or less per twenty-four hours in a case of suspected Simmonds disease are a strong supporting factor in the diagnosis. Low values are also recorded for urinary reducing steroids and for blood corticoids. Low values for all these steroid estimations are found in Addison's disease. In primary myxoedema, Fraser and Smith found values varying from zero to 1.7 mg per twenty-four hours, an observation which we would confirm in some but by no means all cases. Administration of thyroid to these cases is followed by a return to a normal excretion of 17-ketosteroids.

The serum values for sodium, potassium, and chloride rarely approximate to those found in Addison's disease, but the Kepler test of adrenal function not infrequently gives values as low as those found in Addison's disease. The reason for this is the marked inability of the patient with Simmonds' disease to excrete a water-load, a function dependent on the glucocorticoid and not on the mineralocorticoid activity. The serum values for sodium and chloride may be normal, but may be low, sometimes even as low as, or even lower than, those found in Addison's disease. This is not due, however, to an abnormal loss of sodium but to hydration and haemodilution following cortisone deficiency. In contrast with the severe phases of Addison's disease, the serum potassium values are not raised. The Kepler test is not without danger in these circumstances as drowsiness, headache and even coma from water poisoning may follow ingestion of large volume of water. The overnight fast in preparation for the test may induce hypoglycaemic symptoms as well.

Renal salt loss and potassium retention, characteristic of Addison's disease, is extremely rare in Simmonds' disease, despite the secondary adrenocortical failure. This is now explicable by the discovery that aldosterone, the most potent mineralocorticoid, differs from the other adrenal steroids in that its rate of secretion is not directly related to the degree of ACTH stimulation. Therefore failure of anterior pituitary function is associated for many months with a normal output of aldosterone but later, as actual atrophy of the adrenal cortex develops, the rate of secretion falls to subnormal levels.

Natural History

Severe cases may live a twilight existence for many years before a fatal crisis supervenes. The length of history, despite the degree of disability, is in sharp contrast to the often catastrophically short history of untreated Addison's disease. However, the patient with well-developed anterior pituitary failure is always likely to succumb to intercurrent infection or to become grossly psychotic. Chronic dementia may mask the endocrine nature of the disease and lead to certification.

Variations in natural history depend on the degree of pituitary damage, a point well illustrated by ischaemic necrosis of the gland. Following such a severe post-partum haemorrhage that complete anuria ensued, one patient failed to lactate and her pubic hair failed to regrow for two months. Tests of pituitary function indicated both thyroid and adrenal insufficiency, yet convalescence was uneventful and she made a complete recovery with resumption of normal menstruation within four months of labour. She represents the mildest type of temporary pituitary insufficiency, which would not be recognized clinically without an intensive follow-up. In two other patients the only permanent endocrine dysfunction was amenorrhoea with extreme atrophy of the uterus and lower genital tract. However, the pituitary is not always involved in terms of gonadotrophin secretion. One of our patients resumed menstruation when her hypothyroidism and adrenocortical insufficiency were treated. She conceived successfully and, during pregnancy, remained well in the absence of hormonal therapy. Within three weeks of a normal delivery, clinical and biochemical evidence of pituitary insufficiency was apparent once more.

The relapse is noteworthy because Sheehan and Murdoch have suggested that pregnancy in the course of the disease is followed by spontaneous cure. Obviously this is not an invariable rule, but spontaneous recovery can occur in the absence of pregnancy as illustrated by a patient who made a complete recovery after treatment for a period of five years. However, such an event is very unusual.

Partial but permanent lesions do not involve all pituitary hormones to the same extent. Occasionally, failure of ACTH or thyrotrophin secretion is the only severe deficiency, but, as a general rule, gonadotrophin and growth-hormone secretion are affected with preservation of the more vital control of adrenal and thyroid. Thus young patients display dwarfism and sexual infantilism in the absence of thyroid and adrenal failure.

Recently more attention has been focused on the symptomatology and physiopathology of hypopituitary crises. Not only are these episodes likely to end in death unless immediately recognized and energetically treated, but the underlying disturbances of function are an acute exaggeration of those responsible for the chronic symptomatology of the condition and therefore illustrate the basic disorder of hypopituitarism. In a protected stable environment the body's primitive metabolic arrangements continue to function slowly in the absence of the pituitary but they are deprived of the necessary range of activity and adaptability which is normally provided by the stimulus of the adenohypophysis as an essential to good health. Consequently a breakdown in this limited homeostasis will follow even minor changes in environment and lead to the severe symptoms of a crisis. Trauma, infection, starvation, and excessive cold can all be the precipitating factors. Operations on the pituitary or adjacent areas are now not uncommon causes of crisis in patients already suffering from panhypopituitarism due to neoplasm in some cases the preoperative evidence of pituitary insufficiency is slight and the operation, by acutely inhibiting the remainder of pituitary function, will be followed by the most severe disturbance we have also seen operations on other sites such as a colporrhaphy, cause crisis by virtue of the stress imposed on an inefficient endocrine system. All types of infection, varying, in our experience from an infected tooth socket to gastroenteritis, induce a crisis in the same manner. It must also be remembered that panhypopituitarism renders a patient extremely sensitive to morphine and barbiturates; even routine dosage of these drugs can be followed by prolonged stupor. Lastly a crisis may signify the terminal breakdown of metabolism after a slowly progressive downhill course.

The symptoms of crisis are less variable than the causative disturbances of physiology. Refusal of food, resentment at any interference, querulous complaints, commonly of arthralgia, give way to increasing lethargy and prolonged sleep. Stupor follows, sometimes interrupted by short maniaceal outbursts often associated with hallucinations. The last stage is one of deep progressive coma. The patient may lie flaccid with absent reflexes or curled up, responding violently to examination. Bradycardia is usual and may be extreme. The blood pressure is often unrecordable and the radial pulse absent. However, hypotension is not necessarily an early sign. An important and often neglected sign is the extremely low body temperature-often unrecognized because the thermometer has not been shaken down to its lowest level. Crisis following cerebral surgery can be differentiated from loss of consciousness due to cerebral injury by the absence of localizing signs in the central nervous system. But differentiation is not always easy. It is not enough to confine one's thoughts to traumatic causes of post-operative stupor and the possibility of hypopituitarism must always be borne in mind.

The disorders of physiology underlying the coma of Simmonds' disease can be identified as:

1. Hypothermia.
2. Cerebral anoxia.
3. Water intoxication.
4. Hypoglycaemia.
5. Electrolyte disturbance.

However it is seldom that one noxious factor can be isolated as the cause of a particular coma. In some, hypothermia is dominant and consciousness returns on gently heating the patient in others hypoglycaemia, apart from its obvious role in producing acute states of unconsciousness, is associated with slowly progressive stupor. Yet administration of glucose is not always followed by a return to consciousness when the blood sugar is again normal. Water poisoning with coma may follow directly on a water-load, but it is seldom realized that patients with hypopituitarism are very easily overloaded with fluids and this is a common feature of many crises. The lowered serum sodium due to haemodilution must be distinguished from that of true sodium depiction. However, such Addisonian electrolyte changes are rare unless severe vomiting has preceded the coma. Cerebral anoxia may be induced by hypothermia or hypoglycaemia and hypotension will exaggerate it. Postural hypotension is a common cause of more transient attacks of faintness rather than stupor.

All these changes are due to a combination of thyroid and adrenal failure. Hypothyroidism, apart from its role in hypothermia, is seldom vital; indeed it may protect the body from the effects of adrenal failure because the administration of thyroid or even, as in our experience, the injection of thyrotrophin may raise the metabolic rate and precipitate a crisis. This does not occur if cortisone has been given concurrently. Glucocorticoid deficiency is undoubtedly the most important factor of all; the administration of cortisone or hydrocortisone in hypopituitary crisis produces results which are far superior to any other form of treatment. It is interesting that the electroencephalographic abnormalities, which are characteristic but not specific of a crisis, are corrected by cortisone but disappear some time after return of the clinical state to normal. We have also observed this sequence of events in Addison's disease treated with cortisone but there is no correction following dexoycortone.

Diagnosis

Amenorrhoea, weakness, apathy, poor appetite with some loss of weight, bradycardia, hypotension, low basal metabolism and temperature, and hypersensitivity to cold, are present in a characteristic case; and frequently these symptoms follow a parturition associated with severe haemorrhage. It is now accepted that gross loss of weight is not a cardinal feature of the disease and the maintenance of normal nutrition is the rule rather than the exception. However, a loss of 4 to 8 lb. in weight is common and we have observed a gain in weight only in exceptional cases when hypothyroidism has dominated the picture.

It is important to remember that many cases are examples of an incomplete syndrome, and may well be missed unless the condition is kept in mind as a sequel of complicated parturition. Amenorrhoea, for example, was formerly considered to be an invariable feature, but this is not so, and undoubtedly cases have even become pregnant. However, the presence of normal menstruation makes the diagnosis much less certain. We attach importance to bradycardia, but it is claimed by other observers that it is not invariable. The same applies to low blood pressure, and the basal metabolism is not necessarily markedly lowered.

Simmonds' disease may be due to neoplasms or granuloma of the pituitary gland, and it will be remembered, therefore, that parturition is not the only cause, and that the disorder may also occur in men. If the condition starts in childhood, e.g. a slow-growing destructive craniopharyngioma, infantilism will be the background on which the adult syndrome will be superimposed.

The disease is often insidious in onset, even when due to a post-parturition thrombosis, but it may be acute and fatal, e.g. haemorrhage into a chromophobe adenoma. On the other hand, it may be present and pass unrecognized for thirty or more years.

A number of conditions will be separately considered in the following differential diagnosis, and in some it will be indicated that there we are dealing with a question of nomenclature rather than differential diagnosis:

Differential Diagnosis

This includes:

(1) Addison's disease. From the fact that both in Addison's and Simmonds' disease the adrenal cortex is functioning poorly, much of the symptomatology is common to both diseases'. Pigmentation is usual in Addisons' disease and is widespread, usually including the mucous membranes; but in acute cases, or in fair people, pigmentation may be minimal. In Simmonds disease pigmentation is absent and pallor of the skin is often a striking feature. Bradycardia is rare in Addison's disease and the basal metabolism is not appreciably lowered except in crisis. Pubic and axillary hair is seldom absent in Addison's disease, and menstruation is not infrequently normal.

(2) Myxoedema. This diagnosis is often erroneously made. Thyroid insufficiency is one feature of the disease but not the whole clinical picture. The 17-ketosteroids are below 2.0 mg per day in both conditions. The blood sugar is usually not low in myxoedema, there is a slower fall in blood sugar after intravenous insulin, but a normal or slightly delayed subsequent rate of recovery of blood sugar values. Pubic and axillary hair is not lost. Examples of Simmonds' disease have been described under the title of 'pituitary myxoedema' - a confusing term which should riot be used.

Myxoedema will respond dramatically to thyroid, whereas in Simmonds' disease the response is only partial and sometimes the patient is made worse. A more experimental approach will show that the iodine uptake of the thyroid will respond to thyrotrophic hormone in Simmonds' disease, whereas in myxoedema it is completely uninfluenced, the thyroid being unable to respond.

It is important to realize that severe untreated myxoedema of many years' duration will result in a depression of pituitary function. The rise in thyrotrophin secretion which follows destruction of the thyroid is succeeded by a gross fall in the output of this hormone, together with a diminution of gonadotrophin secretion. The subsequent administration of thyroid extract is followed by a return to normal secretion of both these hormones.

(3) Anaemia. In Simmonds' disease the blood picture may be normal, but anaemia of moderate degree is the rule. Some 50 per cent. of cases have achlorhydria. These findings, together with the pollor of the skin, which is disproportionate to the pinkness of the mucosae may lead to a diagnosis of anaemia, without recognition of the endocrine condition.

(4) Anorexia nervosa. This condition is a neurosis and not an endocrine disorder. Autospy findings are quite different from Simmonds' disease in that the endocrine glands are normal apart from involution of the ovaries and uterus. The importance of anorexia nervosa as a differential diagnosis to Simmonds' disease has receded, now that it is clear that cachexia is not a cardinal part of the clinical picture of pituitary destruction.

Amenorrhoea occurs early, due to the mental disturbances mediated by the hypothalamus. At the stage gonadotrophin secretion is still present. In the later stages of inanition gonadotrophin secretion diminishes or ceases. The fall in metabolic rate is related to starvation and not initially to thyroid hypofunction, as radioactive iodine uptake by the thyroid is normal; later a raised blood cholesterol and a low radiactive iodine uptake indicate secondary hypothyroidism. In marked contrast to Simmonds' disease the patient remains intensely active, often with obsessional traits, despite the extreme cachexia. Anorexia is of course an early and predominant feature. Body hair tends to increase over a rough dry skin, although in the later stages pubic hair may become scanty. It is apparent from Leyton's studies in starvation in prisoners of war that amenorrhoea, imoptence, bradycardia, hypotension, low basal metabolic rate, and some lowering of the blood sugar result from inanition. Certainly a depression of pituitary function accompanies these changes, but it is best to avoid the term "functional Simmonds' disease".

Treatment

Surgical conditions, such as intracranial neoplasms, require surgery, but the majority of cases need hormone substitution therapy, and the latter is also called for after surgical hypophysectomy.

Since nearly all the endocrine glands are affected, it is difficult to decide in any one case which form of therapy use, and it is technically and practically impossible to employ complete replacement therapy. Our own experience with several cases is as follows:

Cortisone

The availability of cortisone acetate, for oral use, or intramuscular injection, has marked a signal advance in the treatment of Simmonds' disease. Previous experience had shown that testosterone, for either sex, was of great efficacy in the restoration of strength and well-being. But those patients who have changed from testosterone to cortisone have been amazed at their new state of well-being. The oral administration of 12.5-37.5 mg per day (tablet once to three times daily) is dramatic in its effect and renders the patient less prone to crisis after infection or hypoglycaemia on fasting. The use of adrenocorticotrophin is more logical for hypopituitarism, but the disadvantage of repeated injections (even if the long-acting ACTH gel is injected once or twice weekly) makes it less suitable for maintenance therapy. However, adrenocorticotrophin is of use in initial therapy, and we are impressed by the responsiveness of the adrenals even if they have been inactive for years. However, we administer both adrenocorticotrophin and cortisone with considerable caution to the long-standing case of Simmonds' disease as we have observed that these hormones may induce a temporary but severe psychosis, usually of the manic type. Careful adjustment of the dose allows long-term therapy to continue. In states of crisis, intravenous injection of *50* mg of hydrocortisone, prepared specially for this route of administration, is preferable to other forms of therapy. Cortisone intramuscularly provides the necessary supportive therapy.

Testosterone

We have found testosterone propionate by injection (e.g. *25* mg on alternate days) or implantation (0.4 G. of testosterone) a very useful therapeutic measure. Oral administration of methyltestosterone, 5-10 mg three times a day, is also effective, not only for men but for women, in whom the secretion of adrenal androgens, which is common to both sexes, is very low, as judged by urinary excretion. This makes testosterone a logical substitution therapy. Further, androgens are protein anabolic hormones, producing nitrogen retention, increasing strength and weight, and preventing osteoporosis.

In the male, already on cortisone therapy, testosterone is necessary to restore potency, penile erections, and a normal volume of ejaculate. In the female, large doses have the disadvantage of producing facial hirsutes, acne, and a deepening voice, but small doses in conjunction with cortisone stimulate protein anabolism and offset the catabolic action of cortisone.

Thyroid

Thyroid extract or L-thyroxine by mouth helps partially in some patients, but in others proves harmful and may even precipitate a crisis if given in large doses. It should therefore be used with caution, commencing with small doses, and it is best deferred in severe cases until general improvement is made by other means. An initial dose of thyroid extract, ½ gr. daily, or L-thyroxine, 0.05 mg daily, should be doubled after 2 weeks and, after a similar interval, the maintenance dose of 2-3 gr. thyroid extract can be reached. We have noted that patients already taking thyroid require some increase in dosage if they are treated with cortisone.

Oestrogens

Oestrogens by mouth may not be well tolerated, but by injection or subcutaneous implantation they proved helpful generally, apart from the possibility of restoring the uterus to normal size and producing a bleeding. They should be given in large doses, e.g. 5 mg oestradiol benzoate injected daily. Restoration of fluid to the subcutaneous tissues appears to be a good effect.

The problem of dyspareunia from an atrophic vagina is solved by oestrogens. This important point is seldom considered before treatment, because of the patient's complete loss of libido. When normal sex desire returns with treatment some patients are too reticent to complain of pain or intercourse.

DeoxycortOne acetate (DOCA) is never required. Salt loss is seldom a feature of Simmonds' disease, and can usually be met by a high salt diet. Cortisone itself causes little salt retention but continued aldosterone secretion makes mineralocorticoid therapy unnecessary. Indeed prednisone and prednisolone can be used for their potent glucocorticoid properties despite the absence of salt-retaining power. Thyrotrophin is of diagnostic use but it is not recommended in therapy. Gonadotrophins are likewise of no practical importance.

Treatment of Crisis

Early diagnosis and the increase of glucocorticoid dosage in anticipation of factors such as operation or infection, will do much to diminish the incidence of crisis. When such as event has occurred, treatment must be guided by the dominant physiological abnormality. Hypothermia is always important, and should be countered by gentle heating of the patient; drastic methods with heat cradles are dangerous. A warm bath is advocated by Sheehan and Summers despite its obvious practical difficulties. *Hypoglycaemia* can be corrected rapidly with intravenous dextrose (50 per cent) and frequent glucose drinks should be given later to prevent a subsequent fall in the blood sugar. In rare instances sodium depletion will require the intravenous administration of normal saline, but at all times the fear of water intoxication should limit the volume of intravenous fluid.

Undoubtedly glucocorticoid therapy is of paramount importance in all cases. Intravenous administration of hydrocortisone (as the 'free alcohol' or as the hemisuccinate) should aim at an initial dose of 50 mg to be followed by a continuous intravenous infusion delivery of 10 mg hourly. Intramuscular or oral cortisone can be given from the outset in the milder case or started when the condition is improving : about 100 mg daily are required. The slow response of the adrenals to ACTH makes this hormone of little use in crisis. The immediate administration of thyroid extract or its equivalents is dangerous. Glucocorticoid therapy should always be started first. Hours later, triiodothyronine, 20 μg, three times a day, can be given if hypothyroidism appears to be severe.

DIABETES INSIPIDUS

Diabetes insipidus is a disturbance of water balance, characterized by primary polyuria and secondary polydipsia, due to a destructive lesion of the posterior lobe of the pituitary gland or the adjacent part of the hypothalamus. An experimental puncture lesion of the tuber cinereum, or nucleus supraopticus, is followed by atrophy of the posterior pituitary lobe.

Cushing stated that: 'Its secretory product (*pars nervosa*) is unmistakably derived from the investing pars intermedia whose cells become basophilic when ripened and under nervous impulses from hypothalamic nuclei, the basophil cells invade the pars nervosa and become transformed into "hyaline bodies", which pass into the infundibular cavity'. However, experimentally it is clear that diabetes insipidus can occur in the presence of a normal pars intermedia, and that the antidiuretic hormone can be extracted from pars nervosa (posterior pituitary) but not from pars intermedia. Fisher, Ingram, and Ranson showed that the essential lesion was anywhere in the supraoptic tract, and Richer reported that the diuresis preceded excessive intake of fluid. The diuresis will continue for a while even if fluid is completely withheld. The recent application of histochemical techniques has shown that the hormones of the supraoptico-hypophyseal tract are actually produced in the upper part of the tract, passing downwards to be released into the circulation from the posterior lobe of the pituitary; the function of this lobe is one of storage and secretion but not synthesis of hormones. Excessive quantities of antidiuretic hormone are found in the urine in normal animals subjected to water deprivation or to emotional stimuli. The amount of antidiuretic hormone is greatly reduced by a water-load so that 'water diuresis may be fitly and accurately described as a condition of physiological diabetes insipidus; and there can be little doubt that the antidiuretic secretion of the neurohypophysis is a hormone in the physiological sense, its liberation being continuously governed by the contemporary concentration of chloride, and possibly of other osmotically active substances, in the arterial plasma'.

Verney's conception of the supraoptico-hypophyseal tract as a regulator of blood osmolarity, responding to an increasing osmotic pressure by the release of antidiuretic hormone, must be expanded to include the overall control of antidiuretic hormone released by nervous impulses from the hypothalamus. Harris has shown that electrical stimulation of the hypothalamus results in secretion of antidiuretic hormone. Furthermore nicotine applied directly to the supraoptic nuclei produces the same effect. Even injection or inhalation of nicotine (from a cigarette) will cause hormone secretion; a physiological observation which has led to the diagnostic use of nicotine when a water diuresis has been induced in a patient with possible diabetes insipidus.

The chemistry of posterior pituitary hormones has now been revealed by the brilliance of du Vigneau *et. al.*, who not only identified vasopressin and oxytocin as two distinct but closely related cyclic polypeptides, but actually synthesized the two hormones. Vasopressin is the antidiuretic hormone. Its site of action is the renal tubule, thereby regulating the renal excretion of water. Despite rather conflicting experimental work there is no evidence that vasopressin exerts any direct action on electrolyte excretion in man.

The renal effect of vasopressin is modified by the action of the adrenal cortex and thyroid; the hormones of these glands are necessary for the full development of polyuria when the secretion of antidiuretic hormone is stopped (i.e. by section of the supraoptico-hypophyseal tract). Coincident damage of the anterior and posterior lobes of the pituitary does not cause full diabetes insipidus because the secretion of adrenocorticotrophin and thyrotrophin is diminished as well as the secretion of vasopressin. Under these circumstances the administration of hydrocortisone and thyroxine is followed by the appearance of gross diabetes insipidus. Similarly thyroidectomy or removal of the anterior pituitary lobe ameliorates severe diabetes insipidus. If the supraoptico-hypophyseal tract is left intact and the anterior lobe of the pituitary destroyed, renal elimination of a water-load is impaired and water poisoning may occur. The same situation arises in Addison's disease. It is of interest that the maintenance of body water balance is related to glucocorticoid and not mineralocorticoid hormones.

Incidence

Diabetes insipidus may be familial, and then occurs in young people, males more commonly than females. It may, however occur at any age.

Aetiology

The causes of diabetes insipidus are as follows:

1. Familial.
2. Idiopathic.
3. Tumours adjacent to hypothalamus or pituitary.
4. Inflammatory lesions in the parapituitary area, e.g. encephalitis lethargica, basal meningitis, syphilis.
5. Fractured skull or surgical trauma to supraoptico-hypophyseal tract.
6. Xanthomatosis (Schuller-Christian disease).

Clinical Picutre

The essential feature is the passage of large quantities (10 litres a day) of pale urine of low specific gravity (usually less than 1.004); and good experimental evidence indicates that this is the primary disorder, the resulting unquenchable thirst being a secondary phenomenon. The tissues become dehydrated; there is no obvious perspiration; and the skin and mucous membranes are very dry. The faeces are hard and desiccated, and the patient constipated. Nocturia prevents sleep.

Course and Progress

The natural history is dependent on the causative lesion. The physiological disturbance itself is benign and, in the absence of a lethal cause, the prognosis is very good. However, it is important to realize that not a few cases of so-called idiopathic diabetes insipidus later show evidence of an intracranial tumour as the origin of the disease. Hence the initial prognosis should always be guarded.

Some psychological disturbances may derange the hypothalamic control of body water; episodes of extreme polyuria and thirst alternating with a suppression of urinary output and water retention. It may be inferred that temporary inhibition of secretion gives way to an excessive secretion of antidiuretic hormone, an event which is in accord with the experimental evidence of increased antidiuresis in dogs who are frightened.

Diagnosis

The differential diagnosis is as follows:

1. Diabetes mellitus—glycosuria.
2. Chronic nephritis-albuminuria, renal casts, and hypertension.
3. Neurosis or hysteria.
4. Caffeine idiosyncrasy-this runs in families and polyuria ceases if water only is drunk.
5. Nephrogenic diabetes insipidus-renal tubular failure to resorb water. Seen in babies. Uninfluenced by vasopressin.
6. Hypercalcuria-gross polyuria associated with high urinary calcium excretion. Seen in rare cases of hyperparathyroidism.

In practice the only difficulty is diagnosis lies in the distinction of diabetes insipidus from hysterical polydipsia. The most reliable diagnostic procedure at the moment is the administration of nicotine when a water diuresis has been induced. Prompt cessation of the diuresis indicates an intact supraoptico-hypophyseal tract while a continued diuresis indicates diabetes insipidus.

Treatment

Vasopressin (Pitressin), 10-20 Units, in 1 ml aqueous solution, injected subcutaneously, is effective. Its duration of action is only a few hours and an injection of 1 ml (5 Units) vasopressin tannate in oily solution has proved of greater convenience, the effect of a single injection lasting for twenty-four hours owing to slower absorption at the site of injection. A dried powder of posterior pituitary, e.g. *Piton,* or *Di-Sipidin,* is also effective when used as a nasal snuff. The dose is 25-50 mg. three times a day. The patient learns well enough to estimate the required dose without weighing. Excessive dosage may cause a feeling of faintness, or intestinal spasm, and in one patient it caused ureteric spasm and dysuria. Vasopressin sclution by the nasal route, as a spray, is also used. Voluntary or compulsory restriction of fluid is illogical, since the primary trouble is excessive excretion, not intake. In severe cases the patient will drink any fluid obtainable, even his own urine, and will stop at nothing to get fluid.

Thyroid Diseases Due to Hormones

Several thyroid antigens are recognized including thyroglobulin, thyroid micorsomes, surface and other cytoplasmic thyroid antigens. Autoantibodies against these antigens may be primary, that is involved in the pathogenesis of the disease, or secondary to the thyroid damage. The only primary thyroid autoantibodies known are those to thyroid stimulating hormone receptors. These may stimulate or block the growth and metabolism of the thyroid cells. The other autoantibodies are probably the result of extensive damage and not involved in

Thyroid stimulating hormone (TSH)
1
2
4
3
Increased metabolism
Increase growth
TSH receptor

	Antibodies which act via TSH receptor	Disease in which antibody is present
1.	Thyroid stimulating antibodies (formerly LATS)	Graves disease
2.	Thyroid metabolism blocking antibodies	Myxoedema (some cases)

3.	Thyroid growth stimulating antibodies	Graves disease with gortre Simple goitre Refractory Hashimoto's Thyroidits
4.	Thyroid growth blocking antibodies	Myxoedema (soem cases)

Fig. 2.1. Surface of thyroid cell showing actions of the primary antibodies in autoimmune thyroid diseases.

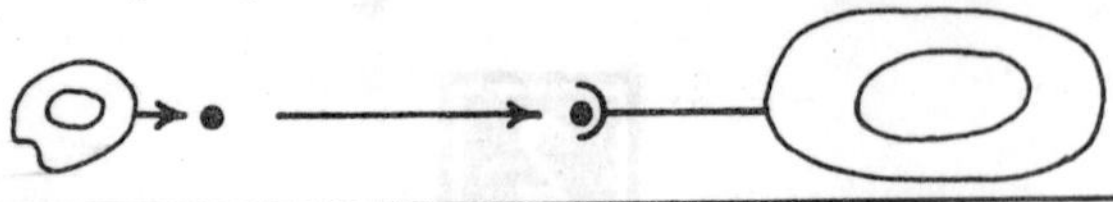

1. *Endocrine cell*	2. *Hormone Receptor*	3. *Hormone Target Cell*
THYROGLOBULIN THYROID MICROSOMES Grases disease Hashimoto's thyroiditis Myxoecema	INSULIN- Insulin reactions Insulin resistance	INSULIN RECEPTORS- Insulin resistance
		AcCh RECEPTORS- Myasthenia gravis
PANCREATIC ISLET CELLS- Type I Diabetes mellitus ADRENAL CORTEX Idiopatoic Addison's disease		TSH RECEPTORS- Graves' disease Myxoedema Endocrine exophthalmas
STEROID PRODUCING CELL. Gonadal insufficiency GASTRIN-PRODUCING CELL- 10% of Type B gastritis		GASTRIN RECEPTORS- Pernicious anaemia (Type A gastritis)

Fig. 2.2. Examples of autoantibodies in endocrine and other organ-specific autoimmune disease with their clinical outcomes. AcCh = acetylcholine; TSH =thyroid stimulating hormone.

TABLE 2.1. MECHANISMS OF AUTOIMMUNE DAMAGE

Mechanism	*Disease*	*Associated autoantibodies*
Stimulating antibody	Graves' disease	Thyroid stimulating immunoglobulin
		Growth stimulating immunoglobulin
	Exophthalmos	Exophthalmos-producing immunoglobulin
Complement-dependent lysis	Myasthenia gravis	Acetylcholine receptor antibody
Opsonizing antibody	Autoimmune haemolytic anaemia	Red cell antibody
	Idiopathic thrombocytopenia	Platelet antibody
Blocking antibody	Pernicious anaemia	Gastric parietal cell surface antibody
		Intrinsic factor antibody
	Myxoedema	Thyroid blocking immunoglobulin
	Infertility (some cases)	Sperm antibody
	Insulin resistant diabetes	Insulin antibody
		Insulin receptor antibody
Cell-mediated killing [T cells; ? K cells]	Hashimoto's thyroiditis	Antibodies to thyroid surface antigens

pathogenesis. Descriptions of the tests used to demonstrate autoantibodies to each antigens are given. Due to the complexity of the assays, tests for antibodies to thyroid surface antigens are not carried out routinely at present, though those for TSH receptor antibodies are available through regional centres. Currently, the most widely available and clinically useful antibody tests are those for antibodies to thyroglobulin and thyroid microsomes.

TABLE 2.2. INCIDENCE AND RELATIVE STRENGTH OF ANTIBODIES TO THYROID ANTIGENS COMMONLY DETECTED IN VARIOUS THYROID DISEASES

	Antibodies to	
Thyroid disease	Thyroglobulin	Thyroid microsomes
Thyrotoxicosis		
Graves' disease	Low titre	Low titre
Hot nodules	-ve	-ve
Goitre		
Hashimoto's thyroiditis	Low titre	High titre
Simple goitre	-ve	-ve
De Quervain's thyroiditis	Transient low titre	Transient-low titre
Carcinoma	-ve	-ve
Thyroxine deficiency		
Primary myxoedema	Low titre	High titre
Normal population		
Males	7%	8%
Females	15-20% Low titre	10% Low titre

Case 1

A 29 year old lady presented with a 3-month history of increased sweating and palpitations with weight loss of 7 kg. On examination, she was a nervous, agitated woman with an obvious, diffuse, non-tender smooth enlargement of her thyroid, over which a bruit could be heard. She had a fine tremor of her fingers and a resting pulse rate of 150/minute. She had no evidence of exophthalmos. A maternal aunt had suffered from 'thyroid disease.

On investigation, she had a raised serum T_3 of 4.8 nmol/l (NR 0.8-2.4) and a T_4 of 48 nmol/l (NR 9-23). Measurement of her thyroid stimulating hormone (TSH) showed that this was low {2.3 mu/1 (normal < 7.0)). The biochemical findings pointed to primary thyroid disease rather than pituitary over activity. Circulating antibodies to thyroglobulin (titre 1/320) and to thyroid micorsomal antigens (titre 1/3000) were detected by passive haemagglutination. A diagnosis of *autoimmune thyrotoxicosis* (Graves' disease) was made. She was treated with an antithyroid drug, carbimazole, to control her thyrotoxicosis, and surgery was not required.

Thyrotoxicosis

Thyrotoxicosis is a common condition with a prevalence of about 20 per 1000 of the population. It can occur at any age but the incidence peaks in the third and fourth decades. It is about five to ten times more common in women than men. Thyrotoxicosis is most commonly due to *Graves' disease* or to *local hyperactive single* or *multiple* nodules in the thyroid gland (toxic adenoma or nodular toxic goitre respectively). The presence of autoantibodies to thyroglobulin or to thyroid microsomal antigens confirms an *autoimmune process,* i.e. *Graves' disease.* Those patients who have high titres of antibodies (particularly to thyroid microsomes) are the ones most likely to proceed to myxoedema, as these *antibodies reflect diffuse damage to the thyroid cells* with release of the intracellular antigens.

There are several pieces of *indirect evidence that Graves' disease is an autoimmune disorder;* these include: (1) infiltration of the thyroid by lymphocytes; (2) the presence of autoantibodies to thyroid antigens; (3) an increased incidence of thymic hyperplasia which characterizes many other autoimmune disorders; (4) an increased risk of thyroid disease in the first degree relatives of patients with Graves' disease; and (5) associations with other autoimmune diseases including myasthenia gravis, pernicious anaemia, rheumatoid arthritis and Hashimoto's thyroiditis.

Direct evidence that a circulating factor was responsible for Graves' disease. Long-acting thyroid stimulators (LATS) were found in the sera of some patients. LATS were originally measured by a difficult bioassay and were found in only one-half of the patients with active Graves' disease. Eight years later, LATS were shown to be an IgG antibody. Sera from 90% of patients with Graves' disease contain IgG antibodies which bind to receptors for thyroid stimulating hormone (TSH) on the surface of human thyroid cells; some of these antibodies stimulate the thyroid cell (thyroid stimulating antibodies) whilst others block by competitive inhibition. These assays are difficult to perform and are not routine.

Two of every 1000 pregnant women are thyrotoxic; occasionally, such pregnancies result in *neonatal Graves' disease.* This is due to transplacental transfer of thyroid-stimulating IgG from mother to fetus. The neonatal disease can be severe. Affected babies have a goitre, exophthalmos, feeding problems, pyrexia and tachycardia and may develop heart failure unless treated promptly. Fortunately, spontaneous recovery gradually occurs over 2-3 months, as the maternal IgG is metabolized at a rate consistent with its half-life (i.e. 3 weeks).

The degree of thyrotoxicosis in Graves' disease is not related to the size of the goitre; indeed, 10 % of patients do not have an enlarged thyroid. *Thyroid growth stimulating immunoglobulin* (TGI) has been demonstrated in the sera of patients with Graves' disease with goitre, and in some patients with non-toxic goitres. In contrast to the thyroid stimulating immunoglobulins (TSI) which causes hyperthyroidism, these antibodies correlate with goitre size but with the production of T_3 and T_4. It is probable that these antibodies react with different epitopes on the two chains which make up the TSH receptor molecule.

Half of the patients with Graves' disease develop *exophthalmos;* this may precede, coincide with or follow the hyperthyroid phase. (It may even occur occasionally in association with Hashimoto's thyroiditis or primary myxoedema.) Exophthalmos is the result of two pathological processes: a myositis affecting the eye muscles and a proliferation of retro-orbital tissue. The myositis is accompanied by infiltration of lymphocytes, and the sera from affected patients contain antibodies which bind to eye muscle extract; some of these antibodies cross-react with other orbital antigens as well as thyroid antigens. Whether they are primary or secondary autoantibodies is not yet known. Reports of successful treatment using plasma exchange with immunosuppression suggest that antibodies may be involved. Positive leucocyte migration inhibition tests have also been obtained when leucocytes from patients with endocrine exophthalmos were cultured with eye muscle or retro-orbital connective tissue extracts. Attempts to stimulate orbital fibroblast cultures with immunoglobulin from normal and exophthalmic patients will determine whether or not such immunoglobulins stimulate fibroblast growth and division.

A few (3-5%) patients with Graves' disease develop pretibial myxoedema; they tend to have exophthalmos as well. Pretibial myxoedema refers to well-demarcated, subcutaneous thickening of the anterolateral aspects of the legs; these areas do not pit on pressure, and are shiny and reddish brown in appearance. The development of pretibial myxoedema is not related to the duration or extent of the hyperthyroidism. *Its pathogenesis is unknown although fibroblast- or fat-stimulating immunoglobulins have been postulated* which could stimulate receptors in the dermis.

The genetic aspects of Graves' disease remain obscure though a positive family history of hyperthyroidism is found in one-half of the patients with Graves' disease. There is 50% concordance in monozygotic twins and less than 5% in dizygotic twins. This indicates that although hereditary determinants are important, non-genetic factors are also involved, as the concordance for monozygotic pairs is not 100%. Caucasian patients with Graves' disease have an increased incidence of HLA-DR3, an antigen associated with several other autoimmune diseases, suggesting it may be close to a susceptibility gene for this type of disease.

Graves' disease can be treated by antithyroid drugs, radioactive iodine or surgery. Immunosuppressive therapy to reduce levels of the causative antibodies has not yet proved feasible, although plasmapheresis plus immunosuppression has been 'successfully used to treat acute severe exophthalmos (sometimes called 'malignant exophthalmos'). There is some evidence that carbimazole (an antithyroid drug) has an immunosuppressive action.

A 39-year-old woman presented with a large painless swelling in her neck. The enlargement had been a gradual process over 2 years. She had no other symptoms and felt generally well. On examination, her thyroid was diffusively enlarged and had a rubbery consistency. There were no signs of thyrotoxicosis or of thyroid failure.

Thyroid function tests showed that she was euthyroid; T_3 was 1.2 nmol/l (NR 0.8-2.4), T_4 was 12 nmol/1 (NR 9-23) and TSH was 6.3 mu/1 (normal < 7.0 mu/1). However, her serum contained antibodies to thyroglobulin (titre 1/320) and to thyroid microsomes (1/64000).

This patient had *Hashimoto's thyroiditis*. The goitre was huge, and she was treated by partial thyroidectomy; the goitre did not recur, and the patient has remained euthyroid for 4 years.

Hashimoto's Thyroiditis

Hashimoto's disease is much more common in women than in men and is probably now the commonest cause of goitre in the UK. At presentation, 75% of patients are euthyroid, 20% are hypothyroid, and the remaining 5% are hyperthyroid and have a disease which closely resembles Graves' disease (known as 'Hashitoxicosis'). About 50% *of patients eventually become hypothyroid due to destruction of the thyroid gland.* Hashimoto's thyroiditis is familial and associated with other organ-specific autoimmune diseases.

The initiating cause of Hashimoto's thyroiditis is unknown. The goitre results from lymphocytic infiltration, thyroid growth stimulating antibodies and occasionally increased TSH levels. The infiltration consists mainly of CD8 positive T cells and B lymphocytes which may form lymphoid follicles with plasma cells. The presence of circulating T lymphocytes sensitized to thyroid antigens (demonstrated by lymphocyte transformation and leucocyte migration inhibition tests) has led to the suggestion that these cells may play a major role in the thyroid damage. Evidence from animal experiments supports this view.

Table 2.3. Evidence for an Autoimmune Aetiology in Hashimoto's Thyroiditis

1. Demonstration of serum autoantibodies which stimulate the growth and division of thyroid cells.
2. Lymphocytes, sensitized specifically to thyroid antigens, are present in the circulation.
3. Prominent lymphocyte infiltration of the thyroid.
4. Induction of experimental, cell-mediated autoimmune thyroiditis by injection of thyroid antigens.
5. Association of other autoimmune diseases is given individuals and in families.

Thyroid tissue taken from a hemithyroidectomized rabbit was mixed with Freund's complete adjuvant and injected back into the same animal. The histological lesion produced in the thyroid resembled Hashimoto's disease. Experimental thyroiditis could be *transferred to other rabbits by lymphocytes,* but not by serum; diseased animals responded well to immunosuppressive therapy. This evidence suggests that cell-mediated immune mechanisms are at least partially responsible for experimental thyroiditis. The precise pathogenesis of Hashimoto's thyroiditis is therefore unclear; it appears that both thyroid growth stimulating antibodies and T lymphocytes specifically sensitized to thyroid antigens (presumably surface antigens) are involved though which, if either, is the primary abnormality is unknown.

The differential diagnosis of Hashimoto's thyroiditis includes simple goitre and subacute (de Quervain's) thyroiditis. The latter usually presents with bilateral painful tender enlargement of the thyroid gland, a low grade fever and general malaise. De Quervain's thyroiditis may be of infective origin since the condition often follows a viral illness. Antibodies to thyroid antigens are usually transient and of low titre; high titre antibodies to thyroid microsomes suggest considerable thyroid damage, and the patient may ultimately develop myxoedema. It is interesting that 70% of the patients with this rare subacute thyroiditis have the HLA antigen B35, suggesting that susceptibility to this disease-is also partly governed by the major histocompatibility complex.

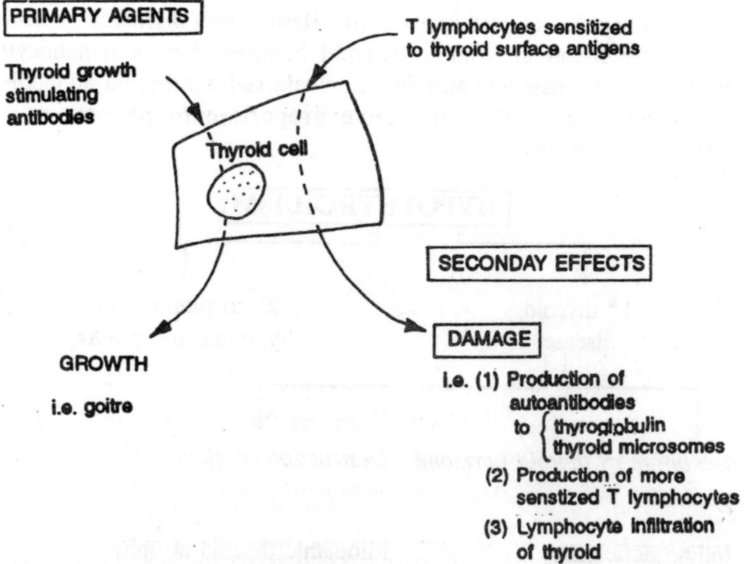

Fig. 2.3. Proposed pathogenesis of Hashimoto's thyroiditis.

Case 3

A 41-year-old woman complained to her doctor that she "always felt cold', and that she had become increasingly clumsy, Although she made no other complaint, her husband had noticed increasing physical and mental lethargy in his wife in recent months. One of her sisters had thyroid disease and her mother suffered from pernicious anaemia. On examination her skin was dry, and her hair was coarse and brittle, Her pulse rate was 58/min, with a blood pressure of 140/70. Her tendon reflexes showed a markedly delayed relaxation phase.

Clinically, she had *hypothyroidism* and this was confirmed by thyroid function tests; her serum T_3 was 0.4 nmol/l (NR 0.8-2.4), T_4 was 4 nmol/l (NR 9-23), and TSH was 12.1 mu/l (normal < 7.0 mu/1). High titres of autoantibodies to thyroid antigens were found in the patient's serum; antithyroglobtilin antibodies were positive to a titre of 1/640, and antibodies to thyroid microsomes to a titre of 1/128000 (haemagglutination assays). This patient therefore had*primary myxoedema* and she was treated with replacement doses of L-thyroxine.

Primary Hypothyroidism (myxoedema)

The term myxoedema is usually applied to the severe form of hypothyroidism in which deposition of mucinous substances leads to thickening of the skin and subcutaneous tissues. There are several causes. Idiopathic thyroid atrophy, like Hashimoto's thyroiditis, is more commonly found in women. Thyroid biopsies show a lymphocytic infiltration, fibrosis and atrophy. Conventional antithyroid antibodies are present in roughly the same proportion of patients as in Hashimoto's thyroiditis.

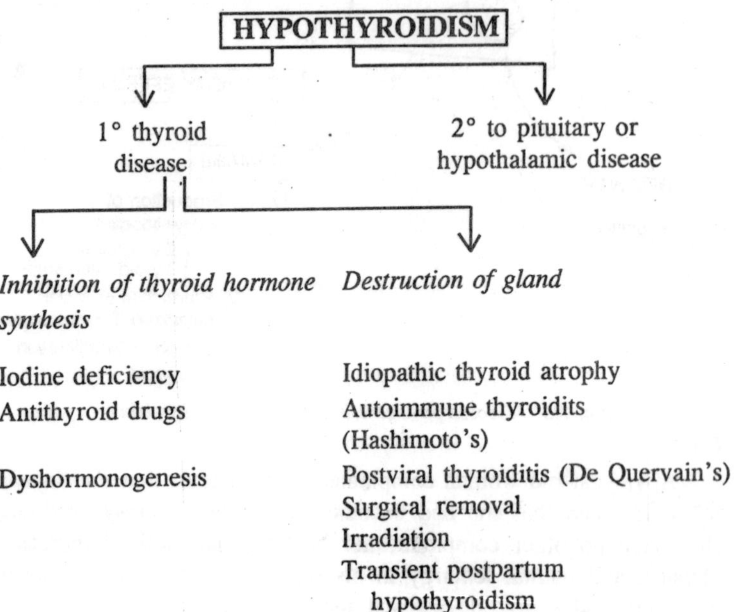

Fig. 2.4. Causes of hypothyroidism.

The pathogenesis of myxoedema is most interesting. Just as there are antibodies which stimulate thyroid cell metabolism (in Graves' disease) and those which stimulate growth (in simple and Hashimoto's goitre), so there are antibodies in primary myxoedema that block both growth and probably metabolism. These appear to be primary antibodies which react with TSH receptors and the reason for their production is unknown.

Transient postpartum hypothyroidism is usually due to reactivation of quiescent thyroiditis and occurs 3-5 months after delivery. It is often associated with a goitre. Most patients improve spontaneously over several months, but in the presence of high titre antibodies to thyroid microsomes such a remission is unlikely.

HYPERTHYROIDISM

The term 'hyperthyroidism' indicates hyperactivity of the thyroid gland and hypersecretion of its hormone. Thyrotoxicosis is used clinically as a synonym for hyperthyroidism. In this country the name of R.J. Graves is often attached to the disease, as he described three cases in 1835. On the Continent the disease is associated with Basedow, who gave a detailed description of the condition in 1840. However, the first clinical description of the disease was published in 1825 by C.H. Parry, a Bath physician. 'Few diseases can have had more synonyms and none more eponyms'.

A useful clinical classification divides thyrotoxicosis into a primary and a secondary variety. In the former, the symptoms are noticed at the same time as the thyroid gland becomes enlarged; in the latter a symptomless goitre has been present for some years before toxic symptoms become apparent. Primary thyrotoxicosis is also known as exophthalmic goitre, because exophthalmos is so characteristically a feature; and secondary thyrotoxicosis as toxic adenoma, because the gland may show single or multiple adenomas and is frequently nodular. It must, however, be recognized that many pathologists, while recognizing the characteristic uniform hyperpiasia in primary thyrotoxicosis, and the tendency to nodular adenomatous formation in secondary thyrotoxicosis, also find many intermediate and mixed types of thyroid pathology which they are quite unable to divide into two distinct types or to correlate with the clinician's differential diagnosis. Moreover an enlarged thyroid that is smooth and uniform on clinical examination may subsequently be found to contain several adenomata, whereas an apparently nodular goitre may show lobulation and diffuse hyperplasia on section.

Studies with radioactive iodine have shown that in diffuse hyperplasia and in adenomatous glands the hormone secreted in normal in quality but excessive in quantity. Autoradiographic techniques have demonstrated that secretory activity is spread diffusely in the majority of adenomatous glands but there are a few examples of secretory activity being confined to the adenoma, the rest of the gland being relatively inactive. Thus, a true toxic adenoma can exist, but it is a rare occurrence.

Secondary thyrotoxicosis usually affects patients over the age of 40; in consequence cardiac manifestations often dominate the clinical picture. A permanent cure will follow adequate subtotal thyroidectomy, but the response to radioactive iodine or antithyroid drugs is less satisfactory than in the primary variety.

Incidence

Thyrotoxicosis is much more common in women than in men,

the proportion being 8 to 1. It is most frequent among young women but may occur at all ages. A familial incidence is not infrequent in primary thyrotoxicosis but is not seen in the secondary type.

Pathology

There is diffuse hyperplasia of the thyroid in primary thyrotoxicosis. The cells are of high columnar type spreading in folds into the centre of each vesicle. Active mitotic division is discernible in many cells and the vesicles contain little colloid. The interstitial tissue shows increased vascularity and, some cases, areas of small round-cell infiltration. Although cellular hyperplasia is present throughout the gland, it is usual to find focal areas of intense hyperplasia corresponding, on autooradiography, to the areas of maximum hormone production. This patchiness of an otherwise diffuse process can be exaggerated until the thyroid appears to contain multiple adenomas of hyperplastic cells separated by bands of fibrous tissue. In contrast to this is the rare case of the solitary toxic adenoma, in which cellular hyperplasia is confined to the adenoma, and the surrounding glands contain inactive cells. This can be classified as secondary thyrotoxicosis because the excessive activity arises in a previously inactive adenoma. It is more common in secondary thyrotoxicosis to find areas of cellular hyperplasia with colloid adenomata and some fibrosis.

Death from thyrotoxicosis is so rare that the limited amount of autopsy material has not provided any consistent pathological findings. Foss and others concluded that there was no structural alteration that could cause death, but they found that in ten of their eleven autopsies, the liver showed patchy necrotic changes. Means confirmed these findings and commented that there was no structural change in the adrenal glands despite the clinical evidence which suggested that adrenal insufficiency might cause death in thyrotoxic crisis.

Aetiology

The cause is unknown, but psychical trauma, sexual maladjustments, or infection frequently precede or initiate the symptoms. Emotional stimuli may act via the hypothalamus and the pituitary thyrotrophic hormone, and experimentally the latter does produce thyroid hyperplasia and hyperthyroidism. However, it has not been unequivocally demonstrated that thyrotoxic patients have a high concentration of thyrotrophic hormone in their blood; this may be due to the fact that the hyperactive thyroid has an increased capacity to inactivate thyrotrophin, as shown by Rawson's experiments on thyroid slices incubated with thyrotrophin. Moreover in Graves' disease, the tendency of the residual portion of the thyroid gland to undergo hyperplasia suggests that it is stimulated by some agent produced outside the gland itself. The most likely agent is the pituitary thyrotrophic hormone.

Werner claims that the thyroid is autonomous in thyrotoxicosis and not influenced by the pituitary, because administration of thyroxine suppresses the radioactive iodine uptake of the normal thyroid but not of. the thyrotoxic gland. The validity of this claim is extremely doubtful because the effect of exogenous thyroxine must depend on the amount by which it alters the total circulating thyroid hormone; the large amount of hormone circulating in thyrotoxicosis will not be altered significantly by the addition of a dose of thyroxine which is sufficient to cause a large increase in the normal amount of circulatory thyroid hormone. Moreover we have not found such a clear-cut distinction between normality and thyrotoxicosis when we have employed these techniques of suppression.

However it is obvious that the normal reciprocal relationship of thyroid and pituitary is disturbed in thyrotoxicosis. The level to which the concentration of circulating thyroxine must rise before it inhibits the output of thyrotrophin is variable and dependent on the hypothalamus. This organ could so alter the sensitivity of the pituitary to thyroxine that the secretion of thyrotrophin could continue at a normal rate despite an abnormally high plasma thyroxine concentration; thyrotoxicosis would then result without any excessive pituitary secretion. The degree of thyroid hyperactivity would still be controlled by the pituitary in that an even greater rise in circulating thyroxine would cause suppression of thyrotrophin secretion from a pituitary only sensitive to very high concentrations of thyroxine. The maintenance of a 'feed-back' control, albeit at excessive levels of thyroxine concentration, is consistent with the waxing and waning of untreated thyrotoxicosis. If the thyroid was indeed autonomous one would expect thyrotoxicosis to pursue a steadily progressive course; the natural history of the disease does not fit with such a concept.

Physiological enlargement of the thyroid is not uncommon at puberty, at the menopause, or during pregnancy, and may proceed to characteristic exophthalmic goitre. Sexual difficulties may precipitate, or cause, hyperthyroidism, by virtue of a close gonadal thyroid, or gonadal-pituitary, interrelationship, but more probably they constitute only another form of psychical trauma or psychoneurosis. The influence of infection is suggested by the disease appearing for the first time during an acute infection, but this may be more apparent than real, since infection is known to aggravate a pre-existing hyperthyroidism.

Since psychical trauma and infection are of such common occurrence it must be postulated that thyrotoxicosis is unlikely to follow unless there is a thyroid diathesis. This view receives some support from the familial incidence of the disease and we have seen three sisters, living apart, who all reacted to an emotional crisis by developing thyrotoxicosis. In fact thyrotoxicosis should be classed in the wide group of psychosomatic diseases. However, it would be unwise to conclude that hyperthyroidism might not be in some cases a spontaneous outburst of endocrine activity for which we have not yet found an adequate explanation.

Clinical Features

General

Fear, anxiety, restlessness, and instability are the characteristic symptoms, but initially the patient may only show a vivacity and dynamic spontaneity-almost an accentuation of pleasing feminine characteristics-and the slight exophthalmos, which gives a glint, and a coquettish look to the eye, is not unattractive. These symptoms are associated with an over-activity of the sympathetic nervous system, which is sensitized by thyroxine.

The cardinal symptoms are exophthalmos, tremor of the hands, tachycardia with palpitations, fatigue, loss of weight, and thyroid enlargement. The tremor is noticed by the patient on holding a pen or pouring out tea, but it is only obvious to the examiner if the patient holds her hands out with the fingers separated. The fine tremor and accompanying hypotonia will then be apparent. The thyroid enlargement is best detected if the examiner stands behind the sitting patient and runs his hands forwards on either side of the neck. Both lobes and the isthmus are enlarged, but one lobe is often larger than the other. Ausculation over the gland will detect a bruit in most cases. Very occasionally thyrotoxicosis can be present in the absence of a palpable thyroid. This usually occurs in men whose necks are thick, but the gland may be retrosternal.

Cardiovascular

The heart rate and pulse rate are almost invariably raised and, in contradistinction to some forms of functional tachycardia, the rapid rate persists during sleep. As the stroke volume and arteriovenous oxygen difference are usually unchanged, the increased heart rate is in part due to the increased oxygen demands of a raised metabolic rate. But thyroxine has a direct stimulatory effect on the heart so that the heart rate is above that required by the metabolic rate. Experimentally, injections of thyroxine increase the sensitivity of the heart to adrenaline, so that this is probably true in thyrotoxicosis also. Younger patients suffer from a persistent sinus tachycardia, accentuated by emotion and exercise. Older patients are more liable to paroxysms of tachycardia, either in regular rhythm or with auricular fibrillation. The effects of age on the heart make it intolerant of thyroxine stimulation, and persistent auricular fibrillation is common, leading in some cases to heart failure but rarely associated with marked constitutional changes of thyrotoxicosis. The response of these cases to digitalis is poor.

Gross peripheral vasodilatation causes a marked increase in pulse pressure with an increase in systolic and a considerable decrease in diastolic pressure. The pulse may be collapsing in character and capillary pulsation is sometimes visible. The vasomotor system is unstable, and paroxysmal vasodilatation is shown by flushing of the face and neck in a warm atmosphere or during excitement, as also occurs at the climacteric.

Electrocardiographic changes occur in some *30* per cent. of patients and characteristically consist of tall P and T waves, and low or slurred R waves, findings which have also been reported with a high sympathetic tone. A prolonged P-R interval may also be found. Cardiac enlargement is found radiologically in some 30 per cent. of patients. It is usually to the left, and the pulmonary arc and right auricle may be prominent-giving the so-called ham-shaped shadow. The association of auricular fibrillation and goitre must always raise the suspicion of thyrotoxicosis. But the absence of confirmatory physical signs often makes it difficult to decide whether an increase of thyroid function is responsible for the cardiac arrhythmia. The basal metabolic rate is not of diagnostic value as it is raised in any form of heart failure, but techniques using radioactive iodine will give an accurate measure of thyroid activity.

Ocular Signs

There are a number of classical signs, descriptive of ocular abnormalities in thyrotoxicosis, which arc of historical and examination interest:

Von Grafe's Sign

On looking down slowly, the upper eyelid lags behind, so that the white sclerotic becomes visible above the pupil.

Joffroy's Sign

On looking upwards, there is no wrinkling of the forehead (occipito-frontalis muscle).

Stellwag's Sign

Absence, or infrequency, of blinking. *MMus' Sign.* Inability to converge, or sustain convergency.

Dalrymple's Sign

Wide palpebral fissure.

It is advisable, however, from the point of view of aetiology and of prognosis, to differentiate two conditions: upper lid retraction and lid-lag, and exophthalmos. The former is manifested by the relationship of the upper edge of the iris to the upper eyelid, and the latter by the relationship of the lower edge of the iris to the lower lid, in both cases the more severe degrees being shown by an intervening white sclerotic area. Upper lid retraction is produced by cervical sympathetic stimulation (contraction of Muller's palpebral muscle) or by sympathomimetic drugs (e.g. adrenaline) which act on the neuromuscular junction, even when the sympathetic nerve is sectioned. Thyroxine sensitizes the end-organ to such stimulation as it does in other sites, e.g. the heart. Experimentally, upper lid retraction is usually, but not invariably, associated with dilatation of the pupil. Sectiori of the cervical sympathetic nerve is followed by ptosis and enophthalmos. The fact that the pupils in thyrotoxicosis are not usually dilated does not contra-indicate the sympathetic mechanism of upper lid retraction, since such experimental dissociation can be produced by appropriate dosage. Both experimentally and clinically, the, condition may be asymmetrical in degree, or completely unilateral for a period, so the additional factor of local responsiveness must be postulated. Thyroid feeding occasionally produces lid retraction, but it is rarity. It is important to remember that abolition of the thyrotoxicosis will abolish upper lid retraction and lid-lag; the latter does not occur with myxoedema.

Exophthalmos is a different story, and a more complex one. Experimentally, in some species, it may be produced in moderate degree by thyroid feeding or sympathetic stimulation. It is probable that this is true also in man, although actual records of it resulting from thyroid therapy show that it is exceptional. However, sympathetic nerve sensitivity produced by thyroxine may play a part in thyrotoxicosis, by the contraction of intraorbital smooth muscle, producing exophthalmos and also obstructing venous return, with resulting oedema of orbital muscles. Clinical experience, however, shows that such sympathetic nerve stimulation is not the major cause, since, unlike upper lid retraction, abolition of thyrotoxicosis by radical measures does not abolish and may even increase the expohithaalmos. Some measure of improvement may be obtained if cases are treated early enough, e.g. by thyroidectomy, and this slight improvement is probably a measure of the small part played by sympathetic nerve stimulation, after sensitization by thyroxine.

A further discussion of exophthalmos will be found in the chapter on malignant exophthalmos.

Metabolism

The essential action of the thyroid gland is an acceleration of metabolism, as was first shown by Magnus Levy in 1895. With expophthalmic goitre the basal metabolic rate is always raised. But, in about 10 percent. of cases, the increase is not sufficient to elevate the metabolic rate above the upper limit of the normal range.

The increased metabolism is evidenced by the negative nitrogen balance, the loss of weight, and the increased appetite, which often becomes ravenous; patients may nevertheless progressively lose weight owing to the preponderance of catabolism over anabolism. The liver is depleted of glycogen, the fat depots of the body tend to disappear, and the negative nitrogen balance, together with creatinuria, indicate the breakdown of muscle tissue. Another manifestation of increased metabolism is ability to stand cold and an intolerance of heat. Some degree of pyrexia is not infrequent, especially with slight infections. Hyperglycaemia and glycosuria are not uncommon, being probably due to the acceleration of glycogenolysis in the liver. Intestinal absorption of sugar is also facilitated by thyroxine. However, true diabetes mellitus is probably not more common among exophthalmic goitre patients than among normal individuals.

The blood cholesterol values may be subnormal, e.g. 80 mg. (normal 150 to 220 mg. per cent.), in contrast to the raised values in myxoedoma. Excretion of sodium and chloride (in sweat as well as in urine) may also be increased, and this may partially explain the loss of strength, disproportional to the wasting. Muscular weakness may also be due to a myasthenic element, and in some cases true myasthenia gravis, responsive to neostigmine, is associated with thyrotoxicosis.

Calcium and Phosphorus Metabolism

Demineralization of the skeleton and softening of the bones in hyperthyroidism was first observed by von Recklinghausen in 1891 while doing an autopsy. Although spontaneous fracture in thyrotoxicosis is infrequent, rarefaction of bones is not uncommonly seen during systematic radiographic examination of thyrotoxic patients; and the negative calcium balance revealed by biochemical studies draws attention to the frequency of a disturbed calcium and phosphorus metabolism in thyrotoxicosis.

Most of the original biochemical work was carried out by Aub and his collaborators, who found normal serum calcium and phosphorus values (occasionally slightly lower than normal), but a negative calcium balance, with the calcium loss predominantly in the faeces; there is also a moderate elevation of serum phosphatase values. Successful thyroidectomy tended to abolish these findings, although the biochemical reversion to normality was early but the recalcification of bone often delayed. Since a positive calcium balance is found in myxoedema, and since, experimentally, thyroid extract produces a negative calcium balance, it seemed probable that the disturbance of calcium and phosphorus metabolism was entirely due to excessive thyroxine secretion. However, Beaumont, Dodds, and Robertson found that in 50 per cent. of thyrotoxic patients calcium and phosphorus metabolism were normal; there was no relationship between the degree of negative calcium balance and the severity of thyrotoxicosis; and successful thyroidectomy might leave the disturbance of calcium metabolism unchanged. They concluded that there was another factor involved in some cases. This factor might be a coexisting hyperparathyroidism but the blood chemistry and the bone lesion do not support this theory. Studies with radioactive calcium show an increased rate of both deposition and resorption of bone in thyrotoxicosis. In some cases thyrotoxicosis is associated with a post-menopausal osteoporosis, in which lack of sex steroids may be an aetiological factor.

Behaviour and Emotion

The patient is restless, anxious, unable to relax and prone to emotional outbursts. An intense desire to be doing something all the time is frustrated by constant fatigue and lack of concentration. Neurotic tendencies are exaggerated, and occasionally acute psychosis arises, usually of a manic type.

Sex Function

Disturbances of menstruation and pregnancy in thyrotoxicosis might be anticipated from the evidence discussed in the physiological section. Menstruation is often normal in mild degrees of thyrotoxicosis, but in more severe cases oligomenorrhoea or amenorrhoea occurs in more than 50 per cent of such patients. A return of normal menstruation after thyroidectomy is usual but not invariable. Menorrhagia is a rarity. Impotence in males may be met with and may respond to testosterone.

In pregnant animals it is physiological for the thyroid to enlarge under the stimulus of thyrotrophin. Similarly the thyroid gland becomes palpable in some 30 per cent. of pregnant women, and the basal metabolism is raised in most women in the last trimester of pregancy to plus 35 per cent, but clinical hyperthyroidism is-not usual. Nevertheless, thyrotoxicosis does occur in a small number of pregnant women, and it would appear that pregnancy may be a precipitating factor. Marine found that there was a relative iodine deficiency during pregnancy and that minute amounts of iodine usually prevented or controlled thyroid enlargement. It is interesting to note that when thyrotoxicosis becomes evident during pregnancy, the thyroid enlargement may be nodular or diffuse, and histological section may show a nodular colloid goitre with areas of glandular hyperplasia: when pregnancy supervenes on a pre-existing hyperthyroidism, the latter ondition may not change in severity or may be ameliorated.

For more severe cases methylthiouracil or carbimazole may be necessary. Subtotal thyroidectomy can be performed safely but is seldom necessary. If the thyrotoxicosis is very acute and severe, operation is advisable.

In many instances patients become pregnant when receiving methylthiouracil in the long-term treatment of thyrotoxicosis. Under these circumstances the disease appears to be ameliorated in pregnancy, so that the patient's thyroid function remains normal despite a decrease in the dosage of antithyroid drug, and she will usually pass through the last weeks of pregnancy without treatment. It is advisable always to decrease the dose of any of the thiouracil group of drugs during pregnancy and to discontinue their use in the later stages because their continued use makes the foetal thyroid goitrous and occasionally transient hypothyroidism is seen in the new-born baby. As thiouracil (and its derivatives) is excreted in milk, no mother receiving this drug should suckle her child.

Gastro-Intestinal Tract

Gastro-intestinal symptoms, of which diarrhoea, abdominal discomfort after meals, and nausea are the commonest, occur in some 30 per cent of patients. Intractable vomiting may precede a crisis. Epigastric pain may simulate that of gastric ulcer, and occasionally the latter is a complication. Upper abdominal pain may rarely by sufficiently acute and severe in its onset to simulate an acute abdomen, but in one such case hyperaemia of the pancreas was found on laparotomy. Achlorhydria is not infrequent, and there is radiological evidence of increased tone and movement in both the small and large intestine. All these changes may be produced experimentally by thyroid feeding, and tend to disappear after a successful thyroidectomy for thyrotoxicosis. Atrophic gastritis may be found at autopsy. Occasionally the presenting features are gastro-intestinal, this constituting a variety of *forme fruste*.

Pretibial Myxoedema

This curious condition is not associated with hypothyroidism, but occurs under the same conditions as exophthalmic ophthalmoplegia and is found in association with it. A mucinous infiltration causes symmetrical indurated swelling on the front of both shins just above the ankle. The skin may be puckered like pigskin or reddened, suggesting inflammation. Very occasionally clubbing of the toes and fingers with a periosteal reaction accompanies the condition.

The skin changes are not influenced by the systemic or local administration of thyroid, or any other substance.

Other symptoms

Troublesome perspiration, sometimes very profuse, results from sympathetic nervous stimulation and increased metabolism. This is associated with a pathological thirst, which may never be adequately satisfied, especially in warm weather.

Crisis

An acute exacerbation of all the symptoms may occur in very hot weather, with infection, or after thyroidectomy performed with inadequate medical preparation. The manifestations may be predominantly cardiac (extreme tachycardia), cerebral (acute mania and delirium), or gastro-intestinal (diarrhoea, vomiting, and abdominal pain). In each type, profound collapse and muscular weakness is found and the condition can be fatal. Hyperpyrexia may occur and abdominal pain can be so severe as to stimulate an acute abdominal catastrophe.

THYROTOXICOSIS IN CHILDREN

'This condition is comparatively rare less than 1 per cent. of all cases of thyrotoxicosis occurring in children under 12 and 4 per cent in children from 12 to 16 years old. There is therefore an abrupt rise in incidence at puberty, which, like pregnancy and the climacteric, may precipitate thyrotoxicosis. There is a familial incidence in thyrotoxicosis, and Cockayne believed the thyroid diathesis to be an irregular Mendelian dominant. The case of Osterreicher, in which a woman with chronic thyrotoxicosis gave birth to 10 children, of whom 8 subsequently developed thyrotoxicosis, is, however, an extreme example of its familial incidence. A positive family incidence of thyrotoxicosis, including adults, is found in some 20 per cent. of all cases, but it rarely involves more than 2 or 3 members of the existing generation. In juvenile thyrotoxicosis, girls are affected about five times more frequently than boys. The treatment is the same as for adults, except that in relatively mild cases symptomatic treatment is more likely to be successful than in adults, and an expectant attitude is often justified.

Diagnosis

Usually this is obvious clinically to an observer not lacking in awareness of the condition, but occasionally one of the symptoms may be so obtrusive as to hide the underlying thyrotoxicosis. In these circumstances the term *forme fruste is* used, a name originally applied by Marie in 1883 to those forms of thyrotoxicosis in which exophthalmos and enlargement of the thyroid were minimal or clinically undetected. In such a typical case, as in other instances of *forme fruste,* the initial diagnosis may be congestive heart failure, auricular fibrillation, diabetes mellitus, gastro-intestinal disturbance, osteoporosis, idiopathic wasting, psychoneurosis, psychosis, peripheral oedema, generalized pruritus, myasthenia, gravis, or progressive muscular atrophy.

A detailed differential diagnosis of all these conditions would serve less purpose than a plea for increased awareness of the possibility of an underlying thyrotoxicosis, especially since the majority of these conditions are possible manifestations or complications of thyrotoxicosis. True myasthenia gravis and progressive muscular atrophy are rarely present, but may be simulated. A form of the latter apparently directly related to the thyrotoxicosis is called chronic thyrotoxic myopathy, and another variety, usually fatal, acute thyrotoxic bulbar palsy. Hypertension associated with a considerably raised diastolic pressure is unlikely to be due to thyrotoxicosis, although some cardiologists claim otherwise. In this, as in other conditions, mentioned above, the abolition of thyrotoxic symptoms by successful thyroidectomy is often disappointing in its failure to relieve a coincident but not directly related condition. True myasthenia gravis associated with thyrotoxicosis, and responding to neostigmine, may, however, be appreciably relieved by thyroidectomy, and this may be explained by the resulting involution of a coincident thymus and lymphoid hyperplasia, since thymectomy is of value in myasthenia gravis.

Occasionally a case of idiopathic coma turns out to be of thyrotoxic origin, and we have seen one such case in which autopsy findings were those of thyrotoxicosis, and there was hyperaemia of the brain and meninges, but no other explanation of the comatose condition. The patient had probably had the thyrotoxicosis for some time, but without seeking medical advice, and died in a state of coma of acute onset, within a few hours of admission to hospital, without any clinical history being available. Zondek has also described such cases.

Anxiety state is often mistaken for hyperthyroidism, especially as there may be a coincident enlargement of the thyroid gland. The tachycardia, however, is more variable than that of thyrotoxicosis, and the sleeping pulse rate is normal. There is also an absence of other features of thyrotoxicosis, and loss of weight is rarely a feature, although, of course, anxiety states may coexist with thyrotoxicosis.

Rarely, patients with thyrotoxicosis show pigmentaton of the face, and body, due to an excessive deposition of melanin, histologically indistinguishable from that of Addison's disease, although the mucous membranes are never involved. It seems, however, that the adrenal cortex is not functionally disturbed in such cases, but very occasionally there is a coincidence of thyrotoxicosis and Addison's disease in the one patient.

When the clinical diagnosis is uncertain help may be obtained by laboratory aids, particularly the estimation of basal metabolic rate and measurement of various phases of the iodine cycle by radioactive iodine.

Determination of the basal metabolic rate requires careful preparation of patient, who must be fasting and tranquil. Sedation is usually necessary. Serial determinations are of far more value than a single measurement. In about 10 per cent. of thyrotoxics the initial basal metabolic rate is not raised above the limits of normal, but confirmation of the diagnosis is obtained by noting a fall in the rate after iodide medication.

Radioactive iodine techniques are playing an increasing important role as diagnostic aids, but the variety of apparatus used makes it impossible to have a uniform standard. Therefore each centre has to define the limits of normality and the physiological significance of the technique used.

Estimation of protein-bound iodine is fraught with technical difficulties and is available in very few laboratories. Blood cholesterol determinations are of some value in that a level of over 200 mg. per 100 ml, takes the diagnosis of thyrotoxicosis very unlikely.

Course and Progress

The natural course of the disease is gradually downhill, but waves of remission and exacerbation occur. Apart from any specific treatment, recovery occasionally occurs and even myxoedema may eventually develop.

Treatment by radical measures produces a cure in a large proportion of cases. A small percentage, perhaps 5 per cent, are never fully controlled or relapse soon after each period of treatment. Even in those who are greatly improved some residual evidence of a pre-existing hyperthyroidism may remain, e.g, exophthalmos, auricular fibrillation, or neurotic symptoms. Weight-gain after treatment may be excessive and is related to the alteration in energy balance, caloric intake exceeding the demands of a lowered metabolic rate. Finally subtotal thyroidectomy or radioactive iodine therapy may be followed by permanent myxoedema.

Treatment

In the last ten years wide practical experience has been gained in use of antithyroid drugs and radioactive iodine. At the same time more adequate medical preparation has led to improved results from thyroid surgery. Consequently the treatment of thyrotoxicosis can be considered in relation to each patient rather than as a rigid routine applied regardless of individual requirements.

The dominant position of iodine in the therapy of thyrotoxicosis has been usurped by other methods, although it retains an important role in the preparation of patients for thyroidectomy. However, we should examine what Means has called 'that remarkable phenomenon, the specific response of the patient with thyrotoxicosis to iodine', because it remains a dramatic treatment whose mechanism is still poorly understood.

The clinical facts are clear: iodine does not lower the metabolic rate of the normal subject, but produces a rapid inclination of symptoms in the thyrotoxic patient together with a slowing of the pulse, a rising body-weight, and a falling metabolic rate. The decrease in metabolic rate is as rapid as that occurring after thyroidectomy (without pre-operative iodine therapy). However, there is little correlation between degree of response and dose of iodine. Maximal response is brought about by 2 min. of Lugol's iodine daily so that no greater response can be elicited from doses ranging up to 90 min. a day. The minimal effective dose is, of course, far is excess of the daily iodine requirements for hormone synthesis. The beneficial effect is maximal after two to three weeks but later the effect gradually wears off. As Means says, iodine has 'no effect on the duration or direction or progress of the disease; it affects at any one time merely its intensity'.

The failure of iodine to modify the action of thyroxine indicates that its therapeutic action is directed to the thyroid or pituitary. The diminution of cell height and reaccumulation of colloid in the thyrotoxic thyroid treated with iodine is good evidence of decreased activity, either from a diminished output of thyrotrophin or some interference with its action on the thyroid. Rawson's experiments on the *in vitro* inactivation of thyrotrophin by iodine led him to conclude that iodine interfered with the action of thyrotrophin in the thyroid. His conclusion was supported by Mason and Dedman who investigated the iodine response of the rat, by measuring the uptake of radioactive phosphorus by the thyroid. The thyroidal uptake of phosphorus has been shown to be an index of thyroid response of thyrotrophin. These workers found that iodine decreased the phosphorus uptake of the intact rat's thyroid towards the lowest normal level but never to the low values obtained after hypophysectomy or thyroxine administration. Rats with a high normal uptake (i.e. under maximum normal thyrotrophin stimulation) had the greatest fall in thyroidal phosphorus uptake after iodine; but rats with lower initial uptakes had a smaller decrease. Thus the effect of iodide depended on the activity of the pituitary-thyroid axis. The full response to iodine was not directly dependent on dosage and was obtained six hours after administration. After one month of iodine treatment the effect was not so great.

The effect of iodine on the rat's pituitary-thyroid relationships was very similar to the effects of iodine in man. Further experiments showed that, in the hypophysectomized rat, iodine did not alter the response of the thyroid to injected thyrotrophin, given in doses usually used for assay work. However, the crucial experiment was the production of a high thyroidal phosphorus uptake (of the same order as found in the most active of intact rats) by injecting thyrotrophin into the hypophysectomized rat. Under these conditions iodine did prevent the full action of thyrotrophin on the thyroid. The logical conclusion is that iodine prevents the thyroid from giving a maximum response to the stimulus of thyrotrophin. One does not have to postulate any interference with the pituitary secretion of thyrotrophin.

Thiouracil Group of Drugs

In the section on thyroid physiology it has been indicated that thiouracil acts by preventing the synthesis of thyroxine. The hyperplasia of the thyroid that results from thiouracil is produced by excessive secretion of thyrotrophic hormone and may be associated with considerable enlargement of the thyroid. Blood iodine studies show that the use of thiouracil is followed by a fall in the protein-bound iodine to normal or subnormal limits.

Thiouracil was replaced in clinical practice by the less toxic and more potent derivatives, methylthiouracil and propylthiouracil. More recently, related compounds with the same action, carbimazole and methimazole have proved even more effective. Carbimazole is at present the best of the range.

In view of the potential toxicity of these drugs it is advisable to use the minimum initial dose that is likely to be effective. Methylthiouracil or propylthiouracil in a dose of 50 mg. four times a day, or carbimazole *(Neo-Mercazole)*, 10 mg. three times a day, will be suitable for the first three weeks of treatment.

Initial clinical improvement is shown by diminished perspiration, diminished tremor and excitability, gain in weight, and general well-being. Slowing of the pulse rate is sometimes delayed. Excessive lid retraction tends to disappear but exophthalmos may persist or increase, as might be expected from the increased secretion of thyrotrophin. For the same reason the size of the goitre may increase and the gland become more vascular. Nevertheless continued therapy over many months is often associated with a regression in the size of the goitre and the exophthalmos.

The possibility of increasing the exophthalmos and the size of the goitre is a disadvantage of thiouracil therapy but the frequency of these complications may be greatly diminished by regular administration of the minimum effective dose of the drug.

A method of maintaining a constant level of circulating thyroid hormone is the combined administration of methylthiouracil and L-thyroxine, 0.05 mg three to four times daily. It has the added advantage of not requiring frequent adjustments in the dosage of the antithyroid drug.

The increasing vascularity of the thyroid with thiouracil therapy is a particular danger if subtotal thyroidectomy is ultimately considered. Administration of iodide will diminish the vascularity, and such therapy is always required prior to operation.

The toxic effects of thiouracil are shared by the more recently discovered derivatives, although the incidence of toxic reactions is now very low. Agranulocytosis is the most serious toxic effect, its onset being so sudden that routine blood counts do not give prior warning. Other manifestations of toxicity include *thrombocytopenia*, generalized enlargement of lymph glands and spleen, fever, nausea, and dermatitis. This catalogue appears extensive but the low incidence of toxic reactions with carbimazole enables it to be used with little risk to the patient. Although sensitivity to these drugs is usually manifested in the first two months of their administration, toxic effects can occur later. All patients should be warned to report any physical illness or sore throat, in case the symptoms are due to agranulocytosis, but it is obviously harmful to give the impression that the therapeutic agent is an unusually dangerous drug. Moreover it must be remembered that leucopenia and splenomegaly can occur in untreated *thyrotoxicosis*, in which case thiouracil will cause a rise in the white cell count and a regression in the size of the spleen.

Thiouracil derivatives may be used as an efficient pre-operative measure or as long-term treatment for thyrotoxicosis. In the latter case treatment should be continued for six to eighteen months. Experience has shown that short-term treatment is followed by immediate relapse in a high percentage of cases, but a prolonged course is far less likely to be followed by a prompt return of thyrotoxicosis. After the initial phase, during which thyrotoxicosis becomes controlled, the dose may be reduced gradually to a quarter or one-third of the initial amount, and therapy continued at that level.

There is no doubt that the majority of patients experience full relief from thyrotoxicosis when treated with thiouracil derivatives. These drugs are less effective in secondary thyrotoxicosis, the response to treatment being far less predictable than in primary *Graves' disease*. Apart from this the goitrogenic effect of thiouracil-like drugs hinders rather than helps the treatment of an adenomatous goitre or one that is causing pressure symptoms.

Although this type of medical treatment offers the patient an excellent chance of being rid of the disease for a considerable period of time, a five-year follow-up from the cessation of an adequate course of treatment reveals a relapse rate which is considerably in excess of that following expert subtotal thyroidectomy. Relapsed thyrotoxicosis will respond to carbimazole perfectly satisfactorily, but the patient may be unwilling to undergo further medical treatment. The decision to use long-term therapy with antithyroid drugs or to use them as preoperative treatment depends largely on the quality of the surgery available and the patient's own inclinations. No dogmatic statement can be made on this subject, which must be decided according to the particular circumstances of each case.

An alternative medical treatment, which has gained favour because of the absence of toxicity, is the administration of sodium or potassium percholorate. This drug acts like thiocyanate in its inhibition of the thyroidal idodide-collecting mechanism. Thus thyroid functin is curbed by depriving the gland of its raw material as compared with the inhibition of hormone synthesis by the thiouracil group of compounds.

Perchlorate has a transient action requiring three doses a day to continue inhibitin of the thyroid's iodine uptake; 300-800 mg. per day is a sufficient amount to control thyrotoxicosis in most cases. The response of teh disease is less rapid and less predictable than after carbimazole. Moreover perchlorate cannot be used in conjunction with iodidee therapy, which makes it unsuitable for routine pre-operative use. These disadvantages offwet its lack of toxicity and, although we have observed some good results in long-term therapy, we do not consider it superior to carbimazole.

Thyroidectomy

Subtotal *thyroidectomy* is indicated in the following types of case: (1) Secondary thyrotoxicosis. (2) When pressure symptoms are present, or the thyroid enlargement is very considerable. (3) As elective therapy in primary thyrotoxicosis, as it gives a reasonable chance of eventual cure without prolonged treatment.

The risks of operation are increased if a previous thyroidectomy has been performed, particularly if the recurrent laryngeal nerve has been damaged. Similarly the presence of auricular fibrillation or heart failure is a contra-indication to immediate operation, and requires adequate medical treatment before surgery can be considered. Satisfactory results are more difficult to obtain by surgery if the thyroid is not definitely enlarged. Increasing exophthalmos is likely to be aggravated by thyroidectomy, but the post-operative administration of thyroid extract helps to minimize this risk.

For mild cases of thyrotoxicosis pre-operative preparation with iodine alone is sufficient. Iodine is usually given in the form of Lugol's iodine, 5-10 min. thrice daily, for 14-21 days prior to operation, as this is the period in which maximum amelioration by iodine can be produced. Postponement of operation may mean that the patient escapes from the effect of iodine with the recúrrence of symptoms and the danger of post-operative crisis.

Severe thyrotoxicosis is not fully controlled by iodine alone. As the response to thiouracil derivatives is poor after the administration of iodine, it is a great mistake to give iodine to the severe thyrotoxic, and then discover that it does not control the disease sufficiently to make thyroidectomy a safe procedure. The wiser course is the employment of carbimazole for three to six weeks, accompanied by Lugol's iodine for two weeks immediately prior to operation.

Adequate pre-operative therapy has rendered surgery in skilled hands safe, the mortality being 0.1 per cent. The surgeon removes some seven-eighths of the thyroid gland, leaving a posterior layer that will prevent interference with the parathyroid glands embedded behind. Nevertheless, tetany occasionally supervenes, but serial sections of the removed glands demonstrate that in the majority of such cases the tetany is not due to removal of parathyroid glands and it is therefore probably due to interference with supply. It is usually transitory and its treatment is indicated in the section on etany.

Radiation and Radioactive Iodine

Earlier attempts at destroying, or inhibiting, the thyroid gland by deep radiation were of only ineffective but often produced burning of the skin. Refinements in the technique of deep radiation indicated that thyrotoxicosis could be treated satisfactorily by this method, but external application of radiation has now given way to the use of radioactive

Using the eight-day half-life isotope ^{131}I, good results have been obtained. The vidity of the hyperactive thyroid for iodine allows a therapeutic concentration of the isotope to irradiate the gland from within the overactive cell, while the total body radiation remains very low.

The possibility of long-term carcinogenesis or of gene mutation by radiation is suggested from animal experiments and, although the chance. of such occurrences in the human is remote, it is usual to reserve radioactive therapy for patients over 40 years old. This form of therapy is particularly suitable for thyrocardiac disease and relapsed thyrotoxicosis after thyroidectomy as it is extremely rare for any immediate ill effect to arise. However, Pers has reported a thyrotoxic crisis after radioactive iodine and we have seen the occasional exacerbation of heartfailure. There is some evidence that post-therapy exophthalmos is less likely to occur after radioactive iodine than any other form of treatment. This is true in our experience, and we have treated several cases with severe exophthalmos and have been impressed by the improvement in the eye condition. The clinical response to therapy is slow, so that the severe thyrotoxic must be given carbimazole as an initial treatment. Some authorities prefer this routine, but we do not consider it necessary for the majority of patients. The advisability of radioactive iodine for secondary thyrotoxicosis depends on the size and duration of the goitre. Adenomatous glands do not respond uniformly to radio-active iodine and the large goitre causing pressure symptoms is unlikely to disappear. These disadvantages of radiation therapy must be weighed against the risks of surgery in the individual patient. It must be remembered that radioactive iodine is no way prejudices the later use of thyroidectomy.

The aim of radioactive iodine therapy is to restore normal thyroid function by one oral dose of ^{131}1. At one time multiple small doses were tried but this method is far more difficult to control than the one-dose technique. However, calculation of the dose still remains a problem. The accepted method is based on the thyroid weight, estimated by the clinician, and the thyroidal uptake and biological half-life of a tracer dose. Unfortunately complete evaluation of the iodine cycle in the gland has proved to be of little help in refining the limits of dosage. Moreover the behaviour of the treatment dose can vary widely from that of an initial tracer dose. Correct dosage awaits the perfecting of some measurement of thyroid sensitivity to radiation. At the present moment a single dose of 7-15 millicuries (mainly depending on thyroid size) gives satisfactory results. A second dose can be given after an interval of 4-6 months if the patient's condition has not been fully controlled. Transient myxoedema lasting 2-3 months may occur with eventual return to normal thyroid function, but 10-20 per cent. of patients are rendered permanently hypothyroid. The long-term results over a five-year period are fairly good, but the method is capable of further refinement.

General Medical Treatment

Since, thyrotoxicosis is commonly preceded by, or associated with, an anxiety neurosis, some form of psychotherapy is often indicated. Reassurance and suggestion, and a willing ear, are usually adequate, and more specialized techniques are rarely required. In acute mania associated with thyrotoxicosis adequate preparation with carbimazole should precede thyroidectomy.

Sedation plays an important ancillary role in treatment, and for this, the drug of choice is phenobarbitone, ¼ ½ gr. three times a day. The use of iodine as a therapeutic measure by itself is not now to be recommended in view of the efficiency of alternative treatments. Iodine temporarily modifies thyrotoxicosis but has no effect on the natural history of the disease. Moreover specific methods of therapy become inefficient if iodine has been administered previously for any length of time.

The treatment of auricular fibrillation is the removal of the causative thyrotoxicosis, and before this is secured the administration of digitalis is never satisfactory. However, full digitalization is indicated if heart failure is present in order to achieve some amelioration of the cardiac condition. Subsequent to adequate antithyroid treatment, if normal rhythm does not return automatically, quinidine, 2 gr. three times a day, increased to 5 gr. three times a day, will often be effective within a week.

In a thyroid crisis, whether spontaneous or post-operative, methods of suppressing thyroxine secretion are relatively ineffective. Large doses of iodine have been recommended for many years, but its effect is not dramatic. The thiouracil derivatives, inhibiting further hormone synthesis but not secretion of synthesized thyroxine, are too slow in their action. The breakdown in homeostais during a crisis may be related to adrenal failure. Consequently large doses of cortisone are suggested and we have seen excellent response to such treatment. There is also a very good case for the use of chlorpromazine as a 'cooling' agent, the initial reports show it to be a valuable drug. An oxygen tent in useful as there is a great demand by the tissues for oxygen.

MALIGNANT EXOPHTHALMOS

Definition

A condition of severe exophthalmos, associated with apparent paralysis of the extraocular muscles of the orbit, occurring in the presence or absence of thyrotoxicosis and seldome relieved by the abolition of thyrotoxicosis.

Aetiology and Pathology

Thyroxine administration to man or animals does not produce exophthalmos even when given in massive doses. On the other hand the injection of thyrotrophin hormone does produce exophthalmos in the guinea-pig. This action has been shown to be independent of the thyroid gland and of the sympathetic system. In man, the administration of thiouracil may cause exophthalmos, in the presence of increased thyrotrophin secretion as indicated by the cytology of the thyroid and in association with a marked diminution in circulating thyroid hormone. However, a simple relationship between the amount of thyrotrophin secreted by the pituitary and the degree of exophthalmos cannot be valid as exophthalmos does not accompany myxoedema, a condition known to be associated with an increased secretion of thyrotrophin. Certainly high serum levels of thyrotrophin have been recorded in exophthalmic ophthalmoplegia but no higher than those found in myxoedema and Querido and Lameyer failed to detect any correlation between the serum concentration of thyrotrophin and the degree and progression of exophthalmos. Rawson put forward an ingenious theory to overcome these objections. He showed experimentally that thyroid slices incubated with thyrotrophin inactivated this hormone. The capacity of the thyroid to inactivate thyrotrophin was dependent on the activity of the gland. Slices of thyroid taken from a patient with thyrotoxicosis inactivated significantly greater quantities of thyrotrophin than normal. He considered that an alteration of the balance between secretion and inactivation of thyrotrophin might explain apparent anomalies between estimates of the level of circulating thyrotrophin and the occurrence of exophthalmos. However, the problem is still undecided and is likely to remain so until more is known of the chemistry of thyrotrophin. There is a suggestion from experimental work that the pituitary secretes two types of thyrotrophin; one stimulating hormone synthesis in the thyroid, the other causing exophthalmos. The evidence for the dual thyrotrophin theory is, as yet, inconclusive, but Dobyns and Wilson have put forward most interesting data in support of the existence of an exophthalmos-producing substance secreted by the pituitary as a separate entity from thyrotrophin. Their method of assay, using a minnow, has been rightly criticized by Langford but their concept is supported on different experimental grounds by Adams and Purves. However, Brain concludes that 'there is no conclusive evidence that thyrotoxicosis alone produces exophthalmos, and there is now little evidence that the thryotrophic hormone, at any rate acting alone, is responsible for it'.

As regards the histology of the orbital muscles, Brain, who has differentiated the clinical syndrome, records the observations of Naffziger and Stallard, and further studies by Turnbull. The muscles are enlarged five or more times the normal size; they are oedematous and show loss of muscle structure with fragmentation and destruction of muscle fibres, fibrosis, hyalinization, and round cell infiltration. The 'paralysis' appears to be due to mechanical obstruction to movement in the much-swollen contents of the orbit, and to involve planes of movement rather than individual muscles.

The histological similarity of the round cell infiltration of muscles affected by myasthenia gravis and the occurrence of neostigmine-sensitive myasthenia in association with exophthalmic ophthalmoplegia indicates that some neuromuscular mechanism may be involved. Rundle and Pochin also noted an increase in intraorbital fat, and found no essential difference in the pathology of the orbital contents in malignant exophthalmos or in relatively mild exophthalmos associated with thyrotoxicosis.

Brain has drawn attention to the frequency of shock or emotion in the production of malignant exophthalmos, and Simpson has stressed the potential role of the hypothalamus.

In idiopathic malignant exophthalmos Brain and Turnbull showed that the thyroid gland was not typical of thyrotoxicosis, and there was no constant pathological picture.

Incidence

The disease is most commonly found in middle age, 80 per cent. of Brain's original series being over 40 years of age, whereas in Graves' disease the majority are under 40. In Brain's series the ratio of males to females was about equal, whereas in Graves' disease there are nearly ten times as many women as men affected. In the post-thyroidectomy group Brain found four times as many males as females, which, considering the original incidence of thyrotoxicosis, indicates a marked susceptibility of males to develop exophthalmic ophthalmoplegia.

Clinical Features

There are three major groups:

1. In association with thyrotoxicosis.
2. After thyroidectomy (or treatment with goitrogenic drugs).
3. Idiopathic, i.e. in the absence of any evidence of severe disturbance of thyroid function.

Thyrotoxic Group

Severe exophthalmos may be associated with severe Graves' disease, but rarely, if ever, with secondary thyrotoxicosis. If it is sufficiently severe, paralysis of movement of the eyes in one or more planes follows. It is important to differentiate true exophthalmos from apparent exophthalmos caused by lid retraction.

Post-Thyroidectomy Group

Thyroidectomy for thyrotoxicosis, if successful in restoring the metabolism to normal, usually abolishes lid retraction, but' does not have the same fundamental effect on true exophthalmos, although, if the latter is not too far advanced, there may be some amelioration. In many patients, however, the exophthalmos is not influenced, and in a small percentage it becomes progressively worse. This unfortunate result may be associated with a too radical thyroidectomy and a resulting myxoedematous condition with reduction of the basal metabolic rate to well below normal. In another group the thyrotoxicosis persists in some degree, and in others the basal metabolism is neither raised nor lowered, but the exophthalmos gets worse. The same events can occur after the treatment of thyrotoxicosis with thiouracil-like drugs.

Idiopathic Group

There is frequently a history of shock or emotional stress. The onset is acute, or, more usually, subacute, and one eye is often affected before the other and in different degree. Exophthalmos may precede the ophthalmoplegia or both may develop simultaneously. Diplopia is frequent. The unequal degree of ophthalmoplegia often gives the appearance of a squint. Brain found ophthalmoplegia unilateral in thirteen patients and bilateral in eighteen. The ophthalmoplegia is a paresis or paralysis, not of individual extra-ocular muscles, but of movement of the eye in a particular plane. When the opthalmoplegia is unilateral, elevation is the movement most often affected. The degree of weakness of an ocular movement is usually constant from day to day and does not fluctuate, though a movement may gradually become weaker, or further movements may become involved as the exophthalmos increases.

The exophthalmos is always associated with some oedema of the loose tissues of the upper and lower lids, and if there is much exophthalmos the oedema may be considerable. In such cases there is also oedema of the conjunctiva which gives it an abnormally glistening appearance and causes it to be thrown into folds at the canthi when the patient moves the eye to either side. In severe cases corneal anaesthesia and ulceration may occur. Papilloedema and optic atrophy are rare complications.

Of Brain's series of 31 cases, the thyroid was visibly enlarged in 5 and appeared slightly enlarged on palpation in a further 9. Signs of mild hyperthyroidism were not uncommon, but corresponding symptoms were rarely complained of, and 'the patient's placid appearance, in spite of the exophthalmos, was in striking contrast with the anxious expression of the typical patient with exophthalmic goitre.' In eight patients in whom basal metabolism was investigated the average increase was plus 25 per cent. However, there is a very obvious discrepancy between the severity of the exophthalmic ophthalmoplegia and the mildness of any hyperthyroidism that may be present. Simpson suggested that the thyroid gland in these cases is relatively refractory to the thyrotrophic or hypothalamic stimulus. Small light-brown freckles, and areas of cutaneous pigmentation on the face, neck, and hands, were not uncommon.

Course and Prognosis

In almost all cases the exophthalmos and ophthalmoplegia, having reached their maximum in a few months, either remain stationary or partially subside, in either case leaving the patient with considerable disfigurement and double vision.

T`reatment

Apart from the good results of giving thyroid extract in appropriate dosage to those patients in whom the condition has followed too radical a thyroidectomy with resulting hypothyroidism, and low B.M.R. the treatment of malignant exophthalmos, is, on the whole, disappointing, and often quite useless.

Brain found deep radiation of the pituitary region to be unsuccessful, and thyroidectomy for those patients with a raised B.M.R. to be rarely beneficial. The latter is not surprising if the primary stimulus is directly hypothalamic or thryotrophic. Attempts to inhibit a pituitary thryotrophic stimulus by oestradiol in women and testosterone in men are similarly not very effective. The physiological inhibitor of the secretion of thryotrophic hormone is thyroid extract, and that can only be given in large quantities if the basal metabolism is low and not raised. Thyroid extract or thyroxine will diminish the exophthalmos in some cases, or check its progression in others. Although this treatment is seldom curative, continued administration may well prevent malignant exophthalmos. One of our patients, whose proptosis was controlled by thyroid extract, stopped treatment of her own accord and within a few weeks she developed the most severe form of malignant exophthalmos. The systemic administration of cortisone has proved to be ineffective but, on occasion, cortisone drops applied to the eyes may diminish the inflammatory signs but will not influence the exophthalmos. Direct irradiation of the orbits is of benefit in some cases, especially those with marked congestive and inflammatory changes. Malignant exophthalmos can, to some extent, be prevented by avoiding overdo-sage and intermittent treatment with thiouracil-like drugs, avoiding thyroidectomy in the presence of actively progressive exophthalmos and the immediate post-operative administration of thyroid extract to all those who undergo thyroidectomy when the degree of exophthalmos is marked. From the surgical point of view, eyesight can be saved by protecting the cornea with a tarsorrhaphy. Orbital decompression, as suggested by Naffziger remains an excellent operation in very severe cases, but is, of course, a major surgical procedure, not to be undertaken lightly.

ENDEMIC GOITRE

Incidence

Goitres, or thyroid enlargements, occur in a high percentage of the population children and adults, in many geographical areas throughout the world. In parts of Switzerland the incidence was as high as 90 per cent. before the prophylactic use of iodine.

It is perhaps not generally realized that the goitre problem in Great Britain and Ireland is a serious one. Thus the Goitre Sub-Committee of the Medical Research Council stated that in England and Wales it was estimated that there were some 500,000 cases of thyroid enlargement in persons of ages 5 to 20 inclusive. In Oxfordshire goitre was present in 37 per cent. of girls, in the Isle of Wight 36 per cent., in Durham 34 per cent., in Somerset 28 per cent., and in Devon and Cornwall 18 per cent. The incidence among boys was about 30 per cent. of that among girls. The Medical Research Council in Ireland reported that in the South Riding of Tipperary 50 per cent. of the children were goitrous, and at the Cashel Industrial School 90 per cent. Sir James Berry drew attention to the high incidence of goitre in South Wales, particularly in Glamorganshire.

The world distribution of endemic goitre shows a predilection for mountainous area. The Alps, the Himalayas, and the Andes have areas where goitre is very prevalent. The most modern and thorough investigation of the problem was the recent survey in endoza, where all the resources of isotope techniques were utilized with great success to provide a definitive study on a population about to undergo oitre prophylaxis on a huge scale.

Aetiology

Chatin observed that in certain areas of the Alps the food, soil, and water were eficient in iodine, and even suggested that iodine might be of use prophylactically. agner-Jauregg, of Vienna, recommended the general introduction of iodine in t as a prophylactic measure against goitre in endemic goitre areas. Theodore Kocher, Berne, believed that there was a goitre-producing substance in the water and that it uld be destroyed by boiling. McCarrison, in India, showed that there was not an solute deficiency of iodine, but that water contamination and/ or vitamin deficiency uld produce endemic goitre.

Nevertheless the iodine deficiency (relative or absolute) theory seems to offer the plest and most consistent explanation of endemic goitre, and has the following facts support it:

(1) the soil and water usually have a low iodine content; (2) the blood has a subnormal iodine content;

(3) the incidence of goitre has been reduced from 90 to 10 per cent by the prophylactic use of small quantities of iodine (e.g. in Zurich).

Against the iodine-deficiency theory is the fact that in some endemic areas the ne content of the water and soil is normal. A relative iodine deficiency may, however, produced by complicating factors: (a) an infection element (contaminated water), (b) high calcium content of the water, (c) a goitrogenous substance, e.g. cabbage and ethylcyanide, (d) a vitamin deficiency. An increased physiological demand for iodine, g. puberty, pregnancy, and menopause, may reveal or aggravate a geographical iodine ficiency.

According to Marine a relative or absolute iodine deficiency results in thyroid erplasia (possibly via the pituitary thyrotrophic hormone). If the iodine deficiency is porarily abolished by an increased supply of iodine or a diminution of physiological and, the gland (or a portion of it) involutes to the colloid resting phase. A further ne deficiency produces hyperplasia, and a sequence of phases of hyperplasia and involution produce adenomas. Ultimately exhaustion atrophy may result.

The response of the thyropituitary axis to iodide deficiency is an attempt to preserve optimum production of iodine-containing hormone in the absence of sufficient iodide. increased output of thyrotrophic hormone will not only enlarge the cell mass available hormone synthesis but also increase the individual cell's capacity to concentrate 'de from the blood. The degree of goitre depends not only on the amount by which plasma inorganic iodide concentration is lowered but also on the demands of the y for thyroid hormone. At any time the restriction of iodide supply may limit hormonal uction to suboptimal values, but increased demands for thyroid hormone will also lead to hypothyroidism when the thyroid cannot increase its hormone production in the absence of sufficient iodide.

The iodine-deficient goitre exhibits extreme avidity for radioactive iodine, but this can be decreased by the administration of thyroxine, which acts by suppressing the pituitary secretion of thyrotrophin. Administration iodide does not curb the gland's avidity for radioactive iodine in the short-term experiment, as it takes some time to replenish the body's store of iodide. If the mechanism for synthesis of thyroxine is still functioning well, the giving of large quantities of iodide is followed by its rapid conversion to thyroxine so that the circulation is suddenly flooded with an excess of hormone. Under these circumstances thyrotoxicosis of acute onset is produced. Such an event was noted in the early days of iodide therapy in Switzerland and Austria and was labelled jod Basedow. As the state of iodine deficiency, the function of the thyroid, and the dose of iodide given must all correlate at a critical state to produce such thyrotoxicosis, the condition is excessively rare and of academic importance only in this country.

Pathology

According to the physiological phase (and past phases) at the time of section, areas of hyperplasia, colloid involution, or adenomatous formation may predominate or occur in different portions of the gland. The distribution of such areas has been attributed to variability of the blood and lymphatic supply. Exhaustion atrophy (associated with cretinism and myxoedema) is also a terminal sequence; microscopic examination reveals desquamation and degeneration of the lining cuboidal cells, with fragmentation and irregular staining of the nuclei, a loss of colloid material, and an increase of fibrous stroma.

Clinical

At all ages the incidence of endemic goitre is much higher in women. They are susceptible than men to minor degrees of iodine lack, probably because of menstruation and pregnancy. In areas of severe iodine deficiency the total incidence of goitre is very high and the sex ratio is about one to one. But in other areas, with a lower total incidence, the proportion of women to men is increased markedly. In this country women heavily outnumber the men affected by goitre. It is of interest that of a family brought up to adult life in a goitrous area of Somerset, the three girls remained goitrous on moving to another environment, but the two boys, whose goitres were always smaller than their sisters', became normal on living in an area of adequate iodine intake.

The effect of the female sex cycle is illustrated by the appearance of the goitre at puberty and its increased size with menstruation or pregnancy. Goitres are noted in children only when iodine deficiency is relatively severe. Goitrogenic factors in the diet may exacerbate the iodine deficiency, as illustrated by two sisters living in Derbyshire. The one with a goitre had a passion for vegetables, particularly cabbage, which she ate in remarkable amounts. The other with no goitre had refused to touch vegetables from earliest childhood.

The puberty goitre is more common in endemic areas but slight or moderate diffuse enlargement of the gland at this time should be regarded a physiological, since it may disappear entirely after some years or may be obvious only during menstruation. In a few cases the thyroid may enlarge considerably and thyrotoxicosis may supervene. Similarly the long-standing goitre may be associated with normal thyroid function until the climacteric, when thyrotoxicosis arises.

In the majority of cases in this country there is no gross disturbance of thyroid function, but mild degrees of hypothyroidism are met with. Endemic cretinism was once common in Switzerland, but not in this country. There is an increased incidence of deaf-mutism in goitrous children.

If the goitre is multilobular and large, pressure symptoms in the neck may be troublesome. The main complaint of the patient is the very reasonable one that the goitre is both uncomfortable and unsightly.

Prophylaxis

It is said that the normal requirements of the body are 0.4-1 mg. of iodine per day, and successful prophylaxis is achieved by even smaller quantities, e.g. given as sodium iodide, 1: 200,000 mixed with salt, a total of 18 mg. of sodium iodide in a year may be adequate. Iodine is also given as a chocolate-coated tablet, containing 1/6 gr. (10 mg.), one being given weekly for a year before puberty, and two years afterwards. The giving of iodine in small quantities to pregnant women with goitre will prevent congenital goitres, in the same way as it will prevent goitres appearing in the puppies of thyroidectomized dogs.

The Medical Research Council in Great Britain drew attention to the increased incidence of endemic goitre in 1917-18, as well as in 1943-4, when there was a deficiency of fish and other iodine-containing sea foods. But apart from the securing of appropriate diets in general, and especially in endemic goitre areas, they strongly recommended that iodized salt, containing 1 part of potassium iodide in 100,000 parts of salt should be generally available. With an average daily intake of 10 g. of salt per person, this would provide 0.1 mg. of iodide, or 0.08 mg. of iodine. They stated that 'no illeffects are to be expected from the widespread use of iodine in such concentrations-indeed the bulk of the evidence is to the contrary'; and advised an official pronouncement in favour of its general employment. This seems to be advisable on general grounds, considering the population as a whole.

The dangers of iodide prophylaxis have been hotly debated in the past, sometimes with political rather than scientific fervour. The long-term results of goitre prophylaxis in Switzerland and other areas have amply demonstrated the efficacy of the method, and the dangers of producing thyrotoxicosis only apply to certain circumstances which are so rare as to be disregarded in comparison with the advance in health of the population at large.

Treatment

Small doses of iodine, such as 3 min. of Lugol's iodine daily may assist the involution of the goitre when adolescent or pubertal. Small doses of thyroid extract, ½—2gr. daily, diminish secretion of thyrotrophic hormone with a resultant decrease in thyroid size. This is usually more successful than iodine and should obviously be employed if there is any suspicion of hypothyroidism. In adolescence the association of a colloid goitre with obesity, pallor, sluggishness, and menstrual irregularity often indicates a degree of hypothyroidism. At a later date the histological changes are irreversible so that surgery is necessary for pressure symptoms or to satisfy aesthetic demands.

MYXOEDEMA

Defintion

Myxoedema is a condition of hypothyroidism which may occur

sporadically or be associated with endemic goitre; or, occasionally, it may be a sequel to hyperthyroidism. Myxoedema usually occurs in adults-more frequently in women than in men-but it may occur in childhood., 'Juvenile myxoedema' is a term applied to myxoedema commencing in childhood but not present at birth, the latter being termed 'cretinism.'

The term 'myxoedema' is not applicable to hypothyroidism secondary to anterior pituitary deficiency, as occurs in Simmonds' disease. In myxoedema the essential pathology is in the thyroid gland itself, and its subnormal function cannot be increased by injections of thyrotrophic hormone.

History

Hilton Fagge, physician to Guy's Hospital, who first described sporadic cretinism, predicted that a similar condition would be found sporadically in adult. Though his senior colleague, W.W.Gull, reported five such cases, J. already described the same condition, but had not published his account. The term 'myxoedema' was suggested by W.M. Ord, of St. Thomas's Hospital, because of the excess of mucin found in the skin. Myxoedema was ascribed to thyroid deficiency by Felix Semon, who also concluded that cretinism and post-thyroidectomy myxoedema (cachexia strumipriva) were both due to the same cause. G. R. Murray, of Manchester, successfully treated myxoedema by injetions of a glycerin extract of sheep's thryorid, and in the following year Hector Mackenzie and E. L. Fox independently reported successful therapy with dried thyroid gland, administered orally.

Aetiology

The disease has a prediction for multiparas, and a special incidence at the climateric, when involution and fibrosis of other endocrine glands, e.g. the ovary, may occur. The condition is not due to deficient secretion of thyrotrophic hormone, as there is an excess of this hormone in the blood in myxoedema (just as there is an excess of gonadotrophic hormone at the climacteric), and injected thyrotrophic hormone is without effect. Complete thyroidectomy results in excessive secretion of pituitary thyrotrophic hormone, so that the latter phenomenon in myxoedema must be regarded as secondary to the primary thyroid deficiency.

As myxoedema may occur at any age, including childhood, one might postulate that it also results from a general infection (compare the effect of mumps on the gonads), but there is rarely any clinical evidence of this, probably because of the long latent period.

However, subacute or chronic thyroiditis may cause myxoedema. This is a rare complication of the Riedel type of thyroiditis, but an inevitable event in lymphadenoid thyroiditis, as described by Hashimoto. Although the initial phase of the disease may suggest mild thyrotoxicosis the end-result is hypothyroidism. If partial thyroidectomy is undertaken for pressure symptoms, myxoedema almost invariably follows within the ensuing three months and is clinically severe. It is interesting to note that the majority of patients with thyrotoxicosis who develop myxoedema after operation have lymphadenoid changes in the thyroid. The cause of this curious small round cell infiltration remains obscure, but it is obvious that the finding of such changes-at thyroidectomy must alert the clinician to the probability of later hypothyroidism. Thyrotoxicosis may, in some instances, be followed spontaneously by myxoedema, a sequence of events which may be related to the natural history of lymphadenoid goitre.

Myxoedema can not only be produced by thyroidectomy but also by radiation or antithyroid drugs. Radioactive iodine therapy for thyrotoxicosis may lead to trasient or permanent hypothyroidism. In the treatment of cardiac disease by complete thyroidectomy or massive radioactive-iodine therapy myxoedema is produced intentionally to diminish the work of the heart. Antithyroid agents produce enlargement of the thyroid and hypothyroidism, which are reversible on cessation of treatment. When such drugs as methylthiouracil or carbimazole are used in the treatment of thyrotoxicosis the clinician will be watching for the development of hypothyroidism, but other antithyroid agents are used therapeutically for non-thyroid disease so that their relationship to induced myxoedema is not realized. Para-aminosalicylic acid and thiosemicarbazone, both used in the treatment of tuberculosis, have given rise to goitre and hypothyroidism. A similar thyroid disturbance has followed the use of resorcinol on varicose ulcers, butazolidine in arthritis, and cobalt in anaemia.

Pathology

Apart from endemic goitre, the thyroid gland in idiopathic myxoedema has undergone fibrosis and atrophy. The skin and subcutaneous tissues are infiltrated with mucoid material containing nitrogen. The heart muscle may be similarly affected, and show myocardial degeneration. Degeneration of the coronary arteries is sometimes a complication or concomitant.

In lymphadenoid goitre there is a widespread infiltration of the thyroid tissue with lymphocytes, and little, if any, normal thyroid tissue remains. Fibrosis occurs in the later stages.

Clinical Features

The symptoms are the opposite of hyperthyroidism. The onset is insidious, the patient becoming lethargic, apathetic, and somnolent, with a marked slowing of speech and intellectual processes, and a failing of memory. The condition is half-way towards hibernation, a low basal metabolic rate, e.g. minus 40, with subnormal temperature and sensitivity to cold, being the basis.

There is also a mucoid infiltration of the skin, subcutaneous tissue, tongue, laryngeal mucous membrane, heart, and sometimes the liver, producing a number of characteristic features. The nose and lips tend to become thick and less well delineated, but not comparable to the gross deformity of acromegaly. The lids are oedematous, and the eyes may appear slit-like in the midst of a puffy orbit. Exophthalmos is usually absent in idiopathic myxoedema, but may be present by itself, or with ophthalmoplegia, if myxoedema supervenes upon thyrotoxicosis, e.g. after thyroidectomy. The enlarged tongue may interfere with articulation, and the laryngeal changes result in a hoarse, husky, or toneless voice. The speech, in any case, is slow and sluggish, but this is probably due to retardation of the intellectual processes. Impairment of smell, taste, and hearing may be present. Even with a normal blood count, the facial appearance is pallid, due to the infiltration of the skin, and a malar flush on the pallid countenance may be present. Carotinaemia and a yellow colour of the skin is sometimes met with, and multiple cutaneous xanthomata have been recorded. The hair of the head is dry and lustreless, and falls out. This is also true of the eyebrows, especially of the outer half; and Holbein's portrait of Henry VIII, by virtue of the scanty eyebrows and puffy face, has been said to indicate myxoedema. The pubic and axllary hair may become more scanty than usual, but are usually retained, in contrast to panhypopituitarism, where the pubic and axillary hair disappears. The nails are striated and tend to break. The soft tissues of the hands and fingers become thick and puffy; and the muscles and ligaments. become hypotonic, flat feet being not uncommon and arthralgia a frequent complaint. The shoulders become rounded, and the abdominal walls flaccid and protuberant. Apart from the mucoid infiltration there may be some increase of fat, e.g. in the supraclavicular and suprapubic areas, and above the wrists and ankles. Adiposity is not, however, an essential of hypothyroidism.

In contrast to hyperthyroidism, appetite and thirst are subnormal, and constipation is a constant feature. Achlorhydria is frequent. Menorrhagia is not infrequent. Occasionally amenorrhoea is found.

Cardiovascular System

Pathological changes in the heart muscle and coronary arteries are common in myxoedema, but are not always associated with cardiac symptoms. However, cardiac failure may occasionally occur, and anginal pains are sometimes a manifestation of myxoedema. The pulse rate is nearly always slow, but may become quick if cardiac ailure supervenes. Coronary degeneration and hypertension are complications due to the hypercholesterolaemia, and angina is not infrequent; myxoedema probably accelerates the progress of arterio-sclerotic and other degenerative vascular changes. Since, however, myxoedema following thyroidectomy ameliorates cardiac pain and insufficiency, it ollows that manifestations of these features in spontaneous myxoedema may indicate a greater degree of pathological disturbance than in normal people. This is also suggested y the fact that whereas cardiac symptoms are comparatively rare is spontaneous myxoedema, radiological and electrocardiographic abnormalities are comparatively ommon. Thus, cardic enlargement, as revealed by X-ray examination, is found in more than 50 per cent. of patients. It is usually associated with myxoedematous infiltration of the cardiac muscle, and the condition tends to return to normal on giving thyroid by mouth. There may be a pericardial effusion as well. The electrocardiogram reveals diinution in the size of all the waves; the QRS complex is of low voltage, and the T waves are flat or inverted. Under treatment the P and QRS waves become larger, and the T waves become upright. At the same time the heart size is diminished and pericardial fluid disappears. However, the rise in metabolic rate after administration of thyroid extract may induce anginal pain.

Gastro-Intestinal System

In contrast to hyperthyroidism, appetite and thirst and subnormal, and constipation is a constant feature. Intestinal movements are often sluggish, and intestinal absorption slow. The colon is often grossly distended and enlarged.

Achlorhydria is frequently shown by a fractional test meal. The liver may be enlarged and palpable, probably due to mucinous infiltration, and recedes to normal size on thyroid therapy.

Blood Picture

Possibly, associated with the achlorhydria, a simple hypochromic microcytic anaemia, responding to iron, or a typical Addisonian megalocytic hyperchromic anaemia responding to liver, may occasionally be found associated with myxoedema. There is, however, a third type of anaemia (simple hyperchromic anaemia) which responds neither to iron nor liver, but to thyroid gland (although slowly), which is therefore presumably due directly to the hypothyroidism. Bomford described the condition thus:

This simple hyperchromic anaemia is never severe, the colour index is normal or a little above 1. There is some macrocytosis but no poikilocytosis and no excessive anisocytosis. The reticulocyte count may be normal and there may be achlorhydria. The administration of liver or of iron has no effect on the anaemia, but the anaemia does respond slowly to treatment with thyroid alone, in such doses as are found to keep the patient free from symptoms of myxoedema or overdosage. The rate of response is very slow, the blood count attaining normal levels in from three to nine months.

He regarded the anaemia as a result of a decrease in teh size of the erythron, which takes place in hypothyroidism as a physiologic compensation for diminished need of the tissues for oxygen, and akin to the anaemia which appears in animals exposed to atmospheres of oxygen tension greater than normal. The bone marrow is hypoplastic and sternal puncture shows a reduction of nucleated cells. The serum bilirubin is normal.

Generative Organs

In thyrotoxicosis one often meets with amenorrhoea or oligomenorrhoea, and in myxoedema menorrhagia occurs. Some text-books state that amenorrhoea is the most frequent finding in myxoedema, but we believe this to be incorrect, and due to confusion of myxoedema with hypothyroidism secondary to hypopituitarism. In the latter condition amenorrhoea is the rule, but in myxoedema and excessive and irregular menstrual bleeding is not infrequent. Gynaecologists even give thyroid extract empirically for menorrhagia in the absence of clinical myxoedema and claim good results. In juvenile or childhood myxoedema, however, there is often retardation in sexual development and in the onset of menstruation, unless the condition has been treated with thyroid. Of course, if myxoedema occurs at the climacteric there will be associated amenorrhoea, but this may be preceded by ienorrhagia.

Emotional Pattern and Psychoses

Sluggish mental reactions, poor memory, slow speech, absence of emotional response, and general inertia are characteristic. Neurosis is rare, but psychosis is common enough in untreated cases to make the psychiatrist aware of myxoedema as a possible cause of a psychosis. The latter may be delusional or hallucinatory, or schizophrenic. In early cases there is a good response to thyroid therapy.

Myxodema Coma

In rare instances of severe hypothyroidism the metabolic processes become so slow that the body can no longer preserve a normal temperature. The resultant state may be aptly described as hibernation coma. This event is usually terminal and either follows the progressive course of the disease or is precipitated by infection. Coma is ushered in by gross mental disturbance and accompanied by a profound drop in body temperature and pulse rate. The final state is one of suspended animation usually terminating in death, despite treatment.

Juvenile Hypothyroidism

This condition is rare and, by definition, refers to the condition of myxoedema commencing in childhood but not present at birth, as in cretinism. The symptoms are those of adult myxoedema, but in addition there is deficient growth and delayed sexual maturation. Delay in the appearance of the centres of ossification is associated with epiphyseal dysgenesis. The latter may be mistaken for Perthes' disease, for the child may complain of pain in the hip and the stigmata of hypothyroidism go unrecognized. Young children become mentally backward if the disease remains untreated, but the degree of mental defect is neither so severe nor so irreversible as in cretinism. The disease may present no delayed puberty or anaemia, or any obvious clinical signs of hypothyroidism.

Localized Myxoedema

In hypothyroidism the generalized appearance of myxoedemic skin infiltration may be accentuated by mucinous deposits in various areas, particularly in the supraclavicular spaces. However, there is a separate condition of localized pretibial myxoedema which is associated with thyrotoxicosis and not with hypothyroidism. Consequently pretibial myxoedema is discussed in the chapter on thyrotoxicosis.

Metabolic and Biochemical Changes

(1) Basal metabolism is invariably low, usually in the neighbourhood of minus 40 per cent.

(2) Blood cholesterol is usually raised, sometimes very considerably. Normal values for blood cholesterol average 160 mg. per cent. and any value above 250 mg. per cent. suggests myxoedema. It is rare to find values above 500 mg. per cent., but values as high as 953 mg. per cent. have been recorded, even when the basal metabolism was no lower than minus 38 per cent. There is usually some

relationship between basal metabolism and cholesterol, but it is by no means constant, and some observers attach greater importance to blood cholesterol than to basal metabolism as a measure of the presence, or severity, of myxoedema. Occasionally xanthomatous nodules occur on the face and along the extremities, and in one such case the serum was of a milky character as in lipaemia. There was only a tardy and partial response to thyroid therapy. But as the condition is so infrequent it was regarded as coincidental rather than as part of the myxoedematous syndrome. Nevertheless, thyroidectomy in the dog produces a high level of blood lipoids, as well as cholesterolaemia. Phospholipids and lipoproteins are also abnormal in myxoedema. The sedimentation rate may be raised. From the clinical point of view serial estimations of blood cholesterol are a valuable guide to therapy.

(3) Water metabolism is also deranged, part of the myxoedemic appearance being due to retention of water. This is shown by the puffiness of the eyelids which is worse after lying down and diminishes on standing. Administration of thyroxine causes a water diuresis. Renal handling of water is also impaired; ingestion of a water load is not followed by normal diuresis. This is partly due to associated adrenocortical hypofunction but it can only be fully corrected by thyroxine, not by cortisone

(4) Endocrine glands other than the thyroid become -involved in the general lowering of metabolic rate. Low 17-ketosteriod values indicate depression of adrenocortical function and there may be a delayed adrenal response to adrenocorticotrophin. These abnormalities are corrected by thyroxine. Similarly, gonadotrophin output is diminished but returns to normal as the myxoedema is corrected.

Diagnosis

Clinical diagnosis is suggested by loss of hair of the head, loss of outer half of eyebrows, loss of memory and sluggish mental reactions and speech, hypersensitivity to cold, puffy eyelids, pallor, and bradycardia. Low basal metabolic rate, failure of thyroidal iodine uptake, and high blood cholesterol are confirmatory evidence. The appearance of some women after the menopause suggests mild myxoedema but it is seldom that the diagnosis can be confirmed. It may be that minor degrees of hypothyroidism are missed by the clinician, but this is a doubtful point which is insignificant compared to the misdiagnosis of myxoedema as anaemia or chronic nephritis. In the young adult fatigue may be the only symptom and pallor the only marked sign of hypothyroidism, with the result that anaemia is diagnosed correctly but fails to respond to haernatinics. In the same way a pale puffy face with some albuminuria and a high blood cholesterol suggests Type 2 (Ellis) nephritis. We have seen such a case of hypothyroidism in a young man who also had some ascites. Free fluid in the peritoneal cavity can occur as part of the myxoedematous process and is a confusing physical sign.

Panhypopituitarism is not infrequently labelled myxoedema because of the secondary hypothyroidism. Amenorrhoea, absent pubic hair and axillary hair, extreme skin pallor with a smooth fine texture favour the diagnosis of panhypopituitarism. The response of this disease to thyroid therapy is inadequate and sometimes the condition is aggravated, in contrast to the most gratifying response of myxoedema. Intravenous injection of insulin is followed by a rapid fall in blood sugar and continued hypoglycaemia in panhypopituitarism, while in myxoedema the fall in blood sugar is delayed and hypoglycaemia transient. In both diseases 17-ketosteroid output is low and the Kepler test indicates adrenal insufficiency. Administration of thyroid is followed by an increase in 17-ketosteroid excretion and a return of the Kepler test to normal. No such change occurs in panhypopituitarism.

The use of tracer doses of radioactive iodine to determine the thyroid uptake or the urinary excretion of this element is an advance in diagnostic method. The percentage of the dose accumulated by the thyroid is small and the urinary excretion high. Both the rate of thyroid accumulation and renal excretion is slow. However, these techniques are not always informative in the mild case when the thyroid handling of iodine is not widely different from the normal.

Those workers who have found the estimation of protein-bound iodine to be reliable consider that low values are consistently seen in myxoedema and this estimation is of great diagnostic value. A simple aid to diagnosis is the determination of blood cholesterol, a normal value being almost unheard of in primary myxoedema. Hypothyroidism secondary to pituitary lesions is, however, not associated with a marked rise in blood cholesterol. The most logical test to distinguish between primary thyroid failure and secondary hypothyroidism due to lack of thyrotrophic hormone is the measurement of thyroid radioactive iodine uptake before and after a course of thyrotrophin injections. In the majority of cases secondary failure shows response to thyrotrophin, but in long-standing cases little or no response is found. Therefore the test is not completely specific and the conditions of testing need careful scrutiny.

When there is considerable doubt as to the diagnosis of hypothyroidism the patient's response to six weeks' administration of thyroid will solve the problem. The specific effect of thyroid extract will be observed clearly in this period. If there is no change in physical signs or symptoms, hypothyroidism can be excluded.

Treatment

This is a most satisfactory branch of endocrine therapy. Dried thyroid gland should be given by mouth commencing with one grain daily, and gradually increasing the dose to a maximum of 3-4 gr. It is very rare for any patient to require more than this. It should be remembered that thyroid extract takes at least twenty-four hours to exert its action and therefore need only be given once a day. Whatever the size of the initial dose may be, the patient's response will not be fully evident until therapy has been continued for two weeks. Consequently the dose should only be adjusted every two weeks. If there is any evidence of cardiac disease it is wise to use ½ gr. daily as the initial dose. Too rapid a strain on the heart may produce angina or precipitate failure. The pulse, which should never be allowed to exceed 80 per minute, is the best single criterion of overdosage. However a general appraisal of the patient's physical state and the absence of symptoms is the best guide to a correct maintenance dose. The more severe the myxoedema the more dramatic the response to a small dose of thyroid, so that there is no indication for giving large dose because of severe disease. Most patients attain full health when their basal metabolic rate is still slightly subnormal. Any attempt to increase the dose of thyroid until the metabolic rate achieves normality is likely to produce signs of overdosage. Clinical judgment is far superior to metabolic tests in the treatment of myxoedema.

L-thyroxine sodium is now readily available and has the advantage of standard potency. One grain of thyroideum siccum (B.P.) is equivalent to 0.1 mg. L-thyroxine sodium. Triiodothyronine is five times more potent than L-thyroxine sodium and is quite different in its speed of action. The dose of triiodothyronine will produce a marked effect in a few hours, and its action will diminish in twenty-four hours. It is doubtful whether such a quick action is of therapeutic value except in myxoedemic coma, and it may be a disadvantage from the cardiac point of view.

There is not only a marked difference in the speed and duration of action between thyroxine, triiodothyronine, and its acetic acid analogue, but there may well be a qualitative difference in their effects. In some cases of myxoedema, triiodothyroacetic acid reduces the blood cholesterol and diminishes the myxoedemic appearance yet fails to elevate the metabolic rate. This cholesterolytic action could be of wide therapeutic use if regularly divorced from an increase in metabolism. We have treated an elderly patient with myxoedema and heart block who developed heart failure when given small doses of thyroid which did not alter her appearance of high blood cholesterol. Administration of triiodothyroacetic acid reduced the blood cholesterol to normal, diminished the signs of myxoedema, and had no ill effect on her cardiovascular, system. However, this type of response is far from constant and we have seen marked tachycardia develop within six hours of giving this analogue to a young adult with myxoedema. In her case the adverse effect on the heart preceded any other change. This subject is far from clear at the moment and the effect of thyroxine and related compounds in non-myxoedematious states must also be investigated more extensively. Kurland *et al.* have made an important point in finding that triiodothyronine, but not thyroxine, will elevate the metabolic rate in certain cases of hypometabolism without hypothyroidism.

The treatment of the rare case of myxoedemic coma is very unsatisfactory. The patient's body temperature must be raised slowly by external heating. It is better to stop heat loss rather than to apply strong heat as the hypothermia must be, to some extent, a protection from hypometabolism. Associated adrenocortical failure demands the use of cortisone or hydrocortisone. Lack of adrenal response invalidates the use of adrenocorticotrophin. Triiodothyronine or its acetic acid analogue should be used in preference to thyroid extract or thyroxine. Whatever therapy is used there is a great danger of heart failure terminating the disease despite recovery from the coma.

CRETINISM

Definition

This is a condition of hypothyroidism beginning in foetal life, and becoming manifest at birth or earliest infancy. In contrast, juvenile myxoedema is superimposed on a normal childhood.

History

The endemic form of cretinism has been known since antiquity, and was described by Paracelsus who noted its association with endemic goitre. The only instance of this form of cretinism in England was reported in the village of Chiselborough, Somerset, in 1848 by Norris. The condition ceased to be endemic a few years later. Hilton Fagge distinguished sporadic cretinism by the absence of a goitre, although Curling had previously suspected that the disease might be due to the absence of thyroid function. It is noteworthy that this form of hypothyroidism was identified before the adult form of myxoedema.

Aetiology

Endemic cretinism was found in areas of severe long-standing iodine deficiency where a high incidence of goitre had been present for generations; the goitrous mother giving birth to a goitrous cretin. The control of endemic goitre has led to the virtual elimination of endemic cretinism. Indeed, cretins now born in areas where previously the condition was endemic probably suffer from the same type of thyroid disturbance as the sporadic cretin.

Sporadic cretinism arises either from an anatomical or a biochemical defect of the thyroid; in the latter, the thyroid is goitrous. Congenital absence of the thyroid (athyrotic cretinism) has been recognized for years, but McGirr and Hutchison have pointed out that dysgenesis of the thyroid can give rise to cretinism or apparent juvenile myxoedema depending on how long the function of the small amount of thyroid tissue can provide for the needs of the growing child. The dysgenetic fragment of thyroid is usually ectopic, situated somewhere along the thyhroglossal tract. In some cases the only thyroid tissue present has been in the tongue. We have seen a functioning ectopic thyroid removed from a child, thus causing extreme hypothyroidism as there was no thyroid tissue present in the normal site.

Biochemical defects in an anatomically normal thyroid cause cretinism because the normal synthetic pathway of thyroxine is blocked. This was noticed first by Stanbury and Hedge who investigated a family of sporadic goitrous cretins. There was no lack of iodine in their diet, and their thyroids accumulated radioactive iodine very rapidly. However, the administration of thiocyanate resulted in a prompt discharge of radioactive iodine from the thyroid. As thiocyanate will only discharge iodide from the thyroid, it was apparent that these patients were unable to bind iodide to thyroxine. Thus the block to thyroxine formation was at the earliest stage. Blockage at later stages of hormone production (i.e. from iodinated tyrosines to thyroxine) have also been described and in some cases it is obvious that diiodotyrosine not only leaks from the thyroid but passes into the urine as the de-iodinating enzymes of the body are absent. At least three types of block to hormone synthesis are now known. In all a congenital lack of a thyroid enzyme is the probable lesion, the defect being genetic in origin, occurring with a familial distribution and probably inherited as a single autosomal recessive gene. There may be some connexion with cases of non-toxic colloid goitre in non-endemic areas as in one of our cases both parents had such a goitre from childhood (with no evidence of hypothyroidism) and were deaf mutes.

All cases of cretinism due to defective hormone synthesis develop a goitre. This may not be apparent in infancy but grows to a large size in childhood. Administration of thyroid extract diminishes the size of the goitre in early cases, but the later histological changes are irreversible. Inadequate thyroid therapy may be associated with a gradually increasing size of goitre. The thyroid is composed of masses of cells with extremely little colloid so that the normal vesicular architecture is not seen. Later changes are those of cystic degeneration interspersed with areas of Intense cellular activity. The histological picture suggests great stimulation from thyrotrophic hormone and no doubt this hormone, discharged in excess because the level of circulating thyroxine is so low, is primarily responsible for goitre formation. The situation is entirely analogous to the artificial blocking of thyroxine synthesis by the administration of thiouracil. However, we have observed the sudden development of a goitre in a treated cretin aged 25 years. She had received adequate thyroid therapy since the first year of life and there was no evidence of hypothyroidism, nor was the therapy altered prior to the enlargement of the thyroid. Chromatographic studies on extracts of the patient's thyroid revealed iodinated tyrosines and iodide, but no thyroxine. The histology was identical with that of other goitrous cretins. No explanation is offered for the emergence of a goitre in a patient who obviously had a hereditary disturbance of thyroxine formation but it casts some doubt on the thesis that thyrotrophin is the sole factor in such goitre production.

Clinical Features

These resemble those of myxoedema as both conditions are due to hypothyroidism.

Special characteristic features are the broad nose with flat bridge and wide nostrils, thick lips, open mouth with protruding thick tongue protuberant abdomen with umbilical hernia, supraclavicular pads, and spade-like hands. The coarse texture of a yellowy skin and sparse coarse hair is similar to adult myxoedema. The most important defect is that of intelligence, early diagnosis and treatment being essential to prevent complete idiocy.

The early symptoms are those of lethargy, failure to suck, constipation, and lack of physical progress. The initial store of maternal thyroxine may delay the onset of these symptoms for several weeks. Soon the general delay in development becomes obvious. The fontanelles remain open, centres of ossification appear late and commonly show dysgenesis, and dentition is delayed. *Dwarfism* is marked; it is rare for the untreated cretin to reach a height of 4 ft. 6 in. Although the disorder of maturation is due to lack of thyroid hormone, a major factor in the dwarfism is a secondary failure of growth-hormone secretion. Gonadotrophin secretion is also depressed by the involvement of the pituitary in the general depression of tissue activity; full pubertal development does not occur. *Juvenile myxoedema* is also associated with *sexual infantilism* but with little defect in somatic growth.

The untreated cretin remains a physically undeveloped and mentally deficient child, liable to early death from intercurrent infection and, at all times, leading an apathetic vegetable existence. The degree of mental defect is variable and even early treatment may not save the child from severe mental deficiency. For this reason it has been suggested that in some cases, the mental and the thyroid defects are both primary genetic failures. Deaf-mutism may be an added burden to the stunted mind.

Diagnosis

Clinical diagnosis of the established case is easy but probably too late for full effective treatment. Aids to an early diagnosis are measurement of the serum cholesterol and *electrocardiography*. The results in cretinism are similar to those of myxoedema. X-ray examination of the epiphyses is essential to detect the specific appearances of *epiphyseal dysgenesis.* This is only evident when calcification of the cartilagenous epiphysis has occurred. Instead of a normal single opaque centre of ossification, numerous small foci of calcification are seen; these eventually coalesce to form an epiphysis of irregular shape with poorly defined fluffy margins. Determination of the metabolic rate is not applicable to infants, but radioactive iodine techniques are very useful in elucidating the type of thyroid dysfunction. It must be remembered that a normal uptake of radioactive iodine is found in sporadic goitrous cretinism as outlined in the section on aetiology.

Treatment

Administration of thyroid extract from infancy onwards will usually result in the attainment of an approximately normal child and adult. If treatment has been delayed for some years the only result may be the conversion of a harmless apathetic idiot into a mischievous truculent and troublesome semi-idiot. Nevertheless, excellent results are sometimes obtained when treatment is late and, conversely, early and adequate treatment may be disappointing.

The initial daily dose of thyroideum siccum (B.P.) for the infant (under one year of age) should be 1/8 gm., rising gradually to ¼ gm. or more. Overdosage is indicated by loss of weight, or failure to gain weight, and by *diarrhoea.* It is dangerous to start with large doses or to increase the dose too rapidly. The average daily dose at one year of age is ½ gm., at four years of age 2 gm., and in later childhood 3 gm. There is considerable variation of sensitivity to thyroid in different individuals and sometimes in different phases in the same individual. Apart from the supplementary use of chemical aids, such as blood cholesterol, periodic clinical assessment is essential. As in myxoedema, L-thyroxine sodium may be given by mouth as an alternative to thyroideum siccum but offers no real clinical advantage.

DISEASES DUE TO PARATHYROID HORMONES

HYPERPARATHYROIDISM

Hyperparathyroidism is *primary* when there is an adenoma or, much less frequently, idiopathic hyperplasia of the parathyroid glands; and *secondary* when increased parathyroid secretion exists as a compensatory mechanism maintaining the blood calcium level in various diseases which tend to lower that level.

PRIMARY HYPERPARATHYROIDISM

In primary hyperparathyroidism a secreting parathyroid adenoma causes generalized osteitis fibrosa (von Recklinghausen's osteitis fibrosa), metastatic calcification, renal calculi, and disturbances of calcium and phosphorus metabolism. Largely as a result of Albright's work, it is now recognized that renal calculi may be the only outward manifestation of a parathyroid adenoma.

History

In 1891 von Recklinghausen included a probable case of this disease among an undifferentiated motley of bone disorders, but the first recorded case is said to have been described by Courtial in 1700. The first report of a parathyroid tumour, in a patient suffering from generalized osteitis fibrosa, was by Askanazy in 1904; and in 1906 Erdheim observed enlargement of the parathyroid glands in patients with osteomalacia and supposed the hyperplasia to be a secondary compensatory reaction. However, it is probable that some of these cases were actually osteitis fibrosa and Schlagenhaufer, having found parathyroid tumours in two fatal cases of this disease, regarded them as being the aetiological factor and recommended parathyroidectomy as the correct treatment. Nevertheless, it was not until 1926 that Mandl removed a parathyroid tumour from a patient with generalized osteitis fibrosa and recorded the improvement which followed.

Although MacCallum had reported as far back as 1905 the presence of a tumour of a parathyroid gland in association with chronic renal disease, it was not until 1934 that Albright and Bloomberg drew attention to the frequent occurrence of renal calculi in hyperparathyroidism and pointed out that such calculi might be the only symptoms of a parathyroid tumour.

Aeitology and Pathogenesis

It is not known what, in general, causes tumour formation or primary hyperplasia of the parathyroid glands. Though it has been suggested that the condition can be compared with toxic goitre and is due to excessive secretion of pituitary parathyrotrophic hormone, there is grave doubt that such a hormone has any significance-or even exists. Cases of hyperparathyroidism following pregnancy have been reported. Davies *et al.* have reported two patients in whom hyperparathyroidism appears to have resulted from chronic steatorrhoea; is one of these, two parathyroid adenomata were found so that in this patient at least, 'primary' hyperparathyroidism was caused by the steatorrhoea. A familial aspect may also be of significance; Frohner and Wolgamot found five cases in a single family and suggest that it would not be inappropriate to screen the families of all the cases of hyperparathyroidism.

The excessive secretion of parathyroid hormone leads to a rise in the level of plasma calcium, a fall in that of plasma phosphate, and an increased excretion of calcium and phosphate .urine. This constitutes the biochemical syndrome of hyperparathyroidism.

The increased calcium excretion by the kidney requires increased water excretion, so leading to polyuria and polydipsia-the so-called 'calcium diabetes'. This condition may in fact be mistaken for diabetes insipidus. The excessive excretion of calcium by the kidney leads sooner or later to renal damage; calcium may be deposited in the collecting tubules and give rise to nephrocalcinosis, or renal calculi may be formed, producing nephrolithiasis. The progression of this renal syndrome may lead to death through renal failure without any of the bone lesions of hyperparathyroidism having become manifest. This aspect of the disease, which probably results when the intake of calcium in the diet is adequate to maintain the raised serum calcium, has been called 'hyperparathyroidism-without-bone-disease' by Albright. In the Massachusetts General Hospital, 5 per cent of all cases of renal calculi were found to be associated with hyperparathyroidism and it may therefore be emphasized that all cases of renal stone should have at least a plasma calcium estimation performed in order to exclude this possible cause of the stone. Since the prime cause of death in cases of hyperparathyroidism is renal failure and the prognosis depends mainly on how soon the renal condition is recognized and treated, the importance of detecting the disorder in its earliest phases cannot be over-emphasized.

It seems probable that the bone disease associated with hyperparathyroidism depends . largely upon the availability of calcium, which in turn is determined by the amount of calcium in the diet and the efficiency of calcium absorption from the gut. If adequate supplies of calcium from the gut are not available then the calcium loss from the bone consequent upon the action of the parathyroid hormone is not made good and the manifestations of osteitis fibrosa cystica generalisata appear. Excessive osteoclast activity is probably a direct result of parathyroid hormone action. It leads to decalcification and proliferation of fibrous tissue in the Haversian canals. This is followed by cyst formation and this in turn may be followed by the formation of osteoclasts among fibrocytes that are less differentiated than in the remainder of the fibrous marrow. Osteoclastomata are not malignant and they disappear following removal of the parathyroid adenoma. Because there is an accompanying marked increase in osteoblast activity, a raised level of serum alkaline phosphatase is found.

The parathyroid tumour is single in the great majority of cases but cases have been reported in which there were two tumours. The remaining parathyroid glands may show involution comparable to that found in the opposite adrenal gland when an adrenal cortex tumour is present. Tumours weighing up to 34 g have been reported but the severity of the disease is not related to the size of adenoma and a small tumour weighing only 1 g has been known to produce crippling disease. In a series of twenty-five cases seen at the Lahey Clinic hyperplasia of the parathyroids was found in only one, a single tumour being present in all the others.

Incidence

The disease is usually found in the third or fourth decades but may be present at any age. It is said to-be more common in women than in men but, owing to its rarity, such preponderance is not necessarily encountered in any group of cases.

Clinical Features

The onset is usually gradual and insidious, although the first major manifestation may be sudden and dramatic, e.g. a pathological spontaneous fracture, or renal colic. A not uncommon presentation is a bone tumour which, on section, is seen to be an osteoclastoma; or the long bones, the chest and spine, may become thickened, bent, or deformed. Increasing asthenia and wasting, with muscular and bony pains may be the predominating features and give no obvious indication of the underlying disorder. A more complete clinical picture can be synthesized from consideration of the various systems affected.

Skeleton

The skeleton changes are characteristically well marked and generalized but not necessarily uniform. In some patients, however, the bony changes, as seen by X-ray, may be minimal. The more usual finding of extensive decalcification results in rarefaction and softening of the bones, which become bent and deformed. The lower limbs tend to become bowed, and walking becomes increasingly difficult, the gait being awkward and waddling. In the later stages the patient is bedridden. Osteoclastomata form swellings at the ends and in the shaft of long bones, on the jaw, and anywhere on the skull. The vertebrae tend to be absorbed, and collapse with resulting kyphosis and considerable loss of height. Pathological fractures occur and delayed union is frequent. The jaw may become massive and its deformity leads to displacement and falling out of teeth, but the latter are not decalcified. The bones are osteoclastomatous swellings are often tender, especially upon pressure. Pain in the lower back may be severe. Clubbing of fingers may occur from resorption of the terminal phalanges. It is most important, however, to remember that the bone changes may be quite inconspicuous.

Radiography

All the bones may show great rarefaction, Osteoclastomatous swelling and cyst formation may be seen in various parts of the skeleton. The skull may show a granular appearance and lack of differentiation between the tables. Recent and old fractures of the long bones are revealed. Subperiosteal erosions of the phalanges, and especially of the terminal phalanges, are quite typical radiographic findings in hyperparathyroidism. Loss of the lamina dura of the teeth is also pathognomonic.

Muscles

Hypotonicity of the muscles is present, in contrast to the hypertonicity and irritability of the muscles in the opposite condition of tetany. The patient feels weak and is incapable of muscular effort. Considerable wasting of the muscles is not infrequent. Spontaneous pains occur, simulating rheumatism, pseudo-arthritis, and neuritis, and the muscles may be tender to touch. The joints may be excessively mobile.

Gastro-Intestinal System

Anorexia and intermitfent nausea, with progressive loss of weight, are frequent features. Vomiting may be intractable and is ascribed by Snapper to the hypercalcaemia. Abdominal pains and cramps are met with, and gastric ulcer or appendicitis may be simulated. Constipation is usual. Dry mouth and polydipsia are the result of the polyuria, due to the high calcium excretion.

Heart and Lungs

Dyspnoea and cynosis may result from calcium deposition in the heart and lungs, as well as from bony chest deformities and muscular weakness. Tachycardia is not uncommon.

Blood

The viscosity of the blood is increased. Destruction of the bone marrow may result in a secondary anaemia and in leucopenia.

Nervous System

Though patients may be nervous and irritable, being sometimes confused mentally, organic lesions of the central nervous system are not present. Apathy is not infrequent. Symptoms of tetany may be encountered after removal of a parathyroid tumour; or may rarely be present terminally in hyperparathyroidism complicated by renal insufficiency.

Metabolism

This has already been discussed. The characteristic chemical findings are a raised plasma calcium (e.g. above 11 mg per 100 ml), a lowered plasma phosphorus (usually below 2.5 mg. per 100 ml), and a raised plasma alkaline phosphatase (normal 4 to 8 King-

Armstrong units). There is a negative calcium balance. If renal function is impaired the plasma phosphorus may be normal or raised. In the latter case the plasma calcium values may not be appreciably elevated. Rose, working with C.E. Dent, has described a method for determining ionized calcium and he has fond that the plasma-ionized calcium is always high in primary hyperparathyroidism, even when the total plasma calcium is within normal limits. This is not so in secondary hyperparathyroidism.

Kidneys and Renal Function

Polyuria and polydipsia with nocturia are frequent symptoms and do not necessarily indicate renal disease, being manifestations of the attempt to excrete increased calcium is soluble form. However, since the kidneys are frequently involved in hyperparathyroidism, the first manifestation often is renal, e.g. haematuria, renal colic, renal calculi, or chronic nephritis. The excess of calcium in the blood may be deposited in all the soft tissues of the body or selectively in the kidneys or in the arterioles. When the kidneys are involved the calcium deposition may be in diffusely scattered particles (calcinosis), or multiple calculi, often very large, may form either in the kidney substance or the pelvis, or both. The changes are sometimes found in the absence of gross skeletal changes.

Where diffuse calcinosis is present, the kidneys undergo fibrosis and hyalinization and the ultimate clinical and pathological picture is that of chronic interstitial nephritis. The deposition of calcium in the arterioles may lead to their degeneration and hyaline occlusion. Hypertension develops and may be severe. The patient dies in uraemia or from intercurrent infection. Although no impairment of renal function may be observed at the time of removal of a parathyroid tumour, and although such an operation is usually followed by a complete control of the primary hyperparathyroidism, yet chronic nephritis may develop some years later, and one must assume that initial irreversible changes were sufficiently severe to progress to fibrosis without further calcium deposition. In a case reported by Simpson and Wilson the patient died from renal insufficiency four years after the removal of a parathyroid adenoma, having developed hyperplasia of the remaining parathyroid glands secondary to the renal insufficiency. After removal of a parathyroid tumour, renal calculi may disintegrate rapidly, though this is not always the case.

A further complication of the relationship between the parathyroids and the kidneys is the fact that, in chronic renal disease of any aetiology, parathyroid hypertrophy and hyperplasia may be a secondary effect in an endeavour to excrete the retained phosphorus. Such secondary hyperparathyroidism will be discussed later.

Diagnosis

The disease may present itself in many forms, e.g. rheumatism, spontaneous fracture, a bony swelling (osteoclastoma) of the long bones, jaw, or skull, weakness and fatigability, gastro-intestinal disorder, renal colic, haematuria, or nephritis. Most cases show generalized osteoporosis on radiographic examination but such bone changes may be minimal. The skull frequently gives a characteristic granular radiographic picture and the phalanges show subperiosteal bone resorption. The lamina dura of the teeth is absent. Calcium deposits may be seen in the kidneys and in other viscera. The plasma calcium is raised and the plasma phosphorus is low, while calcium-balance experiments show a negative balance with excessive urinary excretion of calcium. The plasma phosphatase is almost invariably raised. However, an atypical chemical picture as a result of renal disease may cause some difficulty in diagnosis. It was further pointed out by Lui that where hyperparathyroidism is associated with hypovitaminosis D, the plasma calcium may be normal and no calcium may be excreted in the urine. However, the giving of calciferol in adequate dosage to correct the hypovitaminosis will be followed by a return to the characteristic chemical picture of hyperparathyroidism.

Unlike a thyroid adenoma, a parathyroid adenoma is usually not palpable and must be sought for at operation. Rarely, however, such a parathyroid adenoma may even be palpable clincially before operation.

A number of conditions which bear a possible resemblance in one or more clinical, or radiographical, or biochemical features to generalized osteitis fibrosa are considered below:

Albright's Syndrome

This was described by Albright and colleagues under the title 'Syndrome characterized by osteitis fibrosa disseninata, areas of pigmentation and evdocrine dysfunction with precocious puberty in females'. Falconer et al. showed that such precocious puberty also occurred in boys. The main characteristics are: (a) multiple bone cysts which have a distribution suggesting a relation to nerve roots, or to an embryological defect in the myotomes; (b) areas of pigmentation which have a distribution suggesting some connexion with the bone cysts, the pigment being melanin; (c) precocious puberty with premature union of the epiphyses and ultimate dwarfism. In Albright's four cases, the first menstruation was observed at 1, 2½, 3½, and 7 years of age respectively. Normal pregnancy may occur in adult patients. The blood calcium and phosphorus and the calcium balance are normal, but the phosphatase may be jraised. Falconer deserived other features, e.g., massive bony deformity of the head, with resulting optic atrophy; and of the jaw, resembling leontiasis ossea; acromegalic features; enlargement of the thyroid, unilateral exophthalmos, and wide separation of the eyes.

Focal Osteitis Fibrosa

This condition may be found in one or more bones, and its incidence is chiefly in adolescence, although it may appear at any age. The commonest clinical manifestation is spontaneous fracture. General symptoms and constitutional disturbance are absent. The cause is unknown and there is certainly no obvious connexion with the parathyroids, since the calcium and phosphorus levels in the plasma, and the calcium balance are normal. Where several bones are affected the plasma phosphatase may be raised.

Paget's osteitis Deformans

Paget, who described the disease, believed the condition to be inflammatory in origin and, although this is not generally held to be the case today, no aetiological cause, metabolic or otherwise, has been substantiated. Kay, Simpson, and Riddoch observed and investigated thirty-four cases of this disease. Its onset is usually in middle life, although it may be first observed in the third or eighth decade of life. The average age of onset in this series was 46, the youngest 30 and the oldest 60 years of age. There were 18 females and 16 males. A brother and sister and their mother constituted the only example in this series of a familial incidence, but others have observed such familial tendencies in the minority of cases.

The onset of osteitis deformans is usually insidious and the progress gradual. The disease may be limited to one tibia for some years, but more usually is generalized. The vault of the skull is considerably thickened, enlarged, and deformed, and the face seems in comparison to the top-heavy head. Owing to phases of softness of bones, the spine and shoulders bend, and in advanced cases the patient's stance is simian in character. The legs become bowed and may cross over in scissor fashion, so that the patient may become bedridden, contrary to Paget's original observation that 'the limbs, however mis-shapen, remain strong and fit to support the trunk'.

Generalized pains of the bones are common and may be very severe, especially in the legs. Fractures following slight trauma occurred in five of the patients mentioned above. Sarcomatous change in a long bone rarely supervenes. Plasma calcium and phosphorus levels are normal, but a negative calcium balance is not infrequent, and the plasma phosphatase is always raised. No pathological changes in the parathyroids have been recorded. Radiologically, areas of rarefaction and increased density are seen side by side, and a characteristic fluffy, cotton wool appearance may be seen in the pelvis and skull. Complications are arterial degeneration and, rarely, spastic paraplegia or optic atrophy, due to bony compression of,nerve tissue.

Carcinomatosis of Bone

If metastases from an undetected primary carcinoma, e.g. prostate, are numerous, a radiological resemblance to generalized osteitis fibrosa may be observed. However, the chemical picture is not characteristic of hyerparathyroidism, the plasma calcium and phosphorus being normal. The phosphatase is raised, as in most generalized bone disturbances.

Multiple Myelomatosis

The presence of multiple marrow tumours may simulate generalized osteitis fibrosa. Progressive anaemia and cachexia, associated with a high incidence of fractures, are major features. If there is much bone destruction, the plasma calcium may be high and a negative calcium balance exists. The plasma phosphorus is never low. It is normal or above normal when the kidneys are involved. Bence Jones protein in the urine is characteristic.

Osteomalacia

This vitamin D deficiency disorder is a rarity in England but may be found as a result of gastro-intestinal dysfunction not permitting adequate absorption, e.g. chronic steatorrhoea. The plasma calcium and phosphorus are both low, or one may be normal, but never are they above normal. The urinary calcium is low and the faecal calcium high. The plasma phosphatase is raised. As previously mentioned, two cases of chronic steatorrhoea, leading to the development of hyperparathyroidism, have been described by Davies *et al*.

Generalized Osteoporosis Resulting from a Low Renal Threshold

Hunter recorded two such cases, due to the kidneys permitting an excess of calcium to escape into the urine. The serum calcium, however, was not raised and the renal aetiology was put forward as a suggestion.

Thyrotoxic Osteoporosis

The clinical picture is that of thyrotoxicosis, but some 40 per cent of patients show some rarefaction of bones and a negative calcium balance with normal plasma calcium and phosphorus values. Thyroidectomy, or antithyroid drugs, correct the osteoporosis and negative calcium balance, which are related not to the parathyroids but to the increased metabolism of hyperthyroidism.

Senile Osteoporosis

Generalized osteoporosis may be found in senile people, or in younger people confiend to immobility for long periods. The cause is undetermined but the diminution of gonadal secretion, especially oestrogens, has been postulated.

Eunuchoid Osteoporosis

Osteoporosis may accompany the other skeletal deformities found in some cases of gonadal dysgenesis.

Fragilitas Ossium

Multiple fractures occur *in utero,* in infancy, or in childhood. There is no disturbance of calcium or phosphorus metabolism and no known endocrine cause. The sclerotics of the eye are blue.

Course and Prognosis

In the absence of correct treatment hyperparathyroidism is inevitably progressive. Weakness and deformity of the bones eventually render the patient bedridden and intercurrent infection, such as pneumonia, leads to death. Sometimes the kidney lesion is the most severe feature and terminal uraemia results.

Treatment

The condition cannot be controlled medically. If the clinical and biochemical pictures indicate hyperparathyroidism, the neck should be explored and the adenoma removed. The difficulty of the operative procedure is finding the tumour, since sometimes this is deeply embedded in the thyroid gland, or may lie in the mediastinum or behind the oesophagus. Re-exploration, if the first operation fails to find the tumour, is always a far more difficult procedure because of the scar tissue resulting from the previous operation; it is therefore necessary that the surgeon should make every effort to succeed at the first attempt.

It is wise to administer a high calcium diet for two or three weeks before the operation, in order to make good, as far as possible, the depletion of the calcium reserves. The diet, therefore, should be rich in milk, cheese, and eggs; and in addition, calciferol should be administered in a dose of 50,000 Units daily. Careful post-operative attention is necessary, since latent or manifest tetany, due to a pronounced fall in plasma calcium, may occur. This is due to disuse atrophy of the remaining glands, and is most likely to develop in patients with generalized osteitis fibrosa and a high serum phosphatase; it is rare in patients without bony changes. Usually it is only temporary, but in some cases it has led to death. As a precaution against this occurrence, 2-4 G. of calcium lactate can be given three times a day for several weeks and the administration of calciferol should be continued for several months. On the first suspicion of tetany, intravenous calcium gluconate solution, 10-20 ml of a 10 or 20 per cent solution, should be given and repeated, even several times a day, if necessary. Parathormone, should not be given, since it is obviously illogical to mobilize calcium from bones already decalcified. The manifestations of subnormal calcium concentration may be psychotic rather than tetanic, and similarly are abolished when the plasma calcium reaches normal values again.

The more immediate results of operation are a disappearance of pain in the limbs an increase in strength the loss of gastro-intestinal symptoms, and the cessation of polyuria and polydipsia. Recalcification of bone may take several months or more and, although further deformity or fractures are unlikely, the existing malformation may prevent proper ambulation. Osteoclastomata tend to disappear in a few weeks. Renal calculi may disintegrate and be passed as gravel. Chronic nephritis, if of recent onset, may improve-but it may also continue to deteriorate and eventually cause death through renal failure. Cataract or lenticular opacities may occur if calcium is not given in adequate doses after operation. Menstruation, if previously scanty or absent, may return to normal. The plasma calcium falls immediately and the subnormal levels reached may lead to tetany; the plasma phosphorus tends to return to normal and the increased calcium excretion ceases. The plasma phosphatase usually remains raised, only gradually falling after a period of months or more; it is therefore more a measure of the degree and extent of bony change rather than of the excess of parathyroid hormone.

Secondary Hyperparathyroidism

It has been pointed out that in primary hyperparathyroidism the cause of the parathyroid adenoma is usually undiscoverable. In secondary hyperparathyroidism, however, hyperplasia of the parathyroid glands occurs as a compensatory mechanism which helps to maintain a normal concentration of calcium in the body fluids in various conditions in which the level of blood calcium tends to be decreased. Since a fall in plasma calcium leads to increased parathyroid hormone secretion, it follows that hyperplasia of the glands can be expected in those conditions which lead to a reduction in the calcium level-such as rickets, osteomalacia, steatorrhoea, pregnancy, lactation, and long-standing renal insufficiency. The cause of the low plasma calcium in rickets, osteomalacia, and steatorrhoea is insufficient or defective absorption of calcium from the intestinal tract; during pregnancy and lactation it results from the continuous drain on maternal calcium. The increased parathyroid activity removes calcium and phosphorus from the bones and increases the excretion of phosphorus, so that in the blood the calcium level remains normal, while that of phosphorus falls. In the meantime, of course, the bones decalcify. Albright has argued that when, in vitamin D deficiency, the plasma calcium is low and the plasma phosphorus is normal, compensatory hyperparathyroidism has failed to take place; while if both calcium and phosphorus levels are low, increased parathyroid activity has occurred, though in a degree insufficient to raise the plasma calcium to a normal level.

The enlargement of the parathyroid glands, which not uncommonly accompanies chronic nephritis, is considered by Albright to result from the following sequence of events: phosphorus is retained because of the renal failure; this leads to lowering of the blood calcium; parathyroid hyperfunction is the consequence. Were it not for this secondary hyperparathyroidism it seems probable that many patients with renal insufficiency would have severe tetany. Albright has defined a syndrome of 'renal osteitis fibrosa cystica' in which marked renal insufficiency has lasted a long time, with phosphate retention and a high plasma inorganic phosphorus level, a slight reduction in the plasma calcium level, marked acidosis, calcium deposits in the neighbourhood of joints, extreme calcification of the media of all arteries, generalized osteitis fibrosa of all bones, and enormous enlargement of all parathyroid tissue. He further considers that 'renal rickets' is really a variety of this syndrome in childhood, the bone changes being secondary to chronic nephritis and produced by secondary parathyroid hyperplasia.

Acute Hyperparathyroidism

Only seven cases of this extremely rare condition have been

reported. It is caused by a chief-cell adenoma of the parathyroid gland but it differs from *chronic hyperparathyroidism* in so far as the clinical picture shows a very rapid onset of symptoms. These consist of anorexia, vomiting, constipation, pains in the bones, loss of weight, and lassitude developing into increasing drowsiness and asthenia. The abdominal pain may be severe, resembling acute abdominal disease. There is slight fever, with a disproportionately high pulse rate, and there may be evidence of impaired renal function. In some cases there have been multiple *thromboses*. The metabolic disturbances typical of hyperparathyroidism are present, but bony change may be absent. There is widespread visceral and vascular calcification. Death usually occurs after several days.

As cause of death in acute hyperparathyroidism, Oliver has suggested dehydration, loss of electrolytes, and failure of the brain to utilize glucose in the absence of diffusible phosphorus. It is this latter which may be the explanation of the gradual onset of coma. In the case described by Hanes, it was felt that death was due either to severe myocardial lesions or to lack of diffusible phosphorus in the presence of a very high plasma calcium. It is the opinion of Oliver that prompt recognition and treatment of the disease might lead to good results. The treatment recommended consists of a continuous withdrawal of blood from a vein and its replacement by normal saline solution, followed, as soon as possible, by removal of the tumour.

HYPOPARATHYROIDISM

Hypoparathyroidism results from destruction, or operative removal, of the parathyroid glands. The resulting fall in the level of the blood calcium leads to tetany, a condition characterized by prolonged muscular spasms, due to increased neuromuscular excitability.

History

Tetany was first described clinically in 1815 by John Clarke. However, it was not until the end of the nineteenth century that it was brought into prominence as a result of its occurrence after partial thyroidectomy, an operation which was then initiated for goitre. Post-thyroidectomy tetany was produced experimentally by Schiff in 1884 and Horsley in 1885. In the meantime, however, Trousseau had described his sign in 1862 and Chvostek recorded his in 1876. The chemical basis of the parathyroid deficiency was recognized in the early part of this century by a series of workers, especially, MacCallum and Voegtlin. The guanidine theory of Paton and Findlay became popular for some time but was refuted in 1925 by Collip and Clark who showed that guanidine intoxication, which causes symptoms similar to those of tetany, could be produced even in the presence of excess of parathyroid hormone.

Aeitology of Tetany

Tetany can be due to many causes, but the ultimate basis is a fall in the plasma-ionized calcium. Although in alkalosis normal plasma calcium values may be found, there is nevertheless a decreased proportion of ionized calcium.

Interference with, or Removal of, Parathyroid Tissue

1. After removal of a parathyroid adenoma for hyperparathyroidism, most patients have some immediate post-operative symptoms, due to the fall of plasma calcium, but after some days or weeks these tend to disappear and it is assumed that the remaining parathyroid glands undergo compensatory hyperplasia, or return to normal if previously involuted.

2. After thyroidectomy the symptoms may occur at once, or after a latent period of some weeks-the so-called tetania parathyropriva. They may rarely persist in a chronic form. In a series of 277 patients operated on for *thyrotoxicosis*, Lachman found that 14 per cent showed transient evidence of post-operative parathyroid insufficiency. This figure seems a high one, even if only half required any treatment and more recent writers consider that post-thyroidectomy hypoparathyroidism should not occur in 1 per cent of cases under optimum conditions. Tetany is more frequent after total thyroidectomy for cardiac disease, but should not be a deterrent to operation in suitable cases, since it is usually easily controlled. Post-thyroidectomy tetany occurs practically only in women; even allowing for the increased incidence of thyrotoxicosis among women, it is probable that this fact is not without significance.

Since the finding of parathyroid tissue in thyroid glands removed at operation for thyrotoxicosis is exceptionally rare, it has been postulated that post-thyroidectomy tetany is due to interference with the blood supply of the parathyroids. It is also possible that removal of large amounts of thyroids tissue may in itself cause a transient fall in plasma calcium, since the opposite condition of thyroid *hyperplasia* may be associated with an increased urinary excretion of calcium and *osteoporosis*. In a study of post-thyroidectomy metabolism. Robertson found that the urinary excretion of phosphorus falls in cases of tetany following subtotal thyroidectomy for thyrotoxicosis, but is diminished to the same extent even after uncomplicated subtotal thyroidectomy.

Idiopathic Hypoparathyroidism

This condition is considered to be rare, only some 60 or 70 cases having been described in the literature. However, de Mowbray considers that more cases might come to light if the diagnosis were entertained in patients presenting with paraesthesiae, pains, cramps, and spasms in the extremities; in cases of epilepsy; and of cataracts occurring in young people; while cases associated with trophic changes in skin, hair, and nails might be found in skin clinics.- Moreover, three-quarters of the cases of idiopathic hypoparathyroidism reported in the literature have had their onset of symptoms in childhood, so that diagnosis should be considered in cases of infantile convulsions. In these cases of idiopathic hypoparathyroidism the gland cells of the parathyroids are replaced by fibrous or fatty tissue, or show marked round cell infiltration. In some cases the parathyroids are congenitally absent.

Rickets, Osteomalacia (Adult Rickets), Steatorrhoea

In these conditions there is deficient absorption and utilization of calcium. Infantile spasmophilia may also be included.

Pregnancy, Lactation, and Menstruation

The increased demands for calcium in these conditions probably render a latent tetany manifest. Deficient calcium in the diet and deficient sunlight and vitamin D may be the predisposing causes.

Alkalosis

This acts by reducing the ratio of ionized to nonionized calcium. It may result from excessive vomiting or gastric lavage, e.g. pyloric or intestinal obstruction; hyperpnoea, which may be hysterical, voluntary, or due to encephalitis lethargica; excessive alkaline treatment of peptic ulcer; and the use of alkalis in nephritis.

Miscellaneous

The following causes of tetany have occasionally been encountered: infection, in association with deficient diet; epidemic and occupational situations in which the causative factors have probably been deficient diet and sunlight; and dietary excess of phosphorus. This latter is a somewhat theoretical cause in man though in cattle it is well recognized and is presumed to act by depression of the blood calcium level.

Symptoms generally do not appear until the plasma calcium level is below 8 mg per 100 ml, and the plasma inorganic phosphorus level rises to above 5 mg. per 100 ml. In complete aparathyroidism, the plasma calcium may be as low as 4 mg and the plasma inorganic phosphorus as high as 12 mg per 100 ml. The fall in blood calcium level cannot be the whole explanation, for it is well known that patients with hypoparathyroidism may have periods of freedom from symptous, even though the calcium and phosphorus levels of the blood remain the same as those during periods of active tetany. What further factors may be involved in determining the abnormal neuromuscular activity are still largely speculative.

Clinical Features

The presenting symptoms are: Tetany, in some 70 per cent of cases, epilepsy, or generalized convulsions, in over 40 per cent; laryngeal spasm, ectodermal lesions, and failing vision, due to cataracts, each in some 10 per cent of cases. The major manifestations may be classified under seven headings. (1) Paraesthesiae and muscular cramps; (2) convulsions; (3) gastro-intestinal disturbances; (4) respiratory disturbances; (5) neurological disturbances; (6) psychoneurosis and psychosis; (7) trophic disturbances. One, or all, of these manifestations may be met with, and in latent tetany ectodermal trophic changes may be the only clinical manifestation.

Paraesthesiae and Muscular Spasms

The only disturbance in mild tetany may be numbness and tingling of the fingers. A burning sensation sometimes occurs, or the fingers may feel stiff. Cramps of the calf muscles tend to become worse at night. The muscles may be in a state of chronic tonic contraction, and if the facial muscles are so involved, a characteristic facies develops, e.g. a mask-like face with the corners of the mouth drawn downwards and the naso-labial folds accentuated; the forehead may be wrinkled and the eyes wide open. Tonic muscular contractions are occasionally associated with violent and unbearable pain.

Fibrillary muscular twitchings may be localized to groups of muscles, or widespread. Gross muscular spasms are often very painful and the patient then cries out with pain and perturbation. They last for minutes or hours, and may occur many times a day. Characteristically, the muscles of the hands and feet are involved, producing carpopedal spasm. The fingers are flexed at the metacarpo-phalangeal joints and extended at the inter-phalangeal joints, while the thumb is flexed across the palm, producing the obstetric hand. The wrists and elbows may also be flexed, bring the hands across the body. The toes are flexed, the ankle joint extended, and the sole of the foot inverted. Facial and neck muscles are also involved in some patients.

Convulsions

Epileptiform attacks, both 'petit mal' and 'grand mal' are known to occur, even in the absence of both signs, and patients have been treated in neurological clinics for years as idiopathic epileptics. Kowallis, describes an attack in a woman of 32 suffering from idiopathic hypoparathyroidism as follows:

Seizures commenced in the sixth postpartum week and subsequently occurred every two weeks. They were characterized by sudden onset, without warning, at any time of the day or night. There were loss of consciousness, biting of the tongue, clonic movements of all extremities and vesical incontinence. The seizure was followed by a deep sleep. The whole episode involved about an hour. The patient was not conscious of what happened during the attacks, although she remembered the residual headaches and mental depression. After the onset of her convulsions, definite personality changes developed, primarily irritability, stubbornness and forgefulness.

In this case, the plasma calcium was 5.1 mg, and the phosphorus *4.8* mg per 100 ml. In a case described by Himsworth and Maizels a boy of 12, carpopedal spasms or 'grand mal' attacks occurred and were completely controlled by calciferol, providing the plasma calcium was not allowed to fall below 7 mg per 100 ml. Even 'grand mal' attacks were avoided so long as the calcium level remained above 5.5 mg per 100 ml. Characteristic changes may be shown in the electroencephalogram in patients with tetany; there may be abnormal slow waves or epileptic patterns. Apart from headaches associated with epilepsy, typical migranine may be a manifestation of tetany.

Gastro-Intestinal Disorders

Spasm of the gastro-intestinal musculature produces abdominal cramps, pain, and vomiting. Laparatomy has been performed for suspected perforated peptic ulcer, or appendicitis and in fact, ileal spasm has produced a fatal ileus. Spasm of bile passages produces a clinical picture of gallstone colic and, rarely even transitory jaundice.

Respiratory Disorders

Spasm of the larynx is liable to occur, more especially in rickety children with spasmophilia. The attacks and sudden in onset and alarming in their dramatic presentation. Spasm of the bronchial musculature simulates bronchial asthma.

Neurological Disturbances

In addition to the psychiatric disturbances mentioned below, papilloedema, cerebellar dysfunction, and cerebral calcification may be found. At times the changes may mimic brain tumour to the extent of precipitating neurosurgical diagnostic exploration.

Psychiatric Disturbances

In addition to mental retardation, which may be found in juvenile patients with hypoparathyroidism, a variety of psychoneurotic and psychotic changes may be encountered. These include anxiety symptoms, irritability and depression, and impairment of memory and intellectual capacity. More rarely, hallucinations, confusion states, manic-depressive conditions, paranoia, schizoid personality, and dementia may be present in chronic tetany. In a series of eighteen examples of parathyroid insufficiency, no fewer than five were cases of psychosis. This is most commonly of a toxic delirious type, occurring during the first few months of the parathyroid deficiency, and may be its only manifestation. With adequate treatment of the parathyroid insufficiency, the prognosis is considered to be good, although the response may not be immediate.

Trophic Changes

The skin may be dry, rough, and scaly, and there may be various skin disorders, such as dermatitis herpetiformis, pustules, acrodermatitis pustulosa continua, psoriasis, and chloasma. The hair may show diffuse thinning and occasionally even complete loss. The eyebrows and eyelashes may become thin, and there may be some loss of pubic and axillary hair. The nails show fraying, brittleness, grooving, necrosis, and detachment. There have been a number of reports of cases of idiopathic hypoparathyroidism in which the skin, nails, mouth and tongue have been infected with moniliasis. Whittaker *et. al.* have described a syndrome of familial juvenile hypo-adre-nocorticism, hypoparathyroidism, and superficial moniliasis, based on a description of their own patient and twelve similar patients reported in the literature.

When the parathyroid deficiency arises in childhood, the teeth may be defective in enamel and dentine, and the enamel shows transverse ridging. Dental caries is frequent. The teeth may fall out.

Cataracts may occur in tetany from any cause. They may be an early feature in hypoparathyroidism, even in the absence of manifest tetany. They may also develop after tetany has become controlled by treatment. The history or finding of 'senile cataract' in any person below middle age, or after thyroidectomy, should immediately arouse suspicions of hypoparathyroidism.

Diagnosis

This is not difficult in a well-developed case and, once made, the detection of minor manifestations soon follows. Trousseau's sign consists of producing carpal spasm by maintaining a sphygmomanometer above the systolic pressure for 1 to 5 minutes. Chvostek's sign is the production of contraction of a facial muscles by tapping the facial nerve just below the zygoma and in front of the parotid gland. Erb's sign is an exaggerated muscular contraction in response to minimal electrical stimuli.

The plasma calcium level is reduced, always below 8 mg per 100 ml and occasionally as low as 4 or 5 mg per 100 ml. The plasma inorganic phosphorus level is raised, occasionally as high as 10-12 mg per 100 ml. No direct relation exists between the level of the plasma calcium and the severity of the tetany. Severe tetany probably occurs more often in post-operative cases, in which the level falls rapidly to between 7 and 8 mg per 100 ml; on the other hand, in chronic cases, tetany may be absent or only very mild, even when the level is as low as 5-6 mg per 100 ml. The alkaline phosphatase level is usually normal or reduced. In steatorrhoea or rickets, the plasma phosphorus level is normal. Bleeding and coagulation times are prolonged, owing to the low blood calcium. Tetanus is, of course, in no way related to tetany and is an infective condition, following a contaminated wound. Opisthotonos does not occur in tetany.

Course and Course and Prognosis

Hypoparathyroidism can be controlled, but in severe cases the borderline is easily crossed and intermittent attacks of tetany may occur. Tetany, due to disorders such as rickets or alkalosis, can be cured by appropriate treatment of the underlying disorder.

TREATMENT

Acute Attactks

The immediate treatment is the slow intravenous injection of 10 or 20 ml of 10 per cent solution of calcium gluconate. Soon after the intravenous injection the same amount of calcium gluconate maybe given intramuscularly in order to prolong the effect. Calcium chloride, 20 ml of a 5 per cent solution, may also be used intravenously but intramuscular injection may lead to necrosis and ulceration and so should be avoided. As an emergency measure in very severe cases, the intravenous injection of parathormone, in a dose of 20-60 Units, has been advocated. It is doubtful, however, if parathormone has any advantage over calcium; it further demineralizes bones where osteitis fibrosa is already present; it is expensive; it is liable to give rise to reactions; and-it leads to antihormone formation after repeated injections and thereby becomes ineffective. When parathormone is used the behaviour of the plasma calcium must be observed closely in order to avoid overdosage. The early symptoms of overdosage are anorexia, nausea, and vomiting, and later thirst and drowsiness which may proceed to coma. On the other hand, the hypercalcaemia may cause no symptoms at all. Overdosage has to be treated by discontinuing the injections, and lowering the increased viscosity ef'the blood, caused by the hypercalcaemia, by withdrawing a pint of blood from a vein and replacing it with twice the amount of normal saline solution.

When, by reason of the convulsions, the intravenous administration of the drugs mentioned above is difficult, it is necessary to sedate or even to anaesthetize the patient first.

Subacute or Chronic Tetany

The mainstay of treatment is the administration of an irradiated ergosterol derivative, either calciferol (vitamin D_2), or dihydrotachysterol (A.T. 10). These substances are of similar chemical structure, the difference being that calciferol has a double bond between the C9 and 10 atoms. The principal effect of A.T. 10 is to stimulate phosphate excretion in the urine, and it also increases calcium absorption from the intestine. It thus appears to resemble more closely parathyroid hormone in its action than calciferol, which acts principally by increasing calcium absorption, though it does have a weak action on the excretion of phosphorus in the urine. There is also some evidence that both calciferol and A.T. 10 liberate calcium from bone.

In so far as it resembles parathyroid hormone more closely in its action, A.T. 10 is theoretically preferable; on the other hand, calciferol is much cheaper, so that whereas with the latter, an average maintenance dose costs about a shilling a month, with the former the cost is about £1 per month. As regards their effects in controlling symptoms and plasma calcium level, there seems little to choose between calciferol and A.T. 10, though it is possible that the former is more likely to lead to hypercalcaemia in view of the fact that it acts predominantly upon calcium absorption and has a cumulative action in this respect. The initial dose is usually from *200,000* to 500,000 Units of calciferol (or even more) or 3 ml of A.T. 10, daily. The daily maintenance doses are usually from 50,000 to 200,000 Units, or 0.25-1 ml respectively.

It has been observed that some patients with chronic tetany, when taking a dose of calciferol that has been sufficient to maintain their plasma calcium levels, may, for no apparent reason, develop an insensitivity to the calciferol and remain unaffected, even when the dosage is markedly increased. Dent *et al.* made metabolic studies on two patients taking large doses of calciferol while in such a calciferol-insensitive phase. None of the usual metabolic actions of calciferol were manifest. In four patients who had become calciferol -insensitive, a change was made from large doses of calciferol to normal doses of A.T. 10, or of pure vitamin D_3. This led to a rapid disappearance of tetany and a return to normal of their plasma calcium and phosphorus levels. In two patients, in whom the change from calciferol to A.T. 10 or to vitamin D_3 was undertaken while they were under full metabolic control, it was found that the change of treatment coincided with the onset of normal vitamin D action. These authors therefore consider that in many such patients it may be necessary, from time to time, to change the form of vitamin D preparation in order to maintain a continued response.

As a guide to the correct dosage, the Sulkowitch reaction is a useful rough indication of the amount of calcium being excreted in the urine. If the calcium is precipitated as a fine white powder of calcium oxalate, it is probable that the plasma calcium is about normal; if there is no precipitate the urine is free from calcium and the plasma calcium level may be between 5 and 7.5 mg per 100 ml; if there is a heavy precipitate, so that a milky appearance is produced, the plasma calcium may be above 12 mg per 100 mi. Nevertheless, repeated estimations of the plasma' calcium level are advisable, since instances are not uncommon where the plasma calcium is low when the Sulkowitch reaction is positive and it is known that symptoms of acute hypercalcaemia may appear even when there is no excess of calcium in the urine. The ideal use of the Sulkowitch reagent is by the patient herself, since it is easy to carry out, and a heavy positive reaction should warn her to reduce the dose, or to stop taking the drug, and to see her physician immediately; while an absence of any precipitate would indicate the need for an increase of the dose.

In many cases repeated readjustment of the dosage, in response to infection or according to mental and physical stresses and strains, may be necessary, the situation in fact being comparable to that of the treatment of diabetes mellitus.

Although it is true that a high-calcium, low-phosphorus diet may restore the plasma calcium and phosphorus levels to normal, it is unlikely that many patients could adhere to such a diet with sufficient accuracy. On the whole, therefore, it is better not to place patients on a strict diet but to rely on the effectiveness of the vitamin D preparation.

It is however, advisable to avoid an *excess* of milk in view of the fact that it has a high content of phosphorus as well as being rich in calcium. It is likewise generally better to do without calcium salts, since adjustment is much easier if only one variable, namely that of the vitamin D preparation, has to be taken into account.

Pseudo-Hypoparathyroidism

This rare congenital disorder was first described by Albright *et al.* and the total number of cases in the literature is still below twenty. It consists of three independent, most probably genetically determined, disturbances:

1. There is an abnormal peripheral resistance to the action of parathyroid hormone (target-organ failure) which results in all the manifestations of hypoparathyroidism.

2. There is a dyschondroplasia which results in dwarfism and in shortening of some of the metacarpals and metatarsals.

3. There is a tendency to metaplastic formation of bone in the soft tissues.

The manifestations of hypoparathyroidism can be controlled by vitamin D preparations as in hypoparathyroidism itself. There is, of course, no treatment for the other aspects of the disorder.

Diseases due to Adrenal Hormone

Primary adrenocortical hypofunction, or Addison's disease, is an uncommon disease which affects six in every 100 000 of the population. Some cases of Addison's disease are due to destruction of the adrenal cortex by tuberculosis, other granulomatous diseases or carcinoma (primary or secondary): the remaining cases, called idiopathic Addison's disease, are autoimmune in origin.

Table 4.1. Historical Comparison of Causes of Addison's Disease

	Years studied	
	1938-1958	**1962-1973**
Idiopathic	30%	78%
Tuberculosis	60%	20%
Others	10%	2%

Case

A 12-year-old girl presented with vague abdominal discomfort for 6 months. She had noticed occasional diarrhoea but had not passed any blood. She admitted to weight loss (6 kg) and anorexia. Her mother had thyrotoxicosis. On examination, she was obviously pigmented, although she thought this was sun-induced; however, her buccal mucosa and gums were also brown. There were no other physical signs.

She had a low cortisol level and her response to ACTH in a Synacthen test was poor. A diagnosis of adrenal cortical failure was made. X-ray of her abdomen showed no calcified areas in either adrenal gland, and her serum contained antibodies to adrenal cortex, consistent with a diagnosis of *autoimmune adrenalitis.* Her serum also contained antibodies to pancreatic islet cells and thyroid microsomes. In view of the young age at presentation and these serum antibodies, she will be followed at yearly intervals to see if she develops other autoimmune endocrinopathies.

Autoimmune Adrenal Disease

Three-quarters of all cases of Addison's disease are due to an **autoimmune adrenalitis** which affects the adrenal cortex but spares the medulla. Like other autoimmune endocrinopathies, it is more common in women and reaches a maximum incidence between 40 and 50 years of age. Patients' sera should be tested for all organ-specific autoantibodies as 40% of patients have at least one other autoimmune endocrinopathy. The presence of autoantibodies may predict future onset of the disease, so that replacement therapy (or other relevant treatment) can be started promptly.

TABLE 4.2. ASSOCIATION OF 'IDIOPATHIC' ADDISON'S DISEASE WITH OTHER ENDOCRINE DISEASES

Associated autoimmune disease	*Percentage of 'idiopathic' Addison's disease patients with other organ involvement*
Thyroid diseases	19%
Diabetes mellitus	15%
Ovarian failure	8%
Hypoparathyroidism	4%
Pernicious anaemia	2%

Evidence for immune involvement in idiopathic Addison's disease is shown in Table 2.3. The histological evidence is, of course, only suggestive; *an inflammatory cell infiltrate may be the result of the damage rather than its cause.* The presence of antibodies to cytoplasmic adrenal cortex antigens in this disease may also be secondary to damage, although fewer than 5^k of patients with adrenal damage due to tuberculosis have this antibody. Similarly, cell-mediated immunity to adrenal tissue can be demonstrated in about 60% of patients with 'idiopathic' Addison's disease and is probably secondary. Recently, circulating antibodies have been detected which block ACTH-induced adrenal cell growth in vitro; such antibodies are probably primary, pathogenic autoantibodies.

TABLE 4.3. EVIDENCE FOR IMMUNE INVOLVEMENT IN IDIOPATHIC ADDISON'S DISEASE

1. Association with other autoimmune diseases.
2. Presence of autoantibody to adrenal cortex and high incidence of other organ-specific autoantibodies.
3. Diffuse lymphocytic infiltration of adrenal cortex.
4. Evidence of cell-mediated immunity to adrenal cortex antigens.
5. Adrenal failure produced experimentally in animals by immunization with adrenal tissue with transfer by lymph node cells.

The finding of antibodies to cytoplasmic adrenal antigens in some patients with Cushing's syndrome due to nodular adrenocortical dysplasia has led to a search for **stimulating adrenocortical antibodies.** Positive preliminary data are now being followed up with large scale studies.

ADRENOGENITAL SYNDROME

This term was first used (as i.e. *syndrome genito-surrenal)* by the French physician Gallais, and must be considered as a clinical label. It can be defined as a condition of amenorrhoea, or oligomenorrhoea, produced by an excess of adrenal cortex androgenic hormones, as indicated clinically by an associated development of hirsutism. By definition, the disorder as thus described, is limited to females and cannot be recognized as this syndrome before chronological puberty. The term therefore does not include congenital virilism dating from infancy, and it is to be regretted that the term is sometimes used less discriminatingly. The term also cannot include the similar clinical picture occasionally produced by an androgen-secreting ovarian tumour, since the ovary and not the adrenals in such cases is the source of the androgens.

Pathology

The lesion is usually bilateral hyperplasia of the adrenal cortex but a single adenoma or adenocarcinoma is not infrequent. The ovaries are involuted or atrophic, and multiple small cysts are sometimes present, the appearance resembling that produced by injecting, animals with large doses of testosterone. The excess of adrenal androgens inhibits the normal pituitary secretion of gonadotrophins and there is thus failure of follicle development and of ovulation.

Clinical Features

Amenorrhoea (or oligomenorrhoea) combined with the development or increase of hirsutism are two essential features. Chronologically there are two main types, (1) puberty, (2) adult. The puberty type becomes manifest at the age of chronological puberty, e.g. 14, when the hirsutism is noted and the patient in the course of the next few years fails to menstruate, or menstruates scantily and at long intervals. As it is now recognized that the adrenals develop increase activity (adrenarche) at the time of puberty, it is not surprising that one type of adrenogenital syndrome shows itself at this phase. Since the adrenarche may also occur earlier, *e.g.* age 7, partial manifestations may present earlier than puberty time, but the label adrenogenital syndrome cannot be applied before chronological puberty indicates the evolution, or lack of evolution. Failure of the breasts to develop at 14 or so, is another indication of suppression of normal ovarian evolution by the adrenal androgens. There is also absence of widening of the pelvis so that the relative measurements of shoulders and pelvis approximate to that of the average male.

The adult type of adrenogenital syndrome usually manifests itself in the third or fourth decade, but sometimes is met with in the later teens, after a puberty which is normal or nearly normal. It is difficult to understand, in the absence of an adrenal neoplasm, why the adrenals develop excessive androgenic activity at varying phases of adult life in different individuals (apart from puberty, pregnancy, and the climacteric), but that they do so is undoubted and not infrequent : and with gradually increasing androgen manifestations over a number of years.

Acne is another manifestation of excessive androgenic activity in all types of adrenogenital syndrome and this may be very severe, affecting both body and face. Enlargement of the clitoris is similarly explained and adds strength to the diagnosis, but it is by no means met with in all patients as it depends both upon the intensity of the androgenic stimulus and upon the sensitivity or responsiveness of the clitoric tissues.

Hirsutism

The responsiveness of the hair follicles partly determines the degree of hirsutism met with but, in addition, the distribution of hair follicles varies in different individuals. In some women the hirsutism may be almost limited to the face, in milder degrees affecting the upper sides of the face, the upper lip, and chin, as in the adolescent man, but in the more severe it may cover the face to the extent found in the normal adult male. Body hair may be limited to the appearance, or increase, of hair along the linea alba, and a few hairs round the nipple, but it may spread all over the abdomen, be present or increase over the lumbosacral area, and spread from the spine over the shoulders and scapular areas. It is of interest that in the hirsute male, the lumbar area may be free of hair, whereas it is a sensitive hirsute area in the virile female. The pubic hair increases in amount, and hair spreads downwards from the vulva on to the thighs as seen posteriorly. In severe hirsutism, hair spreads over the buttocks, and even in the absence of hair, the skin over the buttocks loses its smoothness and is covered by raised hair follicles and papules. From this it will be seen that the appearance of the patient's limnar area, buttocks, and posterior thighs, as seen from the posterolateral angle is of diagnostic significance. Hair appears, or increase on legs, forearms, backs of the hands, and fingers. Thick eyebrows, perhaps joined by a less intense middle hirsute ridge, and long eyelashes are also manifestations of heightened androgenic activity. The scalp hair becomes thick and coarse and tends to encroach upon the forehead and nape of neck, and greasy seborrhea is often present. Later scalp hair is lost from the top of the head and frontotemporal areas as in the normal male.

Amenorrhoea may be absolute, or scanty menstruation may occur at long intervals. Occasionally long but irregular intervals of menstruation are associated with menorrhagia and anovular menstruation.

Alternations in Body Fat

In the characteristic, or classical, variety of the varilizing adrenogenital syndrome, fat is lost,. particularly from the breasts, abdomen, buttocks, thighs and upper arms, and face-areas in which the normal deposition of fat tends to produce the normal 'feminine' types of contours-and simultaneously muscular tissue tends to hypertrophy, both these effects being an expression of the protein anabolic effects of the excess of androgens. There is frequently an increase in muscular strength. In so far as these processes are reversed by successful removal of an adrenal androgen secreting tumour, there seems no doubt as to the cause, although the metabolic mechanism may be more involved than that of protein anabolism associated with fat catabolism.

In addition to the above, an adipose type of adrenogenital syndrome must be recognized in which not only is there no loss of fat but fat is deposited, especially in the sites mentioned above, with a resulting general increase in weight-sometimes considerable. In so far as some adrenal glucocorticoids influence fat deposition and fat distribution, it seems probably that the adipose type of adrenogenital syndrome is influenced by a simultaneous excessive secretion of adrenal glucocorticoids, although this is not consistently confirmed by hormone assays. Be this as it may, the clinical adipose type must be recognized as existing, and in fact as being the more commonly met with. Its relationship to Cushing's syndrome and adipose gynism will be discussed later. In this type enlargement of the clitoris is relatively rare. The supposition that the adrenals are the cause of the adiposity receives some support from the loss of adiposity that follows subtotal adrenalectomy, or removal of an adrenal tumour, as such loss is not necessarily associated with any evidence of adrenal insufficiency. The relative excess of adrenal androgens and glucocorticoids determine the clinical picture, as these hormones are metabolic antagonists.

Diagnosis

Clinical diagnosis depends upon definition and is not difficult, although the differentiation between adrenal hyperplasia and neoplasia requires accessory aids. Clinically, the following varieties of hirsutism must be differentiated from the adrenogenital syndrome.

Androgenic Ovarian Tumour (usually arrhenoblastoma)

The clinical picture resembles the virile rather than the adipose type. The raised urinary 17-ketosteroids are not diminished by the prednisone suppression test. When in doubt, examination under anaesthesia, and even lower abdominal laparotomy, is prudent.

Stein-Leventhalsyndrome. When adiposity and/or hirsutism are prominent features of this syndrome, the writer considers that the primary condition is adrenal and that there is a confusion of nomenclature. In other words, many patients described under this heading are examples of the adrenogenital syndrome. This is supported by the clinical fact that bilateral ovarian wedge resection does not influence adiposity and hirsutism appreciably, except perhaps with the relatively rare condition of superluteinization of ovaries, luteal tissue having some functional kinship with adrenal cortex tissue.

Pituitary Type of Adrenogenital Syndrome

Hirsutism, acne, and amenorrhoea are recognized complications of acromegaly but it is less generally appreciated that they may be features of even mild giantism, with oligomenorrhoea or anovular menstruation instead of amenorrhoea. Apart from the skeletal structure, this type canbe identical with the adrenogenital syndrome and perhaps should be included as a third group in this syndrome. The pituitary fossa may be enlarged but a pituitary neoplams is rare. The patients are usually muscular and virile but a degree of adiposity may also be met with.

Adipose gynisin

Although this clinical entity may have a spontaneous favourable outcome, the history in retrospect of some patients with the adipose type of adrenogenital syndrome suggests that this disorder is a continuation of the entity called adipose gyms: or a relapse from a remission from this disorder, which starts in childhood. The diagnosi however, in this adult phase is still correctly given as adrenogenital syndrome.

Familial Hirsutism

This condition is sometimes termed 'essential' hirsutism or 'simpl hirsutism or 'genetic' hirsutism or 'racial' hirsutism, it being more common amor Celtic and Mediterranean races. The nomenclature implies that the hirsutism is n associated with other features of adrenogenital syndrome such as amenorrhoea, enlargf clitoris, or adiposity. Theoretically this is a proper differentiation, but in practice it is n an absolute one, especially when one remembers that the adrenogenital syndrome is itself often familial, genetic, and racial, and that when severe acne is associated wi hirsutism it is difficult not to regard both as of androgenic origin; and further, th hirsutism by itself might not become severe until pregnancy, or the climacteric, whi adrenal androgenic activity increases. The absence of raised urinary 17-ketosteroids cannot be an absolute criterion because these values are often not raised in the adrenogenit syndrome, and constitute a poor measure of adrenal androgenic activity. Neverthele it appears valid to say that the distribution of hair follicles is more dense and mo widely distributed in some women than in others, and that they may be more sensiti' to a androgenic stimulus. To state these facts does not solve the problem arising fro the fact that most women will not accept facial hirsutism as being normal.

Treatment

When an adrenal or ovarian androgenic tumour is the cause, the tumour must obvious be removed surgically. Unlike adrenal glucocorticoids tumours, adrenal androger tumours do not usually lead to atrophy of the opposite adrenal gland so that it is n essential to give large doses of cortisone in the post-operative period, as in Cushinl syndrome. Nevertheless, it might be thought prudent to do so.

In the absence of a tumour, bilateral hypertrophy and hyperplasia of the adrer cortex is the probable lesion to be dealt with. Unilateral adrenalectomy is of little use except in those rare cases in which one adrenal only is considerably hypertrophic. Subtotal adrenalectomy is best carried out by removing the whole of one adrenal gland and some seven-eighths of the other. Since the remnant left behind may be sufficient to maintain essential adrenal functions until it has been given time to undergo some hypertrophy, replacement therapy with cortisone or prednisone is advisable and may have to be continued.

Apart from surgery, adrenal androgenic hyperfunction, as measured by urinary 17-ketosteroids, may be suppressed by cortisone by mouth, e.g., 25 mg. three times a day, or by prednisone, 5 mg. three times a day, although not as effectively as in genetic virilism.

The denial of hirsutism in childhood does not necessarily exclude genetic metabolic virilism because the patient may have amnesia for early life. In one such patient, aged 50, a mild operative interference, without protective cortisone therapy, led to acute and fatal adrenal insufficiency. Every patient therefore should be investigated completely before any operative procedure is undertaken.

Prognosis

Removal of an adrenal tumour usually gives an excellent clinical result, although hirsutism of long standing may persist in the absence of raised 17-ketosteroids. Subtotal adrenalectomy is always effective in regard to menstruation and body-weight, but hirsutism is not always alleviated. Chronic suppression therapy with cortisone or prednisone should not be undertaken in the absence of raised 17-ketosteroids and in any case is more likely to benefit amenorhoea and acne than hirsutism. Facial hirsutims and coincident loss of scalp hair may remain a provocative therapeutic problem.

CUSHING'S SYNDROME

A syndrome due to adrenal cortex hyperfunction, hyperplasia, or neoplasia, associated with excessive secretion of adrenal glucocorticoids, and a resulting negative nitrogen balance, and manifested clinically by a type of plethoric adiposity, hypertension, purple lineae distensae, patchy cyanosis, amenorrhoea or impotence, some hypertrichosis, diabetes, osteoporosis, weakness, and psychoneurotic features. The condition can occur at any age and in either sex.

Cushing's original description deserves quotation:

The disorder is characterized by a rapidly acquired plethoric adiposity affecting the face, neck, and the trunk, the extremities being spared. It is associated in women with hypertrichosis and amenorrhoea. Other characteristic features are vascular hypertension, purplish striae distensae of the abdomen, and acrocyanosis with cutis marmorata of the extremities. It is often accompanied by hyperglycaemia, and a peculiar softening of the bones of the skeleton has been commonly found at autopsy. In its extreme forms, the malady has often been encountered in young adults, and the average duration of life in the fatal cases has been something over five years.

In defining the syndrome I have intentionally excluded a mixed syndrome in which the clinical picture is a combination of adrenogenital virilism and classical Cushing's syndrome, because the hyperfunction is associated with an excessive secretion both of adrenal androgens and of adrenal glucocorticoids. I have described this mixed syndrome, as a separate entity, under the heading of mixed adrenal hyperfunction, but it is recognized that this classification of convenience is not absolute. It is necessary, however, since androgens are antagonistic to glucocorticoids e.g. they are protein anabolic and prevent esteoperosis. The inclusion of hypertrichosis in classical Clushing's syndrome is partly justified by Cushing's original description and partly by the fact that some metabolic products of adrenal glucocorticoids are androgenic, but severe generalized hirsutism and other signs of virilism are not compatible with a diagnosis of classical Cushing's syndrome.

History

There is no doubt whatsoever that the clinical picture of Cushing's syndrome has been known to physicians for some fifty years or more: and has been frequently reported under a variety of clinical names, including 'fat bearded diabetic woman': Ercheim, Launois, Turney, Anderson. Achard and Thiers, and Parkes Weber. It was, however, the keen clinical and pathological observations of Cushing, as well as his intensive study of the literature, which resulted in the crystallization and separation of a distinct clinical entity, so ably and dramatically presented in his classical paper of 1932; and to which, in the same year, Bishop and Close appropriately appended his name. Cushing chose an arresting title for his paper, namely, *The Basophil Adenomas of the Pituitary Body and their Clinical Manifestation (Pituitary Basophilism)*. We shall see in the pathology section that this theory of origin could not be sustained.

Pathology

The more immediate cause of Cushing's syndrome is hyperfunction of the adrenal cortex, hyperplasia being more frequent than neoplasia. Hyperplasia, particularly in children, may be simple or associated with multiple adenomata, macroscopic or microscopic. The zona fasciculata is the zone principally involved. It must be recognized, however, that in some well-developed and characteristic cases, the adrenal glands weigh no more than the normal, and the appearance, macroscopic and microscopic, gives no indication of the hyperfunction and hypersecretion which is obvious clinically, by hormone assays, and by the results following subtotal adrenalectomy.

When due to a neoplasm, the whole gland may be replaced by an adenoma or adenocarcinoma, the latter being more common in children; or a narrow flattened streak of adrenal gland may be attached to the tumour. The opposite adrenal gland is frequently atrophied, owing to the suppression of pituitary ACTH secretion by the high concentration of blood glucocorticoids.

Cushing attached more significance to the finding of a basophil adenoma in some patients with his syndrome than did Erdheim before him, and he thought that diligent search, with serial sections, would show an actiologically significant basophil adenoma in most cases. This did not prove to be so and this theory of the primary cause of the syndrome is now discarded.

Crooke found constant changes in the basophil cells of the pituitary gland in Cushing's syndrome, whether the adrenal lesion was hyperplasia or neoplasia, namely degranulization, hyalinization, and vacuolization of the basophil cells. He recorded: the normal cytoplasm, charged with ripe basophil granules, is replaced by a dense homogenous cytoplasm. This may be complete or partial, and vacuolization may occur'. His observations were confirmed by Rasmussen. Since the clinical syndrome is cured by removal of an adrenal adenoma, Simpson concluded that these basophil changes were secondary to the adrenal hyperfunction and reversible and this was experimentally proved by producing such,basophil changes in animals by injections on cortisone or ACTH.

Nevertheless, quite apart from the fact that Cushing's syndrome is occasionally associated with an enlarged pituitary fossa and even with acromegaly, bilateral hyperplasia of the adrenal cortex is probably caused by an excessive secretion of pituitary ACTH, and further back in the link by an initial hypothalamic stimulus, experimental or in man, from third ventricle tumours; and an excessive concentration of plasma ACTH has been found in some patients with Cushing's syndrome. The cellular source of the ACTH is probably of basophil type but Cushing's syndrome has been found with the following pituitary lesions: a basophil adenoma, a basophil carcinoma, a chromophobe adenoma, and an eosinophil adenoma. If there is a primary hypersecretion of ACTH in Cushing's syndrome, the resulting excessive secretion of hydrocortisone would tend to reduce this. It is also necessary to explain why the adrenal response is mainly or entirely glucocorticoid and not equally androgenic. For this, and other more complex reasons, there are some who regard the essential lesion as a primary adrenal cellular abnormality and hypersensitivity to a normal pituitary ACTH stimulus. The innate difficulty of this qualitative conception is the fact that the onset may occur at any age.

It would appear that a primary adrenal adenoma or adenocarcinoma is independent of any abnormal pituitary stimulus: although, as has been considered in the adrenogenital syndrome, it is possible that hyperplasia proceeds to multiple adenomata and that one of these may become large and autonomous, with resulting involution of the others.

Ovary

Whatever the primary cause of Cushing's syndrome may be, the ovaries usually show secondary changes of atrophy or involution. Thus Cushing recorded senile, fibrotic, or atretic ovaries; atretic follicles with no corpora lutea; numerous follicular cysts of variable size and normal germinal epithelium, but no primordial ova; follicular development without ovulation and luteinization. Such changes are characteristic, but occasionally normal ovaries and normal corpora lutea are found. Exceptionally an ovarian tumour, developing from an adrenal 'rest' in the ovary, may in itself produce Cushing's syndrome. Other ovarian tumours may produce virilism but not Cushing's syndrome.

Testes

Atrophy of the spermatogenous epithelium, and of the interstitial cells, with fibrosis, is the usual finding, but normal testes have been recorded.

Thymus

In two males, Cushing's syndrome was associated with a carcinoma of the thymus, but the adrenals were enlarged, and the pituitary basophil cells showed hyalinization. In the majority of cases, however, the thymus gland has been atrophic or completely replaced by fat. In some it has been normal, and in one boy of 19 the thymus was found to be enormous, the adrenals long, thin, and hypoplastic, and the testes atrophic. A basophil adenoma was present in the pituitary. The significance of the thymus as an aetiological factor in Cushing's syndrome remains doubtful. The involution or atrophy of the thymus usually found is in keeping with animal experiments following cortisone administration.

Thyroid

The thyroid gland is often slightly enlarged, but may be small and fibrotic. The epithelium is flattened and colloid is present in the vesicle, and the appearance is that of a resting gland, in keeping with the known inhibition of thyroid function by cortisone.

Parathyroids

These may be normal, or fibrotic, or infiltrated with fat. Occasionally an adenoma may be present, but there was no evidence of hyperplasia or neoplasm in one case showing a marked increase in calcium excretion, and a negative calcium balance.

Pancreas

Although no constant findings have been recorded, and although fatty degeneration of the islets may occur, the pancreas is usually normal, even in the presence of gross diabetes. This is in keeping with the initial steroid character of the diabetes and the later secondary effects on the pancreatic islets in untreated cases. In children, hyperplasia of the pancreatic islet cells has been found.

Kidneys

The kidneys may be normal or may show histological evidence of chronic nephritis; and sometimes the cardiovascular and renal lesions are identical with those of malignant nephrosclerosis. Minute deposits of calcium may be found in the kidney substance and in the calyces-as in hyperparathyroidism. With or without renal lesions, cardiac hypertrophy and arteriosclerosis are not infrequent findings, as might be expected from the fact that hypertension is a common symptom.

Clinical Features

The disorder is four times as frequent in women as in men, and pregnancy immediately preceded the onset in five of the eleven women described in Cushing's monograph. It is commonest in the second and third decades of life, but there is a group in which the syndrome commences at the time of chronological puberty, and it may start in earlier childhood, although this is unusual in the uncomplicated form. A climacteric form of incomplete type has also been described.

In view of the multiple manifestations of excess of cortisone, or hydrocortisone, the disorder may present in a variety of ways, but most characteristically as a change of appearance, with development of the characteristic moon-like fat face, and fatigability, which draws attention to the wider symptomatology. However, the writer has met with cases which presented primarily as diabetes, severe pain in the back from spontaneous fractures of osteoporotic vertebrae, hypertension; polycythaemia, spontaneous subcutaneous haemorrhages, general adiposity, facial hirsutism, amenorrhoea, malignant nephrosclerosis, depressive psychosis, and polyuria diagnosed as diabetes insipidus. It is therefore a condition which needs to be though of in many branches of medicine.

Since massive cortisone therapy has been used in the treatment of collagen and allergic disorders, most of these symptoms, or manifestations, have been produced inadvertently by excessive therapy, demonstrating unequivocally their aetiological basis in Cushing's syndrome. Confirmatory proof has been given by animal experiments.

Adiposity

Clinically, fat is deposited in the face and neck, over the breasts, abdomen, buttocks, supraclavicular and lower cervical areas. In children it is more generally deposited-including even forearms, and legs-but in some adults these parts and even the upper arms and thighs may lose fat. Fat deposition is not always a prominent feature, and even when it is obvious in the face and trunk, an absence of increase in weight suggests a transference of fat rather than a general increase. In some patients, however, there is a considerable and rapid increase in weight and fat. The endocrine basis of adiposity has been discussed in the physiology section and here it will be sufficient to mention some associated indications:

1. The high blood cholesterol, not explained by the mild degree of thyroid suppression that may be present, but reduced to normal by subtotal adrenalectomy, or adrenal tumour removal.

2. Fatty infiltration of the liver, found at autopsy, with concentrations of hepatic fatty acids five times the normal.

3. Hyperglucomeogenesis from protein with conversion to fat and resulting fat deposition.

4. Loss of fat after subtotal adrenalectomy, even when unassociated with adrenal insufficiency.

Lineae Distensae

These are frequently, but not invariably, found, the sites being the lower abdomen and inguinal regions, the loins, the lumbar regions, along the iliac crests, and even the breasts. They may be short narrow lines or long broad zones, bright red or dusky violet. They are rightly regarded as being the result of the stretching and giving way of the skin by accumulation of fat in the underlying subcutaneous areas, and may, therefore, be met with in other conditions in which fat is deposited. However, the rapidity of fat deposition is one factor that tends to their production, the thinness of the skin in Cushing's syndrome is another, and noteworthy is the deep red or purple colour that is associated with the plethora and cyanosis met with in this syndrome, with or withou polycythaemia. Similar coloured lineae are met with in pregnancy and are regarded as physiological, but it is also known that in pregnancy there is a hypersecretion of adrenal glucocorticoids; and because of this and the fact that pregnancy may be a precursor of Cushing's syndrome, pregnancy has been referred to as transient physiological Cushing's syndrome. Of course, the striae of pregnancy eventually lose their red or purple colour, and become pallid. In so far as the red colour depends upon the visibility of the underlying capillary-venous network through the stretched and 'broken' skin-and this vascular network is active in an attempted repair process-it is probable that all white lineae distensae have at one time been red. Nevertheless, the degree of redness and particularly of purple coloration seems to depend upon the concentration of adrenal glucocorticoids, and the rapidity of the process. Adiposity does not seem to be the only factor, since such coloured lineae are sometimes found in Cushing's syndrome when the adiposity is minimal. Following successful operation the red-violet lineae become pale.

It is recognized that red lineae appear in a variety of infections, particularly tuberculosis, mainly in children or adolescents, and' in a number of normal children at puberty, and in adipose gynism or gynandrism, but a hypersecretion of adrenal glucocorticoids is a probable factor in all these conditions or phases.

Other Cutaneous Features

Apart from the coloured lineae distensae, other cutaneous features are thinness of the skin, patchy cyanosis, plethora, subcutaneous haemorrhages, spider-like telangiectases, hirsutism, and acne. The thinning and delicacy of the skin is believed to be due to a general breakdown of tissue protein associated with protein catabolism and a negative nitrogen balance, all due to the excess of adrenal glucocorticoids.

If, however, there is an associated increase in adrenal androgens which are protein anabolic and antagonistic to glucocorticoids, this thinning is minimal and is not found in the mixed syndrome. Cyanosis is met with in patchy form in the face, over the breast, abdomen, buttocks, thighs, and legs and upper arms. Over the thighs and legs, because of its resemblance to a marble pattern, it was called cutis marmorata. It is not unrelated to underlying fat deposition, but there is probably another vascular factor which is not well understood. The cyanosis may be *very* intense. The face has a congested plethoric appearance, aggravated by a tendency to cyanosis and telangiectases, although in mild cases it could be referred to as a ruddy and robust facies. Spontaneous subcutaneous haemorrhages, especially on the upper limbs, give the appearance of heavy bruising, often excessive and of deep blue-black colour, but aetiological trauma is absent or trivial. Capillary friability and a decrease in fibrinogen levels have been found. Purpura, ecchymoses and bruising are also complications of massive cortisone therapy in non endocrine disorders.

Hirsutism is not an essential feature and is usually limited to the face. It may develop on the body but this suggests an associated increase in adrenal androgens, even when not revealed by 'normal' 17-ketosteroid assay values. When cortisone is given in high dosage for non-endocrine cases, any hirsutism that results is usually limited to the face and chin. Acne may also be a feature of Cushing's syndrome, and it is also a complication of cortisone therapy. Both hirsutism and acne may be severe in the mixed type of syndrome, where there is also a high concentration of androgens. In the male, facial and bodily hair may decrease because of the associated hypogonadism and in the adolescent it may not develop, but in the mixed type of syndrome with increased androgens, the facial and bodily hair growth may become more intense. Crops of boils or pustules may be a troublesome feature of Cushing's syndrome, being part of a general susceptibility to infections, particularly staphylococcal.

Hypogonadism

Amenorrhoea is the rule in women. Occasionally, menstruation is present but scanty, and very rarely menstruation may be normal. Swan and Stephenson recorded normal menstruation in a woman of 31, after which there was a period of amenorrhoea, followed by a resumption of normal menstruation on the giving of thyroid. In this case the ovaries were normal at autopsy; more usually the ovaries are found to be atrophic or involuted, or show cystic degeneration. The uterus is usually infantile, and the endometrium thin and atrophic.

In the male, involution or failure of development of the sex organs, and an absence of potency, is the rule. In Josephson's case of a boy of 17, the failure of sexual development led to a initial erroneous diagnosis of Frohlich's syndrome. Hypogonadism in both sexes is due to the suppression of pituitary, gonadotrophins by the high blood concentrations of adrenal glucocorticoids, as is also evident from massive cortisone therapy and animal experiments.

Blood

Polycythaemia is inconstant but nevertheless part of the syndrome. Just as in Addison's disease there is a relative lymphocytosis and eosinophilia, so in the opposite condition of Cushing's syndrome there is an excess of polymorphonuclear leucocytes, a lymphopenia, and a diminution or complete disappearance of eosinophils. The sedimentation rate is usually normal, but may be raised in the absence of obvious infection. An alkalosis, with low blood potassium, and raised blood sodium is occasionally found.

Skeletal Changes

The bones tend to become rarefied and soft. Clinically this is shown by kyphosis and bent shoulders, with resulting lessening of height. Cushing particularly observed that 'nearly all the females appear to have been definitely undersized'. Radiographically the vertebrae are seen to be compressed, and all the bones of the body rarened, as compared with controls. Backache in the lumbosacral region is not uncommon and may be due to compression or spontaneous fracture of vertebrae-as also occurs in ribs, clavicles, and long bones. This clinical picture is quite comparable to that of hyperparathyroidism, but although an increased calcium excretion in the urine has been demonstrated values for serum calcium, phosphorus, and even phosphatase are usually normal. Further, the parathyroid glands, in most cases are histologically normal, but fatty infiltration, slight hyperplasia, and, in one case, adenoma, have been reported. A further analogy with hyperparathyroidism are the fine deposits of calcium which sometimes are found throughout the kidneys, or minute brown calculi in the calyes, and secondary chronic nephritis, with sclerosed glomeruli and calcium deposits. In spite of these similarities it is probable that the hormone mechanism is unrelated to the parathyroids and that it is all secondary to the negative nitrogen balance, determined by the excess of adrenal glucocorticoids, which results in loss of bone matrix so that normal calcium concentrations lack adequate osteoid sites for normal deposition and are therefore in relative excess in the soft tissues and urine.

Hypertension and the Kidneys

High blood pressure, systolic and diastolic (e.g. 220 and 140 respectively), is a frequent finding in Cushing's syndrome. It may occur in the absence of clinical or pathological renal disease or in association with chronic nephritis or malignant nephrosclerosis. Hypertension, probably of adrenal origin, may be regarded as the opposite of the hypotension of Addison's disease. Since an excess of aldosterone is a rarity in Cushing's syndrome, the hypertension is more appropriately correlated with the excess of glucocorticoids and changes in the intima of the blood vessels with associated hypercholesterolaemia. There is no excess of adrenaline or noradrenaline in Cushing's syndrome. Basophilia of the anterior pituitary has been correlated with hypertension in Cushing's syndrome, as also in eclampsia, and Selye described hypertrophy and hyperplasia of the pituitary basophils in experimentally induced stress. Selye also produced hypertension and nephrosclerosis with desoxycortone in rats. Since cortisone, in massive therapy, can produce hypertension in man, reversible by ceasing the therapy, and endogenous excess of cortisone or hydrocortisone is more compatible with clinical facts and hormone assays as the cause of the hypertension.

The kindeys.are not infrequently involved secondary to vascular endarteritic changes, although this explanation is not adequate in the rare complication of malignant nephrosclerosis. In some patients the renal changes are due to minute depositions of calcium throughout the kindey substance, and in the tubules, as may occur in hyperparathyroidism. Evidence of renal disease may not be present in life, or may only be found on special examinations, *e.g.* granular casts in the urine, and poor renal functions test. In some cases, however, as in that of Close, there may be frequency, haematuria, blurring of vision, vomiting, cramps, dyspnoea, drowsiness, and anuria, as well as albuminuric retinitis and intractable headaches. Experimental evidence indicates a more direct relationship between hypersecretion of the adrenal cortex and renal pathology.

Psychoneurotic Symptoms

Depression, with suicidal tendencies in severe untreated cases, has been the writer's experience, often completely reversible with successful surgery. Personality changes are also met with, including mental and emotional aberrations, in some 50 per cent or more of patients. Although depressive states are more usual, maniacal agitation and violence are met with. Personality changes and behaviour patterns, as well as the psychoneuroses and psychoses, have been aetiologically associated with a variety of hormone disorders, although the basic genetic personality influences the type of response.

Thyroid Funciton

This may be normal or decreased, the latter in keeping with the known depressant effect of cortisone on thyroid function and with the histological picture of a resting thyroid gland. The raised blood cholesterol, characteristic of Cushing's syndrome, is found even when thyroid function is normal and its degree is not paralleled by the mildness of thyroid insufficiency. The thyroid gland is diffusely enlarged to a moderate degree in some 50 per cent. of patients, in the presence of normal or decreased thyroid function. Patients with Cushing's syndrome rarely complain of sensitivity to cold or other features of myxoedema.

Exophthalmos

This is not infrequent in moderate degree and suggests a pituitary exophthalmic hormone dissociated from the pituitary thyrotrophic hormones.

Steroid Diabetes

Experimental and clinical evidence leaves us in no doubt as to the potency of the adrenal glucocorticoids as diabetogenic hormones. Nearly all patients with Cushing's syndrome showed a delayed fall of blood sugar values after glucose, some 50 per cent give clinical and biochemical evidence of mild diabetes mellitus without ketosis, and a small percentage present as diabetes, with or withou ketosis, or with a complication of diabetes such as neuritis or retinitis. The diabetes usually has the main characteristics of steroid diabetes, being relatively mild, slowly progressive, and not difficult to control with diet only. Insulin is required by some patients and these are not necessarily insensitive to insulin. Insulin-sensitivity curves indicate incomplete refractoriness to intravenous insulin. The severity of the diabetes usually fluctuates with the severity of the general symptomatology and its degree of control by therapy. In some patient with an adrenal tumour, and high concentrations of hydrocortisone in the urine, the only manifestation was severe diabetes mellitus, which disappeared on surgical removal of the tumour. If a steroid diabetes is allowed to continue untreated, a secondary pancreatic islet-cell degeneration results in a severe pancreatic diabetes. In most patients who have come to autopsy, the islet cells have been found to be normal, but in a few, especially children, the islet cells were hyperplastic, which should be regarded as a homeostatic reaction to the steroid hyperglycaemia, and an explanation of why diabetes is not found in all cases. The potency of cortisone in aggravating diabetes and precipitating ketosis is dramatically demonstrated by its use in patients with combined Addison's disease and diabetes; as also by the fact that cortisone in massive doses has been observed to produce diabetes in nonendocrine diseases.

Polyuria and Polydipsia

These symptoms may be caused by glycosuria or by an excessive calcium excretion. Clinically speaking, they are not infrequent in Cushing's syndrome.

Pigmentation

The pigmentation of the orbits, face, and neck that is sometimes found in Cushing's syndrome, in the absence of any evidence of adrenal insufficiency, must be attributed to an excess of pituitary ACTH or the closely associated pituitary melanocytic hormone. The same must be true of the pigmentation that sometimes follows successful subtotal adrenalectomy, in the absence of any other indication of adrenal insufficiency.

Fatigability

The explanation of this symptom is perhaps not too obvious as an excess of cortisone suggests the opposite of Addisori s disease, where the weakness is immediately remedied by cortisone replacement. However, the excess is associated with protein catabolism and a negative nitrogen balance and clinically there is wasting and flabbiness of the musculature. Weakness may be extreme and possibly other less obvious metabolic factors are involved, e.g. the loss of potassium in the urine and low tissue concentrations of potassium in some cases. In the mixed syndrome, where there is also an excess of adrenal androgens, weakness is not a feature.

CLIMACTERIC TYPE OF CUSHING'S SYNDROME

This condition cannot really be included as a variety of Cushing's syndrome, since amenorrhoea is a normal feature of the climacteric, but nevertheless, many of the other features of Cushing's syndrome can develop at this time, and it may be presumed that development of excessive pituitary gonadotrophic secretion becomes extended to pituitary ACTH secretion and this may be transitory in some, but persistent in other. A patient described by Achard and Thiers presented the more dramatic features, spontaneous leg fracture, diabetes, and hypertension at the age of 71, but, as in many other patients, other features were present in mild form much earlier and in this patient hair on the chin at the age of 9 suggested adrenal pathology. It might be queried whether a slowly progressive disorder occurring over a period of fifty or more years could justifiably be included under the definition of Cushing's syndrome. It must be regarded as the opposite of characteristic and yet cannot be ignored.

Diagnosis

Amenorrhoea, a change of facies in regard to plethora and rounding of cheeks and chin, and a deposition or transfer of subcutaneous fat, are prominent indications of the syndrome. *When the development is* progressive following pregnancy, the diagnosis is even more probable. It is obvious from the clinical description that the syndrome may first present itself to the gynaecologist, the orthopaedic surgeon, the psychiatrist, the vascular renal clinic, or as the plethoric type of diabetic.

Simple urinary assay or chromatography will reveal high values for glucocorticoids and normal values for 17-ketosteroids. Blood glucocorticoids are raised and following intravenous ACTH, 15 Units in 100 ml. of saline, will show a sharp rise within four hours, the adrenals in Cushing's syndrome showing a supernormal hypersensitive response in this respect.

The differentiation between hyperplasia and neoplasia depends upon radiography and hormone suppression tests, remembering clinically that hyperplasia is four times as frequent as neoplasia. Intravenous pyelogram may indicate depression of the renal calyces below an adrenal tumour, so that they lie at right angles to the vertical. Perirenal insufflation of air has given way to the safer procedure of episacral insufflation of air. When successful, the adrenal area is outlined by the surrounding air and an enlarged or neoplastic adrenal is indicated by the shape and the outline of the adrenal shadow.

When the cause of the excessive secretion of adrenal glucocorticoids is bilateral hyperplasia, the giving of cortisone, e.g. 25 mg. by mouth four-hourly or 100 mg. by injection once daily, should result in a significant fall in 17-hydroxycorticoids in the second twenty four hours' collection of urine. However, cortisone itself is partly excreted as 17-hydroxycorticoids and it has been found more satisfactory to use the more powerful prednisone, 5 mg., six-hourly by mouth: or the still more potent fludrocortisone (9-(x-fluorohydrocortisone), 2 mg. six-hourly by mouth. Both prednisone and fluorohydrocortisone are excreted in insignificant amounts as urinary 17-hydroxycorticoids. In the case of adrenal neoplasm, there is no suppression of 17-hydroxycorticoids in contrast with hyperplasia. However, anomalous results occasionally occur both with neoplasm and hyperplasia, so that the tests are not absolute and must be interpreted in conjunction with other evidence.

Albright considers that low values for 17-ketosteroids are an indication of an adrenal adenoma, since the high glucocorticoid secretion results in suppression of pituitary ACTH and consequently of adrenal androgenic secretion; whereas high values for 17-ketosteroids and 17-hydroxycorticoids (glucocorticoids) are suggestive of adrenal carcinoma.

Treatment

When an adrenal tumour is present surgical removal is the obvious course. As the opposite adrenal is usually atrophied the patient is given cortisone (e.g. 100 g. by injection daily) or prednisone, (e.g. 25 mg. by injection daily) for two days prior to operation, on the day of operation, and for one week afterwards, after which the dose is gradually reduced and changed to oral therapy; and may be tentatively omitted after a further three weeks if the clinical condition of the patient suggests that the remaining adrenal gland is functioning adequately.

In the unusual circumstances of the pituitary fossa being enlarged, or where the technique of pituitary radiation has been highly developed, it appears to some to be justifiable to attempt radiation therapy before surgery, in the absence of an adrenal neoplasm, and amelioration or cure is recorded in a varying proportion of patients: 5-40 per cent. Permanent loss of hair over the radiation sites is a hazard even 'n the best centres. The insertion of radon seeds or cauterization of the pituitary by open operation are in the opinion of the writer more hazardous than bilateral subtotal adrenalectomy.

Unilateral adrenalectomy is as useless for Cushing's syndrome, with bilateral hyperplasia, as was hemithyroidectomy for thyrotoxicosis. In fact, it is sometimes followed by exacerbation of symptoms because of excessive compensatory hyperactivity of the remaining gland. Subtotal adrenalectomy, comparable to subtotal thyroidectomy for thyrotoxicosis, is the logical procedure. It was first attempted at the Mayo Clinic, and particulars of their first series of 29 cases were published by Priestley. Six of the 29 patients died in the post-operative period, but the last 10 patients (and a further 9 referred to in a footnote) were operated upon without any mortality, the safety depending upon cortisone becoming available. Of 20 patients followed up, 1 was not improved, and 19 obtained excellent remissions, although in 3 of them there was subsequent recurrence of major symptoms, three, two, and one year after operation. Another 3 of the 19 had chronic adrenal insufficiency, and required substitution therapy with cortisone. The adrenals were removed at separate operations. Two days before the second operation, one day before, on the day of operation, and for three or more days after operation 200 mg. of cortisone acetate were injected intramuscularly, after which the dose was gradually reduced and finally omitted in the absence of adrenal insufficiency. In the case of bilateral hyperplasia, there is really no need to give cortisone for the first adrenalectomy. Neither is cortisone required until the actual day of the second adrenalectomy, but giving the massive injections in oily solution for two days prior to this provides a depot from which absorption takes place gradually during the day of operation-at least, that is the rationalization of the pre-operative therapy while blood cortisone is already high.

In the absence of cortisone therapy, or with inadequate therapy, acute adrenal insufficiency may prove fatal within a few days of operation or a delayed reaction may occur in the second or third week. Manifestations are anorexia, nausea, vomiting, weakness, fever, tachycardia, abdominal pain, muscular and articular pains, hypotension, and pigmentation. Smaller series of patients treated by subtotal adrenalectomy have been published subsequently by several observers, with broadly similar results, including the Guy's group, who advocate simultaneous radiotherapy of the pituitary gland to avoid recurrence. Others have recommended total bilateral adrenalectomy, preferring constant post-operative therapy with cortisone to the risk of recurrence of Cushing's syndrome. At St. Mary's Hospital, Simpson, Robb, and Wynn have not found recurrence to be such a major problem as to warrant the intentional production of a state of severe Addison's disease by bilateral total adrenalectomy. One whole gland has been removed and seven-eighths of another, so that if clinical recurrence is met with and does not respond to pituitary and adrenal radiation, it is known on which side to explore for compensatory growth. In one patient without any evidence of adrenal insufficiency, and with no chronic cortisone therapy, there were no signs of relapse even after two successful pregnancies. Unless unusual difficulties are experienced with the first adrenalectomy, the second is carried out at the same time, using two loin incisions. Cortisone is, at first, given by intramuscular injection but within a few days of operation it may be given by mouth, e.g. 25 mg. four times a day, then twice a day, with further gradual reductions until, in the absence of signs of adrenal insufficiency, it is discontinued. None of the patients have developed permanent adrenal insufficiency, and the occasional pigmentation could be ascribed to excessive secretion of pituitary ACTH that follows the operation. A 0.4 per cent. solution of noradrenaline in normal saline intravenously is rarely needed during operation, or for the more immediate post-operative period. Cortisone has been replaced or reinforced by hydrocortisone (intravenously), hydrocortisone succinate (intravenously), prednisone and fluorohydrocortisone. Peeling of the skin is an interesting post-operative feature that may go on for months, and one patient developed Raynaud's phenomena in the fingers in cold weather. There have been no deaths. Results have been uniformly good, and subtotal bilateral adrenalectomy would appear to be the operation of choice. The more immediate change in the contour of the facies and the prominence of the abdomen suggests that factors other than fat are involved.

Mason has summarized the results of his own series, and communications from others, and concludes that subtotal adrenalectomy is a satisfactory procedure but that the margin of safety between adrenal insufficiency and danger of recurrence is small for patients under 25.

MIXED TYPE OF ADRENAL HYPERFUNCTION

Adrenal hyperfunction involving both the adrenal glucocorticoids and adrenal androgens and producing a mixed clinical picture, with features both of Cushing's syndrome and of the adrenogenital syndrome. It may be caused by adrenal tumour or adrenal hyperplasia. The title is admittedly a clumsy one, even when reduced to the letters M.T.A.H. for brevity, but it is difficult to omit recognition of such a condition under this heading, without excluding from consideration endocrine syndromes which are district variants of Cushing's syndrome and cannot come within the classical definition of the latter, without permitting considerable latitude and qualification.

Further justification for the burden of additional classification will be forthcoming in a consideration of the many contrasting and antagonistic actions of the adrenal glucocorticoids and androgens, and in a consideration of the symptomatology, with illustrated cases, as well as the response to surgical therapy.

Hormone Basic

Although the adrenals secrete many hormones, the two most important groups in this syndrome are the glucocorticoids and the androgens.

Contrasting Actions of Glucocorticoids and Androgens

	Glucocorticoids	*Androgens*
1.	Protein catabolic	Protein anabolic
2.	Negative nitrogen balance	Positive nitrogen balance
3.	Osteoporosis caused	Osteoporosis prevented
4.	Diabetogenic	Nil
5.	Flabby musculature	Strong musculature
6.	Somatic growth inhibited	Somatic growth increased
7.	Skin and hair thin and dry	Skin and hair thick and greasy
8.	Fat anabolism preponderant	Fat catabolism preponderant
9.	Potassium depletion	Potassium retention
10	Thyroid function depressed	Thyroid function increased

In the above table are seen ten contrasting or antagonistic actions. Most of these are related to the fact that glucocorticoids cause a breakdown of protein and protein tissues, with a negative nitrogen balance, and gluconeogenesis from protein. We have seen that this is also the most likely explanation of the osteoporosis of Cushing's syndrome. Osteoporosis does not appear if there is a coincident increase in adrenal androgens which are nitrogen anabolic. The potassium loss from the tissues is partly associated with the protein breakdown but cortisone does produce potassium loss as well as sodium and water retention when given in massive doses, although its analogue, prednisone, is relatively free from these electrolyte effects. Rarely in Cushing's syndrome there is also an associated increased secretion of aldosterone, which is chemically closely related to cortisone.

If hormone assays were a true reflection of the degree of secretion and activity of hormones, it would be relatively easy to predict or interpret the clinical picture from such assays. Unfortunately this is not the case, particularly if one is limited to the urine and to standard methods, of assay. In particular, the 17-ketosteroid values are frequently 'normal' where there is undoubted clinical evidence of excessive androgenic activity. In regard to hormone assays in general, it would be prudency to say that 'normal' values, as for sedimentation rates, do not necessarily exclude disorders but raised values are always significant.

Clinical Picture

Hirsutism in classical Cushing's syndrome, particularly in the absence of an adrenal tumour, is usually slight and limited to the face. In so far as mild hirsutism may be produced by massive cortisone therapy for non-endocrine conditions, cortisone has a mild androgenic activity due to weak androgenic by-products of its metabolism. When, however, hirsutism of the body has become extensive, it is due directly to adrenal androgens. Similar considerations apply to acne, especially when the skin is thick and greasy, because of well-developed sebaceous glands, rather than thin and atrophic. Although the initial action of androgens causes the scalp hair to thicken, become greasy, and grow more densely and rapidly, there is subsequent retraction of hair line in the frontal and temporal areas and loss of hair from the vertex. In some patients, with an excess of both androgens and glucocorticoids, the latter appear to inhibit the androgenic activity of the former, in that facial and body hair is not excessive and in some constitutional mixed endocrine types may even be scarce. In animal experiments, cortisone inhibits the growth of hair follicles.

Hormone influence on somatic growth is most obvious in the period of skeletal growth. There is no doubt that cortisone inhibits skeletal growth (including height increment) and this is a characteristic feature of Cushing's syndrome in childhood and adolescence. On the other hand, and excess of adrenal androgens in virilism or macrogenitosomia praecox is found to cause an increased rate of growth, as well as skeletal maturation, as is also the case when testosterone is used therapeutically in hypopituitarism or hypogonadism in childhood. Therefore in a mixed syndrome in childhood or adolescence the androgens counteract the glucocorticoid inhibition of growth, and the resultant may be a 'normal' rate of growth.

Fat metabolism is complicated and has been discussed more fully under adiposity. Briefly, it is in children that one sees more clearly an obvious general excess of fat deposition from an excess of glucocorticoids, whereas in adults there is often only a shift of fat from extremities to face and trunk. Virilizing androgenic tumours appear to cause a loss of fat so that muscular contours are clearly visible, but both glucocorticoids and androgens produce an increased appetite and food intake. The weakness of Cushing's syndrome is due both to muscle breakdown and atrophy and to potassium loss, in contrast with the excessive muscular strength found with adrenal androgenic tumours, particularly in childhood. In the combined syndrome therefore, muscular weakness may not be a feature. The toal clinical picture will also vary according to whether the adrenal glucocorticoids or the adrenal androgens preponderate, or whether they are equally balanced.

Diagnosis

Diagnosis depends upon definition, and diagnostic tests are described in the section on Cushing's syndrome and on the adrenogenital syndrome.

Course and Prognosis

This condition is often surprisingly slow in its evolution and this may be the case even when an adrenal tumour is the cause. In the absence of an adrenal tumour, it would appear justifiable to be content with symptomatic treatment in mild cases but the fact that an adrenal adenoma might become an adenocarcinoma and give rise to metastases after some twelve or more years should arouse caution and point the need for thorough and repeated radiological and hormone investigations. An increasing proportion of dehydroisoandrosterone, indicates neoplastic changes. The endocrine results of surgery are good but hirsutism may persist in some degree.

Treatment

An adrenal tumour should be removed and the results are usually excellent. The same precautions as in uncomplicated Cushing's syndrome should be taken and cortisone therapy is required. The hirsutism may be persistent in some degree even when the 17-ketosteroids are reduced to low subnormal values by removal of an adrenal tumour and this is even more likely when subtotal adrenalectomy is carried out in the absence of an adrenal tumour. For this reason subtotal adrenalectomy must not be undertaken in this mixed syndrome with promise of complete cure. Nevertheless, in the writer's opinion it is a logical and justifiable procedure in severe cases, and patients are appreciative even when hirsutism is not abolished.

The persistence of hirsutism in some patients, when hormone assays indicate subnormal concentrations of androgens, suggests that once the condition has been produced by androgens, the change may be irreversible, particularly if it has been present for a long time.

The cure or improvement of hirsutism may also be merely temporary, if hyperplasia recurs, as it may do in some patients. The treatment of hirsutism by cortisone or prednisone suppression of adrenal androgens is only mildly effective in these mixed syndromes, as might be expected, although acne tends to be improved and menstruation frequently returns.

Case Histories

Case 1. A. married woman of 29 complained of the following feature of three years' duration arising during or within six months of pregnancy: Redness and plethora of face, hairiness of face and body, greasiness and thinning of scalp hair, acne of face and body, fatness of face and body, bruising, persistent red striae, and amenorrhoea. The hair of the head became thick and greasy; eyebrows very thick and thick black hair grew over the shoulders and spine: B.P. 190/120. It is of interest that this mixed syndrome arose in pregnancy as does Cushing's syndrome. Urinary 17-ketosteroids were high, 33 mg. per 100 ml. as were also the plasma 17-hydroxysteroids, 35 pg. per 100 ml. Bilateral subtotal adrenalectomy was followed by good clinical result, including loss of plethora, acne, hirsutism and adiposity, and return of menstruation.

Case 2. Married woman of 40 with no children, who for twelve years had amenorrhoea, severe hirsutism of face and body, will loss of scalp hair, acne, easy bruising extremely plethoric facies, polyuria, hypertension, 200/140 mm.; polycythaemia, 6.3 million red cells per c.mm. and raised haemoglobin, 19 g. per 100 ml. blood; raised urinary 17-ketosteroids, 250 mg., raised urinary glucocorticoids, expressed as 20-ketosteroids, 6 mg. (normal 2 mg.), raised urinary oestradiol, 600 i.u. (normal 25 to 350). Removal of adrenal adenocarcinoma led to disapppearance of all features except hirsutism. Subsequent relapse and death due to hormone-secreting metastases.

ADRENAL HYPERFUNCTION IN CHILDREN

Bulloch and Sequeira first drew attention to the fact that the adrenals are related to normal puberty, as well as to pathological pseudo-puberty. In modern phraseology, at the age of 14 (11-16) years, the adrenals as well as the gonads develop an increased activity, because of the simultaneous secretion of pituitary ACTH as well as pituitary gonadotrophins; and, perhaps, because of increased sensitivity of the end-organs to the stimuli. This adrenal activity is shown by the fact that the urinary 17-ketosteroids are increased in females as well as males at puberty. Albright applied the term adrenarche to this conception. Simpson extended the idea in two directions: (1) the adrenarche to include adrenal glucocorticoid as well as adrenal androgenic activity; and (2) recognition that in some normal children a preliminary adrenarche starts at the age of 7 (approximately) and proceeds gradually to maximum intensity at 14, or there is a relatively stationary period between the pre-adrenarche at 7 and the puberty adrenarche at 14. These conceptions are based upon a study of large numbers of normal children and children with adrenal disturbances in childhood, and will be found useful in considering major endocrinopathies in childhood. Both in normal and mildly abnormal children, some of the clinical criteria of adrenal androgenic activity are the degree of hair on the face, body, and limbs, greasiness of the skin and scalp hair, with seborrhoea and scurf, thick eyebrows and long eyelashes, darkening of fair scalp hair, increased rate of growth and weight increment, and increased muscular development and strength. It is obvious that these features are accompaniments of normal puberty. However, if the hair on the sides of the face, upper lip, and forehead is excessive, or if hair is present over the shoulders and scapulae, and extensive over the lumbar area, or more than well marked on the limbs, then the indefinite border region between accepted normality and endocrinopathy may have been crossed; or if these androgenic features develop at 7 instead of 14 the query of abnormality is raised, particularly if vulval hair also starts growing. Evolution to adult 'normality' is usual, but in some there persists a tendency to hirsutism with oligomenorrhoea as a post-puberty feature, and in others a more severe androgenic endocrinopathy develops in the second or third decade or following pregnancy or the climacteric.

When the adrenarche is associated with preponderant glucocorticoid hypersecretion, the patients tend to be fat and plethoric.

ADRENAL TUMOURS IN CHILDREN

Bulloch and Sequeira drew attention to adrenal tumours in childhood causing pseudo-sexual precocity in boys, with enormous strength, due to the high secretion of adrenal androgens (Hercules type), to hirsutism and other androgenic features in girls, and also to a plethoric type of adiposity, resembling a condition later termed Cushing's syndrome, but usually combined with an associated excessive androgenic secretion, giving a mixed clinical picture. Lawson Wilkins reviewed the literature and found that up to 1948, there were records of 70 children (53 girls and 17 boys) who had developed an adrenal cortex tumour before the age of 12 years. In three of these cases, the neoplasm occurred in aberrant adrenal tissue in or near the ovaries. It is probable that the published literature on adrenal tumour in children only reflects a percentage of the total number of cases. Of 53 girls, 31 showed virilism, and 22 showed symptoms suggestive of Cushing's syndrome. All the latter were obese and most showed hirsutism and other evidence of excessive androgens, and it is of additional interest that 6 gave evidence of oestrogen secretion probably of adrenal origin. Although 12 showed obvious virilism as early as the first year of life, none showed a persistent urogenital sinus, as is found with congenital adrenal virilism. Of the 17 boys, 12 showed precocious pseudo-sexual development, accelerated growth and osseous development and muscularity rather than obesity. The testes, unlike the penis, were not precociously developed, with two exceptions difficult to explain. Two showed Cushing type obesity. Malignancy and metastases were frequent.

Wilkins' first case was of special interest being an adrenal tumour in a boy of 5 years of age producing gynaecomastia. The breasts began to enlarge at 6 months of age and reached then maximum size at 2 years. Otherwise clinically he was normal except that the bone age was advanced, namely that of 10 years of age. The areolae of the breasts were well developed but not pigmented and superficial veins were prominent. The penis and testes were normal for the age but the prostate was-definitely enlarged, and thought to be hard and fibrous. The 17-ketosteroids per twenty-four hours were 4.1 mg., a figure considered by Wilkins only slightly greater than average for the age, and the oestrogens (5 rat units per twenty-four hours) were considered to be only a questionable slight increase for the age. Histological examination showed hyperplasia of the duct epithelium and very marked peridectal hyperplasia of the connective tissue. Removal of an adrenal encapsulated adenoma led to a return to normal, observed for a period of four years. No further assays are given. The toal evidence is interpreted as indicating an oestrogenic feminizing adrenal tumour.

Wilkins' second case was a malignant but encapsulated adrenal tumour in a girl of 5, producing enlarged clitoris, deep voice, pubic, anal, and upper lip hari, seborrhoea, acne, increased height, bone age, and musculature: all these features noticed at the age of 5. The 17-ketosteroids per twenty-four hours were greatly raised, 22 mg., falling to 2 mg. after removal of tumour. Clinical improvement was followed by relapse and death two years later, as a result of abdominal metastases, with 17-ketosteroid excretion rising to 124 mg. per twenty-four hours. There was no enlargement of the breasts and no features of Cushing's syndrome. No oestrogen assays were recorded but the vaginal smear showed no oestrinization. Since many adrenal tumours in children are malignant, the β-fraction (dehydroisoandrosterone) of the urinary androgens is usually considerably raised but in this case it was only 1 per cent, from which a good prognosis might have been erroneously made: the histology, however, suggested possible malignancy. Prognosis should always be cautious with adrenal tumours in childhood, even when capsulated, and early diagnosis and removal is obviously important.

Other aspects of adrenal tumours in childhood are considered under sexual precocity and pseudohermaphroditism.

VIRILISM IN CHILDREN

When the appearance at birth is normal and the virilism commences in childhood before puberty, the cause is nearly always an adrenal tumour, and the incidence of malignancy and metastases is high. Apart from hirsutism, acne, and seborrhoea, the clitoris is considerably enlarged, the voice deep, skeletal growth and maturation (radiographic bone age) much advanced, muscular development and strength much above normal, and the 17-ketosteroids greatly increased. In the female the urethral and vaginal orifices are separate in contrast to the common urogenital sinus found in genetic virilism and this clinical differentiation is particularly important when a tumour occurs in the first year or so of life.

Urinary 17-ketosteroids are not depressed by giving cortisone to a patient with an adrenal tumour although there are occassional anomalies. In the male the penis is large and the testes small.

When virilism starts between the ages of 7 and 14, and particularly when it is not severe or rapidly progressive, adrenal hyperplasia, rather than neoplasia may be the cause. Further investigation of a large series of cases by modern methods will give us a better indication than we have at present as to what percentage of such patients are simple qualitative hyperplasia and what percentage have genetic metabolic errors comparable to those to be described under the heading of genetic virilism but not so potent as to become manifest until the adrenarche comes into play. This consideration is not meant to conflict with the main differential diagnosis between severe virilism that appears in childhood and is caused by an adrenal tumour and genetic virilism already apparent at birth. The differential diagnosis between adrenal tumour and hyperplasia is dealt with also in the previous adult section.

The difficulties of diagnosis in exceptional cases is shown by the fact that general hairiness at birth may be due to an adrenal tumour, which does not really become manifest until some years later, as in the girl of 5 years of age described by Kolf and Tjiook. Whether this is an example of hyperplasia passing on to multiple adenomata and then a single dominating adenocarcinoma must remain conjectural.

GENETIC METABOLIC VIRILISM

This is due to an innate inability of the adrenals to convert 17-hydroxyprogesterone, a normal adrenala intermediate metabolite, to adrenal glucocorticoids (cortisone and hydrocortisone). This innate defect of adrenal metabolism results in a deficiency of glucocorticoids, and an excess of adrenal androgens, as measured by total urinary 17-ketosteroids, and by assay of the urinary end-products of 17-hydroxyprogesterone, especially pregnanetriol. Since pituitary ACTH secretion is controlled by the blood level of hydrocortisone, the deficiency of the latter results in an excessive secretion of ACTH, and consequent hyperplasia of the adrenals, which then produce an additional secretion of normal and abnormal adrenal androgens.

This theory was invoked by Bartter *et al.*, Bongiovanni *et al.*, and Jailer to explain the clinical and biochemical facts in genetic virilism in females and pseudo-sexual precocity (macrogenitosomia praecox) in their male siblings.

Clinical Features

1. The condition is present from birth, although it is not always obvious to observers until a year or so has elapsed.

2. The hirsutism and muscularity, together with a much enlarged clitoris, are clinical signs of a considerable excess of androgens.

3. The patients are apt to go into Addisonian adrenal insufficiency crisis, either spontaneously, or following extra stress such as intercurrent infections or minor operations. This is mainly manifest in regard to salt and water metabolism some patients even showing a

chro salt craving. Addisonian-type pigmentation and hypoglycaemia are rare, and before their nature was recognized and cortisone became available adrenal crises often proved fatal. Other manifestations are vomiting, anorexia, and diarrhoea, and vomiting may be the presenting symptom. The inherent biochemical defect probably extends to the synthesis of aldosterone (electrocortin) but this has not yet been suggested or demonstrated. Some patients reach middle age without any adrenal insufficiency showing itself and yet go into severe crisis following a minor operative procedure.

Pathology

The adrenal glands in fatal cases were found at autopsy to be considerably enlarged often three times the normal, and sometimes nodular with multiple adenomata, as well as bilateral hyperplasia. The hyperplasia consisted of polyhedral eosinophil granular cells resembling those of the reticular zone.

Hormone Assays

The blood adrenal glucocorticoids when measured as plasma 17-hydroxysteroids,are low, and so are the urinary 17-hydroxysteroids if measured by appropriate methods, e.g. chromatography or Reddy's method. (Confusion was initially caused by failure to realize that normal or high values are given by other methods, e.g. assays of ketogenic steroids, which include pregnanetriol in their total figure.)

Response to ACTH

The blood and urinary 17-hydroxysteroids fail to increase after the injections of ACTH, since the synthetic defect prevents this, but there is an increase in pregnanetriol excretion. Although the excess of pregnanetriol is a metabolic abnormality characteristic of genetic virilism, pregnanetriol is found occasionally in small quantities in normal women and has been found in excess in Cushing's syndrome due to adrenal hyperplasia.

Response to Cortisone

Cortisone in high dosage, or prednisone, results in a decrease of total 17-ketosteroids and of pregnanetriol in the urine, explained by the resulting inhibition of the raised pituitary ACTH secretion. This is accompanied by dramatic clinical improvement, e.g. breast development, maturation of testes, slowing of the rate of maturation and ossification of bones, decreased hirsutism, & c. Bergstrand and Gemzell found an excess of pregnanediol, as well as pregnanetriol in genetic virilism and a fall to normal values after cortisone.

Response to 17-Hydroxyprogesterone

Hormone Assays

The administration of 17-hydroxyprogesterone results in an increased secretion of pregnanetriol (3α-17α-20α-pregnanetriol) in genetic virilism but not in normal patients.

The clinical manifestations of genetic virilism (pseudohermaphroditism) and macrogenitosomia praecox due to the same genetic defect are described in the gonad section.)

CUSHING'S SYNDROME IN CHILDREN

This disorder is rare in childhood, apart from the puberty type, but it may occur at any age, even in infancy; and it is usually, but not invariably, due to an adrenal tumour which is frequently malignant. The symptoms differ from those in adults in the following respects, but must nevertheless be interpreted and determined by the relative and absolute excess of adrenal glucocorticoids over adrenal androgens.

1. Skeletal growth is inhibited by the excess of glucocorticoids.
2. The adiposity is usually more extensive than in adults and may involve the extremities, including even the hands and wrists; the appearance may almost resemble that of a monstrosity.
3. Androgenic features such as acne, seborrhoea, and hirsutism are more prominent, because of the frequency of high androgen secretion by the adrenal neoplasm.
4. Hypertension may be extreme, e.g. an infant of 6 months of age, with a blood pressure of 245/145, followed by death from cardiac failure.
5. Diabetes is rare, and the absence of disturbed carbohydrate metabolism can be correlated with a greater tendency to compensatory pancreatic islet-cell hyperplasia.

Series of cases in children have been reviewed by Marks *et al.*, Chute *et al.* and Melicow and Cahill. The manifestations in some children with adrenal neoplasm is a mixture of Cushing's syndrome and virilism, as might well be expected.

ADIPOSE GYNISM AND GYNANDRISM

This syndrome was first described by Simpson in 1948 and adipose gynandrism in males and as childhood adiposity with some features of Cushing's syndrome in females; and more specifically under the title of adipose gynism in girls and adipose gynandrism in boys respectively in 1950. The term gynism was used for girls because their general configuration is intensely female, whereas the term gynandrism was used for boys to indicate a mixture of female and male characteristics. Pende, in Italy, described the syndrome in girls only, apparently independently. The respective eponyms were used by Maranon in Spain, and by Berardinelli in Brazil, in confirmatory clinical accounts.

Definition

A constitutional familial pituitary-adrenal hyperfunction manifested by a plethoric adiposity, height above normal, delayed puberty in boys, early puberty in girls, elements of feminization in boys and advanced or intense womanly characteristics in girls, characteristic behaviour patterns and attitudes, with a demonstrable increase in - the secretion of adrenal glucocorticoids and a probable increase in the secretion of growth hormone.

Clinical Features

The fact that similar clinical description of the syndrom were made at first independently, by observers in England and Italy, and later by other clinicians, who had seen these illustrated accounts, seems to establish the conditions as a clinical entity. Marquand regarded the condition as of pituitary origin, because of the incidence of familial giantism and diabetes among the relatives, and Prunty in spite of some assay problems described below, concluded that we are inclined to agree with Simpson that there is an underlying abnormality of adrenal cortical function'. The time of onset usually corresponds with early puberty or with the pre adrenarche, e.g. at 7 or 8 years, but it may occur at any age, and is sometimes precipitated by an acute infection, or an operation, e.g. tonsillectomy.

In both sexes the patients are taller than average; the adiposity effects the face, chin, chest breast area, abdomen, buttocks, and thighs in contrast with thin, distal extremities; the face is red or cyanotic, often with multiple spider telengiectases which are also found in the cerbical area and sometimes on the trunk. The general facial appearance is simillar to, if not identical with, that of Cushing's syndrome in childhood and this similarity is heightened by the general type of adiposity, the tendency to a short, thick neck and the forward stoop of the head and neck. The buttocks often resemble the face in colour and may be deeply cyanotic in some-patients particularly in colder weather, and very cold to the touch; cyanosis is also present over the breast and thighs in patchy form, and the marble pattern on the thighs and legs justifies the term cutis marmorata, which latter is frequently found in Cushing's syndrome.

The skin is thin and delicate and in milder cases this contributes to a healthy and beautiful complexion with rosy cheeks. Whatever the cause may be, the eyes also are often beautiful giving the appearance of a lovely face perhaps babyish, attached to a massive body. There is a tendency to easy bruising associated with the thin skin and capillary friability. Red lineae distensae of the trunk are frequent and are identical with those found in Cushings syndrome, showing similar variability in intensity, colour, and distribution. They are not always present and diagnosis may be made before they appear. In both sexes the scalp hair tends to be dry and to come well forward on the front and side of the forehead.

Osteoporosis is not found, partly because of the small excess of adrenal glucocorticoids, partly because adrenal androgens are compensatory. Nevertheless, the forward inclined head and round shoulders, together with a short, thick neck, gives many children an appearance and posture resembling that of Cushing's syndrome.

In both sexes the pelvis is broad in relation to the shoulders and gives a waddling gait, noticeably in the male, and explains in part the usual inability to run or to participate in sports requiring rapid movement. On the other hand, swimming is a favourite sport with high achievement, and the general configuration of both sexes is characteristic of champion swimmers. Muscular strength is variable but it may be considerable, probably when associated with a simultaneous excess of adrenal androgens. The height is some two inches above the average throughout the period of growth and usually above average when the epiphyses have joined, in spite of the fact that the epiphyses join prematurely in the female, associated with a tendency to an early menarche. The radiographic bone age is usually advanced in females and normal or retarded in males. Puberty is retarded in males and descent of the testes is not infrequently delayed. It is of interest that Cushing described a typical example of his syndrom in a girl of 15, with precocious adolescence and menarche at the age of 10, and three years' regular menstruation followed by amenorrhoea; and that Cushing's syndrome with adrenal tumour, in the male, has been associated with delayed sexual maturation and gross adiposity.

The breasts in girls are not only prematurely developed, but to a greater extent than in many normal adults, often giving the appearance of a woman's breast during pregnancy. The areola is especially broad and prominent, with numerous Montgomery's tubercles surrounding the nipple, and tortuous superficial veins may be present. Gynaecomasitia is not infrequent in the male. In neither sex has it been possible to demonstrate an excess of urinary oestrogens, and pituitary or adrenal mammogens must be postulated. Such breasts are met with in cases of adrenal tumour in children. The patchy cyanosis of the emlarged glandular and fatty breast has been referred to as well as the red or purple lineae distensae in this area in some patients.

As regards the nature, mannerisms, and behaviour pattern, both sexes tend to be hypersensitive, emotional (sometimes going pale and sometimes blushing, even over the neck, with little provocation), exhibitionistic, actively social and conversational, artistic, musical, histrionic, sentimental, with close maternal association in males. They are good dancers despite their massive bulk, entertainers, and often very intelligent and gifted. In addition to these elements and the physical points mentioned previously, the gestures of the male, the tendency to high-pitched voices and scanty beard growth, theri flair for clothes and cooking, all tend to justify the term gynandrism. Nevertheless, their gonadal evolution, although delayed, is normal (apart from the tendency to horizontal pubic hair), as is their potency and fertility. Further, the behaviour pattern and attitudes are considerably modified when there is an associated adrenal androgenic excess.

Diabetes is a rarity in the childhood or adolescent phase, but is frequently mentioned in the family history. Diabetes is also a rarity in Cushing's syndrome in childhood, because of the compensatory pancreatic islet-cell hypertrophy. In six cases very carefully studied by Martin and Simpson (unpublished). it was not possible to demonstrate unequivocal abnormalities of carbohydrated tolerance or insulin sensitivity. In another series using the technique of the glucose uptake of the isolated rat diaphragm, an excess of plasma insulin activity was demonstrated in three of twenty cases studied. However, elevated plasma insulin activity was not constantly found in these three patients, so that the significance of these results must be questioned at the present time. Polycythaemia, hypertension, renal casts, and albuminuria are rarities and cannot be considered as an essential part of the syndrome, although occasionally met with, and of interest in relation to Cushings' syndrome.

Development and Family History

Some detailed case histories have been given in previous publications. In both sexes, subsequent development in adolescence may approximate to normality, and for this reason the condition has been interpreted as an intensification of normal puberty. This is a valid supposition, as far as it goes, and incompatible with the broader conception of the normal adrenarche: and study of the syndrome throws much light on normal childhood and puberty, and the wide variation met with. At the time study of individual cases over many years, as well as of family histories, shows that many stigmata remain, even when the general appearance becomes normal, that many patients do not evolve to normality, and that others suffer a relapse in adult life, sometimes without obvious cause but often precipitated by pregnancy or the climacteric. Adiposity, hypertension, diabetes, and gallstones, appear to be significantly frequent in family histories.

In males, in adolescence, there is often in late adrenal androgenic phase, in which general body and facial hairiness is rapidly acquired, together with increased muscularity and strength, a spurt in growth, a broadening of the shoulders, and a loss of fat.

Hormone Assays

Initially J. Bornstein, using the biological method of hepatic glycogen deposition in the adrenalectomized rat, found raised values for urinary glucocorticoids in five patients 71-106 units compared with the normal 32-57 units. R. Gardner found raised values for urinary glucocorticoids using the copper reduction-arsenomolybdate method of Talbot. Prunty found normal values by measurement of the ketogenic steroids and, contrary to Cushing's syndrome with adrenal hyperplasia, no augmentation following ACTH stimulation. Gray *et al.*, using chromatographic methods, found that 'the excretion of compound F was significantly increased above that of normal children; and, in adipose gynandrism, the excretion of an unknown delta A^4-3-ketosteroid, X_4, was also significantly increased'. Later, this substance X_4 was identified as Reichstein's compound U (A^4-pregnene-17-a-20 (3-21-triol-3-11-dione). Delphine Parrott *(1951)* found an increase in plasma ACTH in four out of five patients. Gardner found a variable increase in urinary 17-ketosteroids but Gray and others found no constant difference from normal controls.

Mixed Androgenic Types

Whether or not 17-ketosteroid assays confirm clinical findings, there seems no doubt that in some of these patients there is also an excess of adrenal androgens as indicated by body and facial hairiness, severe acne, thickness of eyebrows and very long eyelashes, great muscular strength, greasiness and seborrhoea of scalp hair rather than dryness, and rapid growth of scalp hair, and nails. The androgenic phase in adolescent males has been referred to. The clinical picture is best interpreted by reference to the previous section on the mixed syndrome in adults. The androgenic element explains the occurrence of especially strong fat men in the family history, e.g. circus weight-lifters and iron-bar benders, and why some of these patients are great athletes, e.g. Rugby players and boxers. In one heavyweight boxer of this type, not hirsute, the 17-ketosteroids were 34 mg., and in a very strong tall adult woman of this type, also not hirsute, they were 32 mg. The absence of hi sutism in these cases suggest an antagonism between androgens and glucocorticoids in regard to hair growth. Two strong athletic brothers, with this mixed syndrome both developed steroid diabetes, as had other older members of the family.

Treatment

There is no specific treatment available. Reduced diet, with or without appetite restrainers, e.g. dexamphetamine, is effective in some degree, as in other endocrinopathies. Chorionic gonadotrophins will accelerate descent of the testicle and testicular maturation, but this will usually happen spontaneously although delayed.

ADRENAL FEMINIZATION

The term is applied to a clinical condition in man, produced by an oestrogen-secreting adrenal tumour and characterized by gynaecomastia, testicular tatrophy, with loss of libido and potency, and deposition of fat, especially on the breast, abdomen, and hips. The condition is rare.

The adrenal-cortex tumour is an adenoma, or adenocarcinoma, and is not distinguishable histologically from other hormone-secreting adrenal tumours; but hormone assays have shown that such tumours in man secrete a gross excess of oestrogens, demonstrated for the first time in the case of Simpson and Joll, and confirmed in a similar case by Roholm and Teilum. The high level of blood oestrogens inhibits the secretion of pituitary gonadotrophins, so that involution and atrophy of the testes follow. Although the urinary androgens of adrenal origin may be normal or slightly raised, impotence and loss of libido is the rule in the presence of a gross excess of oestrogens. The latter also explains the gynaecomastia. Adiposity is not invariable and, when present, must be presumed to have the same adrenal hormone basis as has been considered with other adrenal tumours. A review of adrenal feminization is given by Armstrong and Simpson.

Holl's two cases will be briefly described as illustrating that: (1)

puberty gynaecomastia may be associated with an adrenal carcinoma, which fact throws some light on the probable physiological mechanism of puberty gynaecomastia, and (2) the adipose type in the adult male may be characterized by a feminine appearance and removal of the tumour result in a return to normality.

Case 1. A lad of 15 who for two months had observed progressive enlargement of the breasts, which projected in bud-like fashion, like those of a young girl. The nipples were deeply pigmented. The suprapubic hair was feminine type with horizontal border. Death followed removal of a malignant cortical tumour.

Case 2. A male of 44 years of age with two children. The breasts slowly enlarged, with some pain, and the nipples became large and pigmented. The testes and penis became smaller, libido was lost, and sexual intercourse ceased. The patient became fat and his face took on a soft feminine appearance. The interesting feature in this case however, is that removal of an adenomatous cortical tumour was followed by a return to complete normality.

Simpson and Joll's classical case will be briefly described because of the oestrogen assays before and after operation and following metastatic recurrence:

In a physician of 34, the presenting symptom was pain in the left scapula and hypochondrium. However in retrospect, it was seen that two years before there had been enlargement of the breasts, with general increase of fat deposition; and one year before, diminution in size of the penis and testes, with loss of libido and potency. The adiposity, however, only lasted some months, and was followed by loss of weight. A large malignant corticla tumour was removed from the left side and incomplete clinical improvement ensued, namely decrease in size of breasts and partial recovery of libido and potency. This was only temporary, and relapse followed the development of hepatic and visceral metastases from which the patient died.

The oestrogens, which were exceedingly high at the time of operation, fell to values below normal after operation, and subsequently increased to very high values (3,000 LU., per litre) with the development of metastases. Burrows *et al.* stated that 'an attempt to isolate the oestrogenic hormone from the urine has not been successful, but the results are consistent with the view that the hormone is oestrone'. Urinary androgens were just above normal, as measured by combgrowth assays.

An unusual case of an adrenal-cortex tumour in a male of 25, producing gynaecomastia and hypoglycaemia, was described by Staffieri, Cames, and Cid. Two atypical cases have been described in adult males, in which urinary gonadotrophins were present in excess, apparently secreted by the adrenal tumour. This was evidenced in McFadzean's case by the disappearance of a positive Friedman test after successful removal of a adrenal adenocarcinoma. Chamber's patient died before removal of an adrenal carcinoma was possible and excreted 50,000 mouse units of gonadotrophin per 100 ml of urine; the Friedman test was positive. Gonadotrophins have also been found in excess in a woman with adrenal virilism and disappeared after removal of an adrenal adenocarcinoma. It seems extraordinary and yet established that an adrenal tumour secretes gonadotrophins.

ALDOSTERONISM

A syndrome produced by excessive secretion of aldosterone, with resulting sodium retention, hypokalaemic alkalosis, and alkaline urine; and manifested clinically by thirst, polyuria, nocturia, polydipsia, hypertension, weakness, periodic paralysis, muscular cramps, and tetany, but usually with an absence of oedema. The condition is sometimes referred to as primary aldosteronism to differentiate it from secondary aldosteronism. Which is a compensatory mechanism in oedematous conditions (renal, cardiac, and hepatic) and in saltlosing nephritis. Some cases previously diagnosed as potassium losing nephritis were subsequently proved to be examples of primary aldosteronism.

Incidence

The condition may occur at any age, usually above 12, and in either sex. By June 1957 a total of 16 cases of primary aldosteronism had been recorded, of which 3 were diagnosed only at autopsy.

Pathology

Of the 16 recorded cases, 13 were due to adrenal adenoma. 1 to adrenal adenocarcinoma, and 2 to adrenal hyperplasia. The adenoma usually arises from cells of the zona glomerulosa, but in one patient, the adenoma was thought to consist mainly of zona fasciculata cells. In Buchem's patient with bilateral hyperplasia, each gland weighing 8 g., the fascicular zone was more hyperplastic than the glomerular. In Conri s case the adrenal contralateral to the adenoma showed atrophy of the zona fasciculata. In others the contralateral gland was apparently normal.

The kidneys show arteriosclerosis and a diffuse vacuolar change and hydropic degeneration in the tubular epithelium, proceeding in some areas to necrosis.

Clinical Features

Conn's case was a 34-year-old housewife who complained that for seven years she had been having attacks off intense generalized muscular weakness, with on four occasions, complete paralysis of the lower limbs lasting a few days. She had been quite well between attacks, although polydipsia, polyuria, and nocturia had been present for some years, with a known hypertension of 190/100, and proteinuria. Chvostek's and Trousseau's signs were present. Chalmer's patient, a woman of 43, presented with periodic weakness of limbs and neck and inability to lift the arms or head. Buchem's patient was a boy of 17 who as well as retarded physical and genital development-had had polyuria and polydipsia since the age of 2, but who presented with hypertension (220/150), and papilloedema. The urine in twenty-four hours exceeded 4 litres and the specific gravity was 1.004. The patient of Holten and Petersen was a girl of 13, admitted with a pyrexial infection who, during subsequent observation, manifested attacks of tetany, convulsions, and unconsciousness, with hypertension (195/150) and papilloedema. Mader and Iseri's patient was a negro woman of 33, who had noticed spasma of the hands during pregnancy, and six months later muscle weakness, cramps, paraestesia, restlessness, and nervousness. Milne and Muehrche described two patients, one originally thought to be a potassium-losing nephritis but with a twelve-year history of attacks of hypokalaemic muscular paralysis lasting, on one occasion, as long as twenty-one days; and the other, almost asymptomatic, with mild transient headaches and moderate hypertension, in whom, an electrocardiogram that was characteristic of potassium depletion, led to the discovery and removal of a small aldosterone-secreting adrenal adenoma. Hewllett's patient was a man of 44 complaining of dryness of the throat for three years, but also suffering from period of weakness, polyuria, and headaches, with hypertension for many years. These selected clinical histories give a characteristic clinical picture of this syndrome in its various manifestations and presentations. Although the primary electrolyte action of aldosterone is on sodium retention, the potassium less and hypokalaemia explain many of the clinical manifestations, especially attacks or paresis or paralysis. The paraesthesia and tetanic spasms are caused by potassium depletion and metabolic alkalosis decreasing calcium ionization, the serum calcium concentration being normal.

The tetany does not usually respond to intravenous calcium. The hypertension and asssociated arterial and renal changes are secondary to the sodium retention and are reproducible in animal experiments,. However, the renal tubular defect is a recognized complication of chronic hypokalaemia.

Diagnosis

An awareness of the possibility of aldosteronism is called for in a variety of conditions such as hypertension, nephritis, attacks of muscular weakness or paralysis, thirst, polyuria, and tetany. The serum sodium is only moderately raised, e.g. 145 mEq. per litre, and may be normal, in spite of considerable sodium retention. The serum potassium is usually considerably lower than normal, e.g. 2.0 mEq. per litre. The serum chloride is normal or even low. The salivary sodium/potassium ratio is readily obtained by the flame photometer and may be 1 : 3 as compared with the normal of 1 : 1. An electrocardiogram is typical of potassium depletion. The alkali reserve of the blood is characteristically high, e.g. 34 m Eq. per litre. The urine is usually persistently alkaline but a neutral urine has been recorded. The urine is of low specific gravity and there is striking impairment of urine-concentrating power, but renal excretion and urea-concentration tests are normal and proteinuria slight.

Although the Chvostek and Trousseau signs are positive, the serum calcium and phosphorus are normal, and the signs of tetany are usually not influenced by intravenous calcium but are ameliorated by prolonged potassium therapy. The polyuria and polydipsia and low specific gravity of the urine simulate diabetes insipidus, but they are entirely uninfluenced by vasopressin. Familial periodic paralysis is associated with low serum potassium but not the other features of aldosteronism and analysis of muscle biopsy will show high or normal potassium concentration in the former but low potassium concentration in the latter.

The rare condition of a potassium-losing nephritis, sometimes associated with obvious pyelonephritis and multiple calculi, can be distinguished from aldosteronism by evidence of primary nephritis, a good clinical and biochemical response to high potassium intake (to which aldosteronism is refractory), renal biopsy and the absence of high values for aldosterone in blood and urine.

The final proof of aldosteronism is the demonstration of increased quantities in the blood and urine. The initial step is partition chromatography and then bio-assay of the purified fraction in the adrenalectomized rat, measuring the effect by radioactive sodium and potassium excretion. The normal values for aldosterone are less than 10 pg. per twenty-four hours in urine and less than 0.1 pg. per 100 ml. in the blood; in aldosteronism these values are raised considerably, e.g. three times the normal.

In secondary aldosteronism, nephrosis, cardiac failure, hepatic cirrhosis, oedema, or free fluid are primary features, and the hyperaldosteronism is an endeavour to maintain the extracellular fluid volume. Oedema does not occur in primary aldosteronism. In a case of idiopathic oedema due to capillary permeability to protein, hyperaldosteronism proved to be secondary. The rats condition of primary salt-losing nephritis may be compensated by secondary aldosteronism. Potassium depletion is not a prominent feature of secondary aldosteronism. Hyperaldoteronism, with urinary values ten times the normal, is met with in the third trimester of normal pregnancy but is not related to toxaemia of pregnancy. It is believed to be secondary, to maintain the extracellular fluid volume.

Tomography after episacral air insufflation may reveal an adrenal tumour, when such is the cause of primary aldosteronism.

Treatment

This consists of removal of an adrenal tumour or subtotal adrenalectomy in the rare cases of bilateral hyperplasia. Cortisone postoperatively is not essential as cortisone secretion is usually normal but as partial atrophy of the remaining adrenal has been reported, its immediate post-operative use might be considered prudent. Apart from operation, or where operation has to be deferred, potassium in very heavy doses may be ameliorative, but is rarely really effective, e.g. 600 mEq. of potassium chloride by mouth or 200 mEq. per litre intravenously. These are heroic doses.

ADRENAL HYPOFUNCTION

ADDISON'S DISEASE

A condition of adrenal cortical insufficiency, usually due to tuberculosis or atrophy of the adrenal cortex, and characterized by malaise, pigmentation of skin and mucous membranes, low blood pressure, weakness, loss of weight and fat, anorexia and gastro-intestinal symptoms, abnormal loss of salt in the urine and saliva, a tendency to develop hypoglycaemia, and a liability to go into adrenal-insufficiency crisis spontaneously or as a result of infection or trauma.

History

Addison's disease was first described in 1849 by Thomas Addison, physician to Guy's Hospital, in an address to the South London Medical Society. The paper was entitled 'Anaemia: Disease of the Supra-renal Capsules', since he had not then differentiated the idiopathic anaemia, which was also subsequently named after him. In 1885, however, assisted by his junior colleague, Samuel Wilks, he produced his clinical monograph, *On the Constitutional and Local Effects of Disease of the Supra-renal Capsules*. William Hunter, in 1909, suggested the term Addisori s disease, a very worthy eponym for an epoch-making discovery, that was first received, as is not infrequent, with scepticism and even scoffing, and later acknowledged as the clinico-pathological foundation of endocrinology.

Aetiology and Pathology

The disease occurs in both sexes, is most frequent in the third and fourth decades, and is rare in children before puberty, as it is also rare in old age. Tuberculosis and idiopathic atrophy (necrosis) are the two common causes, and although tuberculosis is still the most frequent basis (60 per cent.), its incidence is tending to lessen with the decrease in tuberculosis generally. Idiopathic necrosis is responsible for some 30 per cent. of cases. Other causes may be regarded as rare and exceptional, e.g. amyloidosis, bilateral carcinomatous metastases, bilateral primary adrenal carcinoma, mycosis fungoides, and histoplasmosis. Prolonged treatment of non-endocrine states with high doses of cortisone produce a chronic latent adrenal insufficiency, liable to become acute and fatal with operative procedure. Acute bilateral adrenal haemorrhage, with adrenal crisis, is associated with some severe infections, particularly in childhood (Waterhouse-Friderichsen syndrome). In genetic virilism severe adrenal insufficiency may be coexistent but generally a latent adrenal insufficiency exists, precipitated by trauma or infection.

In O'Donnell's series of 8 patients with tuberculous adrenal glands, 4 showed evidence of old healed pulmonary tuberculosis, 2 advanced active pulmonary tuberculosis with cavitation, 1 tuberculous osteomyelitis of the lumbar vertebrae, and 1 with no other recognized tuberculous focus. This indicates a rather higher percentage of associated active pulmonary tuberculosis than is generally found.

The tuberculous adrenals are often enlarged and both the cortex and- medulla are almost totally involved in a fibrocaseous and granulomatous tuberculous destruction, with occasionally a few islets of regenerated cortical cells. In parts of the gland there may be found more proliferative lesions, with many tubercles, gian cells, endothelial cells, fibroblasts, and lymphoblasts. Areas of calcification may be found. It is often difficult or impossible to recognize the medulla, macroscopically or microscopically.

The cause of *idiopathic atrophy* is unknown, although bacterial and metabolic cytotoxic agents have been postulated and a comparison with hepatic necrosis made. The glands are very small and difficult, or occasionally impossible, to find. The pathological process is limited to the cortex, the medulla being usually intact, these findings giving pathological support to the fact that the adrenal-cortex steroids are the essential missing elements in *Addisons disease*, and that the absence of adrenaline and noradrenaline plays no part in determining its symptomatology. The cortical layer is very thin, being almost entirely replaced by distended capillaries lying in a sparse, delicate, connective tissue, infiltrated with lymphocytes, plasma cells, and histiocytes, Small areas of surviving cortex and large atypical cells, in the process of regeneration and compensatory hypertrophy may be detected. The histological picture bears a closer resemblance to a toxic necrosis, as, for example, occurs in the liver, than to a simple atrophy. *Lymphatic hyperplasia*, involving the lymphatic glands, the spleen, the thyroid, and the thymus is frequently met with, in keeping with animal adrenalectomy experiments. Although recognizing a tendency to thymic hypertrophy in man, Sloper was unable to substantiate this by weight measurement in his series. Experimentally cortisone cause involution of the thymus and lymphatic glands.

Sloper has made a special study of the thyroid gland in Addison's disease, and found that in nine of twenty-one cases the thyroid showed severe involutional changes. In two patients there was severe atrophy of the thyroid, and in the remainder the thyroid was normal. Lymphoid infiltration of the thyroid is frequent but Sloper noted that the lymphoid thyroids of Addison's disease were typically unenlargeds, on this point differing from the enlarged lymphoid goitres of thyrotoxicosis and *Hashimoto's disease.* The pathological findings suggested that 'in some instances the patient may be approaching a stage of subclinical *myxoedema*, averted in some by the presence of areas of hyperplasia, in others by the number of surviving normal acini'; Sloper was unable to confirm the previous observations of Hinerman that there is invariably an islet-cell hyperplasia of the pancreas, although in two cases he found small *islet-cell adenomata*. The pancreas was usually diminished in weight; and was atrophic in one case with coincident diabetes. The testes and ovaries may be normal or involuted. There was marked fall in the number of pituitary basophil cells and to a less extent of the eosinophil cells. It is perhaps difficult to correlate these pituitary findings with the excess of pituitary ACTH found in the plasma in Addison's disease, but they must be regarded as histologically factual.

The heart is small and shows brown atrophy, but these classical findings are rare in the modern cortisone-therapy era. The kidneys are usually normal, but may show tubular degeneration.

Clinical Features

The first manifestation of Addison's disease may be an acute crisis, but more usually the onset is insidious. Sometimes tiredness and malaise precede the full clinical picture for many years and postmortem evidence indicates that some nine-tenths, or more, of the adrenal cortex must be destroyed by disease to produce the full syndrome. The classical description of Addison still constitutes an excellent clinical picture:

The patient, in most of the cases so far seen, has been observed gradually to fall off in general health; the patient becomes languid and weak, indisposed either to bodily or mental exertion; the appetite is impaired or entirely lost; the whites of the eyes become pearly; the pulse small and feeble, or perhaps somewhat large, but excessively soft and compressible; the body wastes, without however, presenting the dry and shrivelled skin and extreme emaciation usually attendant on protracted malignant disease; slight pain or uneasiness is from time to time referred to the region of the stomach, and there is occasionally actual vomiting which in one instance was both urgent and distressing, and it is by no means uncommon for the patient to manifest indications of disturbed cerebral circulation. A most remarkable and characteristic discoloration taking place in the skin-sufficiently marked indeed as generally to have attracted the attention of the patient himself or the patient's friends. This discoloration pervades the whole surface of the body, and is commonly most strongly manifested on the face, neck, superior extremities, penis, and scrotum, and in the flexures of the axillae and around the navel. It may be said to present a dingy or smoky appearance, or various tints or shades of deep amber or chestnut brown; and in one instance the skin was so universally and so deeply darkened that but for the features the patient might have been mistaken for a mulatto. In some cases the discoloration occurs in patches, or perhaps rather certain parts are so much darker than others as to impart to the surface a mottled or somewhat chequered appearance; and in one instance there were in the midst of the mottling, certain insular portions of the integument presenting a blanched or morbidly white appearance, either in consequence of these portions having remained altogether unaffected by the disease, and thereby contrasting strongly with the surrounding skin, or, from an actual defect of colouring matter in these parts. Indeed, as will appear in the subsequent cases, this irregular distribution of pigment cells is by no means limited to the integument, but is occasionally also made manifest on some of the internal structures. It is observed that in the form of small black spots beneath the peritoneum of the mesentery and omentum-a form which in one instance presented itself on the skin of the abdomen. This singular discoloration usually increases with the advance of the disease; the anaemia, languor, failure of appetite, and feebleness of the heart become aggravated, a darkish streak usually appears upon the commissure of the lips; the body wastes, but without the emaciation and dry harsh condition of the surface so often observed in ordinary malignant disease; the pulse becomes smaller and weaker; gnd witttoat any special complaint of vain or uneasiness, the patient at length sinks and expires.

Pigmentation

The *pigmentation* is an increase of the normal melanin pigment in the basal layers of epidermis. The precursor of melanin in vertebrates is tyrosine, oxidised by the enzyme *tyrosinase* to *dihydroxy-phenylalanine* and through further intermediate steps to melanin. The pigmentation is especially intense in areas exposed to light, pressure, and irritation. The palms of the hands and soles of the feet, however, escape pigmentation, except for the creases at the interphalangeal joints. Almost pathognomonic of the disease is the pigmentation of the mucous membrane of the mouth, involving the inside of the cheeks, the inner lips, gums, and posterior aspect of the palate. In some patients, however, the pigmentation is limited to the skin. Some degree of desquamation of the latter is not uncommon. As Addison himself pointed out, a leukodermic type of pigmentation is occasionally met with, and the correctness of the diagnosis with this pattern of pigmentation has been confirmed *post mortem*. *Idiopathic leukodermia* itself is not of adrenal origin but when coincident with Addison's disease, the pigmented areas become more pigmented, but the leukodermic areas remain white.

Although patient tend to become more pigmented in phases of relapse and less pigmented in periods of improvement, the degree of pigmentation is not necessarily *a* measure of the severity of the disease. In fact, deep pigmentation may be present *for* some time before any other major manifestation of the disorder. On the other hand, precipitate onset and an acute downhill course may be met with in patients with little or no pigmentation. Normally, fair people and those who go red rather than brown when exposed to the sun, have little or no melanin formation in the skin, and so fail to become pigmented, or deeply pigmented, if they should develop *Addison's disease*. Such a failure to pigment may increase the difficulties of diagnosis in such cases.

Since pigmentation is slight or absent in *Simmonds' disease*, in contrast with the average case of Addison's disease, it has been suggested that pigmentation depends upon an excess of pituitary ACTH secretion, which is present in Addison's disease but absent in Simmonds' disease. This view is supported by the development of pigmentation after ACTH therapy for non-endocrine states. In frogs, darkening of the skin, produced by expansion of the mélanophores and dispersion of pigment in them, results from injection of intermedin, especially in the pale hypophysectomized animal. Intermedin will produce darkening of the human skin with development of pigmented naevi.

Intermedin, so named because it is derived from the pars intermedia of animal pituitaries, is also called *melanocyte-stimulating hormone* (M.S.H.) or melanophore-expanding hormone, or chromatophoric hormone, and has been found in normal human blood and inhuman pituitaries; and in increased amounts in Addisori s disease, after bilateral adrenalectomy, in Cushing's disease, and in pregnancy. The anterior lobe of the pituitary is the probable source of chromatophoric hormone in man, and frog-test assays were found by Sulman to parallel assays of corticotrophin by the ascorbic acid depletion test in several conditions. He further found that the output of these hormones, or biochemical complexes was diminished by cortisone, desoxycorticosterone, and aldosterone, all of which diminish pigmentation in Addison's disease.

While ACTH and M.S.H. appear to be closely associated in pituitary extracts, they have been partially separated by chemical processes and M.S.H., unlike ACTH, is stable to alkali. Salassa and colleagues at the Mayo Clinic made the significant observation that an ACTH preparation, injected into a patient with primary pituitary insufficiency, produced stimulation of adrenal function but only slight cutaneous pigmentation, whereas an M.S.H. preparation produced little effect on adrenal function but intense pigmentation both of skin and mucous membranes. From a practical angle it seems justifiable to refer to an ACTH complex, containing M.S.H, being an important factor in determining increased pigmentation.

Gastro-Intestinal System

Anorexia, especially for fatty foods, is usual, often being associated with nausea and vomiting. Anorexia is also an early sign of relapse. Constipation is usual, but diarrhoea, sosmetimes precipitated by a mild purgative, is met with and is serious as it may herald a crisis. The onset of diarrhoea should be regarded as a warning of adrenal insufficiency in a patient previously stabilized on appropriate treatment. Various types of abdominal pain may simulate intestinal colic, gastric ulcer,., gastric perforation, gall bladder disease, and renal disease. This last is suggested by the pain in the loin due to the underlying tuberculous adrenal; and tenderness in the costovertebral angle is often present. Irritation of the overlying diaphragm and adjacent pleura produces pain, referred to the shoulder (diaphragmatic pleurisy) and round the costal margin, the pain sometimes being very severe. *Hypochlorhydria*, or *achlorhydria*, are frequently found in the course of investigation, if looked for.

Respiratory System

Disorders of rhythm end sighing respiration are not uncommon in the more severe phases of the disease. There is also a susceptibility to respiratory infection, and the supervention of bronchitis or pneumonia may precipitate a crisis and prove fatal. Ante-mortem evidence-of active pulmonary tuberculosis is infrequent, and the incidence of Addison's disease in tuberculosis clinics or sanatoria is small.

Muscular System

Muscular weakness and easy fatigability are characteristic. *Asthenia* affects all the muscles, and not one special group of muscles as in myasthenia gravis. There may be considerable muscular wasting and creatinutia. The latter, in contrast with the creatinuria, of myasthenia graves, disappears on treatment with cortical extract. Cramps of the calf muscles are sometimes met with, and may be due to hypochloraemia, although hypoparathyroidism is rarely a coincident condition. The lack of muscular strength is explicable on several grounds: *(i)* general illness; *(ii)* the decrease of adrenal androgens, as indicated by the 17-ketosteroid assays, particularly in women the adrenal are the only source of androgens; *(iii)* the disturbance of potassium metabolism; and (iv) the absence of hepatic glycogen reserves and available glucose for sustained effort.

Nervous System

Inertia, *lassitude*, and *apathy* are common, but there may be periods of restlessness, excitability, and insomnia. Sometimes the patients tend to lie curled up in bed, or to sink down beneath the covering. Involuntary cries and grimaces, and later, delirium, may precede a crises. Negativism, contrariness, and pessimism may be features of the more chronic phases. Psychotic states, depressive and delusional, are also met with, but muss be regarded as rare. The psychoneurotic manifestations, or abnormal behaviour pattern can be ascribed to (1) abnormal loss of salt, since McCance observed depression, apathy and irritability in normal volunteers deprived of salt, (2) abnormal carbohydrate metabolism with phases of hypoglycaemia, and (3) absence of cortisone since cortison will almost immediately produce a return to normal of the abnorma electroencephalogram often associated with severe *Addison's disease*.

Blood Count

Leucopenia, relative lymphocytosis, and eosinophilia are characteristic, being the opposite of the changes found in Cushing's syndrome and of those produced by an excessive administration of cortisone. In the patient with Addison's disease, cortisone will reverse these abnormalities in white cell counts. Hypochromic microcytic anaemia is often found and may be due to achlorhydria but it is also corrected by cortisone. The anaemia may not be obvious initially if there is a degree of haemoconcentration when the patient is first seen.

Plasma Volume and Electrolytes

The basic conceptions are discussed in the physiological section. The absence aldosterone is the most important factor in determining electrolyte and fluid changes Addison's disease although the absence of hydrocortisone is an additional factor. The primary result of aldosterone deficiency is sodium depletion with excessive excretion sodium in the urine and in the saliva, the latter indicating that the renal is not the on mechanism involved. The sodium loss results initially in a decrease in extracellular fluid and plasma volume in an endeavour to maintain plasma concentration of sodium at normal values, but if the sodium loss is severe this compensating mechanism fails and there is a fall in plasma sodium values. In addition to loss of extracellular fluid through the kidneys, some of the fluid passes from the extracellular to the intracellular spaces. This latter is important clinically since treatment with desoxycortone, or fluorohydrocortisone, or aldosterone, can restore a decreased plasma volume even without the addition of extraneous fluids, causing a redistribution of fluid from the intracellular fluid to the extracellular fluid, including plasma. Severe sodium depletion impairs renal circulation so that initial polyuria gives way to oliguria, and even anuria, particularly in crisis.

Sodium depletion leads to the clinical picture of dehydration, and the diminution in interstitial fluid is indicated by a loss of tissue elasticity, a loss of superficial tissue fullness, or turgor, and by a low intra-ocular tension. The deficiency of plasma fluid is indicated by a rise in the haematocrit and in protein concentration and by poor venous filling, the veins being collapsed and difficult to enter with a needle. Even when the vein is properly entered, it will collapse after withdrawing 1 or 2 ml. so that one must be patient and wait until it slowly refills before drawing up a total of 20 ml. The additional fall in blood pressure is also an expression of sodium depletion and a compensatory vasoconstriction leads to cold extremities. Muscle cramps are also an expression of sodium depletion, the serum calcium being normal or raised.

In mild Addison's disease the plasma sodium may be normal, even when the daily excretion of sodium is in excess, but in severe cases the plasma sodium is diminished. The plasma chloride is a much less reliable index of adrenal electrolytic function, as several factors determine chloride values, but a low chloride value is confirmatory. With the increased excretion of sodium there is a decreased excretion of potassium so that plasma potassium values may be normal or raised, the latter only being found in severe adrenal insufficiency. .

Cortisone, or hydrocortisone, has a mild sodium an associated fluid retaining action so that its absence contributes to the electrolytic defects in adrenal-insufficiency. In so far as many patients in severe adrenal insufficiency, and even in crisis, respond dramatically to cortisone only, its influence on sodium and fluid may be greater in this condition than experimental considerations would appear to permit and in particular it may influence considerably the transfer of fluid from the intracellular fluid to extracellular fluid. In Simmonds' disease we have seen that the absence of cortisone results in haemodilution with increase of plasma volume causing lower values for haeamoglobin and plasma proteins; and cortisone causes a diuresis with a correction of this. This phenomenon is found in investigation water-loading in Addison's disease (Kepler test) and is corrected by cortisone but it does not make itself manifest otherwise in Addison's disease and this is probably explained by the coincident absence of aldosterone, which latter is normally present in Simmonds' disease.

The excessive loss of the kation sodium in Addison's disease results in a metabolic acidosis and a lowering of the plasma bicarbonate. This is aggravated by the fact that there is defective ammonia formation by the kidneys in Addisori s disease, as ammonia formation spares sodium loss.

Renal Function

Although adrenalectomy may result in ultimate renal tubular degeneration in animals, and comparable changes may be found in fatal cases of Addison's disease, the disturbance of renal function in Addison's disease is functional rather than organic, except in the terminal phase. It is rare to find any abnormality of the urine except in a crisis, when oliguria is associated with albuminuria and granular casts. The blood urea is raised in severe adrenal insufficiency but this is a consequence of abnormal salt loss and can be corrected by the giving of salt, or by aldosterone. Sodium depletion causes a fall in cardiac output and a reduction in renal blood flow, and the extrarenal uraemia of sodium depletion may even simulated primary renal failure. Since aldosterone stimulates renal tubular absorption of sodium, the sodium depletion of Addison's disease is partly due to the failure of renal tubular function, determined by the absence of aldosterone. However, the abnormal loss of sodium in the saliva indicates that this is not the only factor in a negative sodium balance.

Basal Metabolism and Body Temperature

The basal metabolism is usually normal, or slightly subnormal, in the more subacute phases, or in a crisis. The infrequency of a low basal metabolism in the more chronic phase is a little surprising in view of the frequency of involutional changes in the thyroid gland, described in the pathology section: but the absence of the inhibitory effect of cortisone on thyroid function may play a part. The temperature in Addison's disease is usually subnormal, but these patients are very susceptible to any infection and then easily run a high temperature. These periods of intermittent pyrexia may also occur in the apparent absence of a definite infection. This is also true of phases of increased sedimentation rate without apparent cause but corrected by cortisone. Patients are also very sensitive to cold, in keeping with animal experiments, and adrenalectomized animals die rapidly on exposure to severe cold. Cortisone is protective against low temperatures and the sensitivity to cold is related to the absence of hepatic glycogen stores for carbohydrate metabolism. Certainly cold is one of the 'stress' stimuli to increased cortisone secretion in the normal animal. The extremities of the Addisonian patient are frequently cold to the touch and the fingers may become white or blue when exposed to cold. The phenomenon has been observed by the writer to occur after bilateral adrenalectomy in the absence of major indications of adrenal insufficiency.

Genital System

In the more severe phases of the disease, impotence and amenorrhoea are not uncommon, but in some women menstruation may continue quite normally. It is probable that the adrenals influence the gonads via the pituitary. There is certainly a close relation between the adrenals and the gonads, the adrenals undergoing hypertrophy after castration and secreting oestrogens after bilateral ovariectomy. Pregnancy was rarely met with but it is becoming more frequent and successful since the availability of the cortisone. Two successful pregnancies in one patient, 'with live normal babies, have been recorded.

Since there is a hypersecretion of cortisone in pregnancy in normal women, pre-existing Addison's disease should be aggravated by pregnancy. There may, however, be some initial improvement and this is explained by the fact that the placenta can secrete cortisone. Theoretically the adrenals of the foetus might play a part. Sometimes the extra demands of pregnancy may reveal latent Addisori s disease and in other cases the pigmentation of pregnancy persisted until the more complete picture of adrenal insufficiency became clear some months or years later. In one patient the climacteric increased the intensity of adrenal insufficiency but subsequently there was a large measure of apparent recovery.

Carbohydrate Metabolism

Porges was the first to point out that a low blood sugar occurred in Addison's disease. Wadi described hypoglycaemic attacks in a man of 24 a few days prior to death. His blood sugar concentration was 71 mg. per 100 ml. in the more chronic phase, but 43 mg. and 36 mg. per 100 ml. in hypoglycaemic attacks that were relieved by intravenous glucose. The diagnosis of Addison's disease was confirmed at autopsy, the suprarenal gland being almost completely destroyed by tuberculosis. Snell and Rowntree found that hypoglycaemia was present in the terminal phases. Simpson found blood sugar values to be normal or slightly subnormal in the more chronic phases of Addison's disease but low values in crisis. Before the cortisone era Simpson found the most frequent cause of sudden death to be hypoglycaemic coma. This was a very dangerous complication when treatment was limited to desoxycortone and fatal hypoglycaemia could occur with great suddenness and be fatal within a few hours. These observations are in keeping with experimental knowledge that adrenalectomized animals have little or no hepatic glycogen and will go into hypoglycaemia under the influence of fasting, stress, or infection.

As long ago as 1909, Eppinger, Falta, and Rudinger found flat carbohydrate tolerance curves, suggesting an increased tolerance for carbohydrates in Addison's disease. Simpson found similar curves in some patients, partly explained by the absence of the diabetogenic action of adrenal glucocorticoids, and partly by retarded intestinal absorption.

In contrast with the above, Addison's disease is sometimes complicated by diabetes mellitus. Simpson described three such cases under his personal care and reviewed the literature of a further fifiteen cases, proved by autopsy. The diabetes may precede or follow the clinical evidence of Addisori s disease or the two may coexist from the onset. *Post mortem* the pancreatic lesion is seen to be atrophy of the islets, or reduction in their size, with hyalinization; but the adrenal lesion may be atrophy or tuberculosis. Haemochromatosis involving the adrenals and the pancreas has also been described, and in this metabolic disorder it is known that haemosiderin can be deposited in the liver, spleen, pancreas, adrenals, pituitary, and testes, & c.

Simpson's three cases are worth a brief summary. The first was a boy of 16 who stopped growing at 13 when lassitude developed, and who appeared to be a case of infantilism until pigmentation at the age of 16 led to the correct diagnosis of Addison's disease. On admission to hospital blood sugar levels were low, 50-60 mg. per 100 ml, but in the course of the next few weeks they rose to 250 and 300 mg. per 100 ml., and 10 Units of insulin produced hypoglycaemic values and symptoms. Treatment was limited to cortical extract and the patient died in Addisonian crisis in 1931, autopsy, showing atrophy of the pancreas and adrenals. It is probable that both these lesions were present simultaneously but that the diabetes was initially masked by the Addison's disease. The case also illustrates the instability of the blood sugar in these cases, the extreme hypersensitivity to insulin and liability to hypoglycaemic reactions.

The second case was a male of 37 who developed diabetes mellitus at the age of 11 and Addison's disease twenty-one years later at the age of 32. He died in 1947, at the age of 37, in Addisonian crisis with autopsy findings of atrophy of the adrenals and of the pancreas. The development of Addisons'disease led to a reduction of insulin requirement from 72 Units to 6 Units daily and instability of blood sugar concentrations was indicated by values of 45, 56, 917, and 1,540 mg. per cent.

The third case was a male of 20 who developed Addison's disease and diabetes mellitus in 1947, at the age of 18, the latter obvious four months after the former, but probably present in latent form from the onset. The patient was initially treated by desoxycortone and the special interest of the case was the effect of changing over to cortisone on the diabetes. Cortisone 25 mg. daily produced diuresis, ketosis, and incipient diabetic coma within forty-eight hours and the insulin requirements increased from 8 to 34 Units daily. In this patient cortisone was so powerfully diabetogenic and ketogenic that even with increased insulin the dose of cortisone had to be limited to 12 mg. daily. Another feature in this case. was a raised sedimentation rate of 20 mm. in one hour (Westegren) partially reduced to 8 mm. by cortisone but variable in the absence of obvious infection. The patient continued well for two years and then died in diabetic coma a few hours after admission, his family doctor having stopped insulin forty-eight hours previously because of hypoglycaemic features. The adrenals were atrophic and the pancreas showed atrophy with some 'quite reasonable islets but curious basophil cells scattered throughout'.

Crisis

The term 'crisis' in Addison's disease is applied to an acute phase of the disorder in which the patient is collapsed and sometimes even comatose. Death is imminent unless active specific therapy is available. The patient may pass from a chronic state of insufficiency into a crisis even in the absence of any obvious precipitating cause. More usually, the incidence of intercurrent infection, to which patients with adrenal insufficiency are especially susceptible, is an important factor.

On the other hand, it should be remembered that patients inadequately treated, and therefore liable to enter upon a crisis, are also much more liable to contract an intercurrent infection than are patients receiving adequate therapy. Extra exertion, or mental stress, in the absence of an increase in the dose of cortisone, may precipitate a crisis. A surgical operation, even a minor one, will lead to an adrenal crisis if therapy is not appropriately augmented. In some patients the diagnosis of Addison's disease has only been made after a minor operation or accident produced an adrenal crisis and drew attention to features of the disease pre-existing but not appreciated. Diarrhoea is one of the features of adrenal insufficiency, especially in more severe phases, but it is also true that excessive diarrhoea produced by a drastic purge in a constipated patient may prove intractable and be the immediate precursor of a crisis.

Frequently there is no warning of a crisis, which comes on with great suddenness, but there are significant symptoms of a relatively minor character, which in the writer's experience can be regarded as of a warning nature. Thus the patient may yawn a great deal and stretch himself frequently, perhaps uttering involuntary cries or monosyllabic sighs. The onset and persistence of hiccoughs is an adverse sign. A susceptibility to conjunctivitis should not be disregarded and photophobia may be ominous. An increased sensitivity to cold, or actual shivering, especially if the patient curls himself up well beneath the blankets and refuses to answer question, should quite properly give rise to anxiety as to the state of adrenal insufficiency. In this stage also, there may be an inexplicable tendency to make unpleasant grimaces, and also a degree of irritability and negativeness.

When a crisis has developed, the patient looks dehydrated with sunken orbits and lack of resilience of the tissues; the veins are collapsed and difficult to enter with a needle and blood can only be withdrawn slowly and intermittently, the veins, tending to collapse after each few ml. and refilling only slowly after a pause. These are manifestations of salt depletion and secondary reduced plasma volume with haemoconcentration, increased haematocrit, increased haemoglobin concentration, and increased plasma protein concentration. The plasma sodium is low and the plasma potassium may be raised. Blood urea is usually raised and the alkali reserve is low because of a metabolic acidosis.

The above clinical description of adrenal crisis largely revolves around severe sodium depletion. However, in some patients, hypoglycaemia may cause predominant features, such as convulsions, coma, or peculiarities of behaviour, e.g. irritability, irrationality. The tendency to hypoglycaemia was more frequent in the desoxycortone or pre-cortisone era and in fact was then probably the most frequent cause of death. Even with cortisone, hypoglycaemia is a phenomenon which one must always be on the alert for in Addison's disease. It may happen quite suddenly in a patient who appears reasonably well, as has been described above for the Addisonian crisis, of which it is one important aspect. These clinical observations-emphasizing the importance of hypoglycaemic crises in Addisons's disease-are fully supported by the results of bilateral adrenalectomy in some animals, namely disappearance of hepatic glycogen and fatal hypoglycaemia, as well as by the contrasting diabetogenic action of cortisone.

ASSOCIATED ENDOCRINE DISORDERS

Addison's disease may be complicated by the coincident existence of myxoedema, thyrotoxicosis, parathyroid deficiency and tetany, diabetes mellitus, and acromegaly.

Clinical Diagnosis

A combination of weakness, loss of weight, anorexia, nausea, or vomiting, low blood pressure, and pigmentation of the skin and mucous membrane, is strongly indicative of Addisori s disease, especially when no other organic lesion can be detected. A previous history of abdominal, cervical gland, bone, or pulmonary tuberculosis, or of idiopathic pleurisy, is important supporting evidence, as is also a familial susceptibility to the tubercle bacillus. In patients over 50 years of age metastatic carcinomatosis may rarely involve both adrenal glands, but tuberculous and atrophic adrenal lesions also occur in older people. Some pigmentation of the skin may be present in carcinomatosis without any gross lesion in the adrenals. In a man of 43 under the care of Dr. Cawadias, and seen by the writer, the cause of Addisori s disease of three years' duration was found to be primary carcinoma of both adrenal glands. The sedimentation rate was 70 mm. in one hour.

When the condition is met with in children it may present initially as arrest of growth with fatigability, or as infantilism, and the diagnosis may be missed for months or even two years. It is very rare for Addison's disease to occur before the age of 11 but Welch described such a case in a girl of 9, with weakness and anorexia following an attack of mumps, and pigmentation developing six months later. Mumps and other virus infections apparently may affect the adrenals, the gonads, the pancreatic islets, and other endocrine glands.

In Simmonds' disease, the adrenals are atrophied except the zone (probably zona glomerulosa) which secretes aldosterone, so that apart from salt depletion, the clinical pictures have many points in common, e.g. weakness, fatigability, anorexia, loss of weight, hypotension, and a tendency to hypoglycaemic attacks. However, in Simmonds' disease the face is pale, skin pigmentation is absent or slight, and pigmentation of the mucous membranes does not occur. The reason for this is that the destroyed anterior pituitary cannot secrete the ACTH complex, excess of which is an important factor in producing pigmentation. Bradycardia and low basal metabolism are usual with Simmonds' disease. Amenorrhoea or impotence are early manifestations of Simmonds' disease, but are late or absent features in Addisons' disease. Slight or absent pubic hair is more characteristic of Simmonds' disease but the pubic hair may become thin in chronic Addison's disease. In fact the clinical differentiation of Simmonds' disease and Addison's is sometimes quite difficult and help is required from hormone and bichemical tests, such as the failure to respond to ACTH in Addisons' disease.

Although pigmentation of the skin is almost invariably a feature of Addison's disease, it may be very slight, or even undetected, in fair-skinned people, especially when the onset is acute. Pigmentation of the mucous membrane is usual but not invariable. Rarely the pigmentation of the skin is indistinguishable from that of idiopathic leukodermia. If pigmentation occurs in the mucous membrane of the mouth as well as in the skin, it is almost invariably due to adrenal insufficiency. Such pigmentation has been said to occur in pernicious anaemia, and Addison himself originally confused the two diseases, but neither the writer nor two colleagues, who have examined hundreds of patients with pernicious anaemia, have ever seen pigmentation of the mucous membrane in this disease, although pigmentation of the skin certainly does sometimes occur. In three other conditions pigmentation of the mucous membranes is said to occur: chronic arsenic poisoning, abdonical carcinoma, and haemochromatosis. In the first and-the last of these conditions the adrenal glands are infiltrated with arsenic or with haemosiderin, as are the other organs, and the pigmentation, when present, is therefore an expression of adrenal insufficiency. In abdominal carcinoma, the adrenals themselves may be affected. Pigmentation of the skin only, however, is not uncommon in any form of carcinoma. Apart from disease, pigmentation of the mucous membrane, although perhaps unnoticed until some illness is present, is found in persons in whose ancestry there is a strain of negroid, Indian, Eurasian, or Levantine blood. The racial factor is frequently forgotten, or unknown, but pigmentation may be found in other members of the family. Pregnancy, with vomiting, in such a Addison' disease. Skin pigmentation, however, especially in brunettes, is not uncommon in pregnancy, and is explicable on the basis of the greater demand on adrenal function.

Pigmentation of the skin occurs in pellagra: and a patient with pellagra secondary to gastro-jejunostomy was sent to the writer with the diagnosis of Addison' disease, other features being anorexia, diarrhoea, weakness, anaemia, and wasting. The adrenals, in fatal cases of pellagra, have, however, been observed to be atrophic probably secondary to vitamin deficiency. The skin in pellagra shows sharply demarcated areas of hyperkeratosis. Pigmentation of the skin is a rare complication of exophthalmic goitre, and it is not unlikely that in such cases the adrenals too are affected, if only functionally, by the thyrotoxicosis. It has already been noted that true Addison's disease and thyrotoxicosis can both exist in the same patient. Cutaneous pigmentation, especially of the orbits, may be met with in Cushing's syndrome, the adrenogenital syndrome and in acromegaly, and is attributable to excess of pituitary ACTH.

Hormone Tests

The urinary 17-ketosteroids are almost or entirely absent in Addison's disease in women, because the adrenals are the only source of androgens in the female. This is no differentiation from Simmonds' disease in women as the 17-ketosteroids are also very low in this condition. In men with Addison's disease the testes continue to secrete androgens, so that the 17-ketosteroids are low, e.g. 6 mg. per twenty-four hours, but not absent. Low values for urinary glucocorticoids in both sexes also favour the diagnosis, but paradoxically with some techniques the values obtained are within normal limits and must be regarded as fallacious and non-specific. The same is true of plasma glucocorticoids. However, since the adrenals are destroyed largely or entirely, there is a failure of an increase in urinary 17-ketosteroids or 11-oxysteroids, or in plasma 11-oxysteroids, following ACTH stimulation in Addisori s disease. In Simmonds' disease the involuted adrenals are capable of responding to an ACTH stimulus and the above values all rise. In the more chronic forms of Simmonds' disease the adrenals may have lost their ability to respond to ACTH, but this ability to respond is often restored by cortisone therapy over a period. The ACTH may be given intravenously, e.g. 20 Units in 100 mg. of saline in thirty minutes, or as ACTH gel intramuscularly; neither test can be considered as completely free from danger. With the intravenous route severe allergic reactions may occur and with the intramuscular ACTH gel, contaminated in some preparations with vasopressin, water intoxication has led to convulsions. This is less true of more recent preparations and 40 Units daily for, three days of the gel preparation given intramuscularly is justifiable, providing the patient's condition is not severe, when it is preferable to postpone such tests, after starting therapy, and only to use them if the diagnosis remains in doubt. Coincidental with hormone assays, the effect of ACTH on the blood eosinophils is of some value, their concentrate decreasing by more than 50 per cent in some normals and disappearing altogether in many other normals, but not being influenced in Addison's disease. The results, however, are not necessarily constant and cannot be regarded as in any sense infallible, but rather as one possible indication.

Therapeutic Test

Cortisone, in therapeutic doses of 25 mg. thrice daily by mouth, is rapidly and dramatically effective in both Addison's disease and Simmonds' disease. In these doses such effects are not obtained in other conditions and, if obtained psychogenically, fail to be sustained. The therapeutic test may therefore be regarded as of very great value and is free from danger.

Diagnosis of Pre-Addison's Disease

Careful clinical history-taking in retrospect, in a large number of classical cases of Addison's disease, in which the diagnosis is beyond doubt, has convinced the writer that adrenal insufficiency may be present for as long as two years, and occasionally longer, before the characteristic clinical picture develops-and in the absence of gross pigmentation. Since the symptoms are often vague, e.g. malaise, lack of strength, poor appetite, the diagnosis of a pre-Addison state may be missed or rejected, particularly if the routine tests described above prove equivocal. Nevertheless, the condition must be borne in mind, particularly if there is a history of personal or familial tuberculosis or if the symptoms developed within months of a virus infection. It has been noted that adrenal insufficiency in children can manifest itself initially as infantilism or failure of the normal puberty evolution. Where there are good grounds for a provisional clinical diagnosis, the therapeutic test seems justifiable and a positive indication warrants the continuance of appropriate therapy. The lack of a critical objective approach might lead to the treatment of a number of a non-endocrine psychoneurotic states, but nevertheless the physician should not be guilty of missing a true adrenal insufficiency in its early stages.

Treatment

An aqueous adrenal extract, prepared and found effective on adrenalectomized animals by Swingle and Pfiffner, was first used effectively in Addison's disease by Rowntree and Green in America and by Simpson in England. The extract was injected intramuscularly or intravenously 5-20 ml. twice daily. In spite of its bulk and inadequacy compared with modern therapy it was a dramatic therapeutic advance at that time. The following year Loeb noted that patients in Addisonian crisis resembled some types of surgical shock and found that sodium chloride by mouth or intravenously was of considerable benefit. His observations were confirmed by Atchley and Stahl on adrenalectomized dogs.

The next step was the synthesis of desoxycorticosterone by Reichstein and its first clinical use in Addison's disease by Simpson. The substance was given in oily solution intramuscularly, e.g. 5 mg. daily, or, after some weeks of stabilization, by subcutaneous implantation of sterile tablets, one tablet of 100 mg. for each 1 mg. of desoxycorticosterone (DOCA) injected daily. DOCA corrected the abnormal renal salt loss of adrenal insufficiency and proved more effective than the aqueous extracts or salt; and particularly so when supplemented by aqueous extracts, whose main action was on carbohydrate metabolism. Nevertheless, many patients, often apparently well, died suddenly from hypoglycaemia. More recently, DOCA was prepared as 'crystules' of its trimethyl acetate in buffered isotonic aqueous solution, 50-100 mg. being given intramuscularly and being effective, by slow absorbtion, for four weeks. All these methods of giving DOCA must be proceeded with cautiously, as excessive retention of salt and water and secondary excessive elimination of potassium may follow insidiously from overdosage. The features of this vary, and may be weakness, paresis, anorexia, vomiting, crepitations in the lungs, frothy sputum, oedema, and hypertension. Overdosage should be treated by removing the cause, by giving 100 ml. of 2 per cent. potassium chloride intravenously, and by the very cautious use of a mercurial diuretic, e.g. mersalyl, to eliminate the excess of sodium. Lipoid adrenal extracts containing a carbohydrate reguating action, and liquorice extracts, containing a salt-retaining factor were only of temporary limited interest.

The next real advance was the extraction and partial synthesis of cortisone and related compounds and their availability for the treatment of Addisons' disease. Cortisone (11-dehydro-17-hydroxycorticosterone or Compound E) is effective by mouth and is supplied as tablets of 25 mg., easily divided into two. When swallowed, action is rapid, beginning within thirty minutes and lasting several hours. In practice it is usual to give half the tablet twice daily but some patients can, manage with the total dose once daily. The usual total daily dose is 25-37 mg. but some patients can manage on 12 mg. and a few require 50 mg. This dose may be just above physiological requirements and some patients become adipose if this dose is maintained for long periods. Cortisone, or the closely related hydrocortisone is the most important missing hormone in Addison's disease and replacement therapy with either substance produces a more complete return to normal than any other therapy. Apart from its beneficial effect on physical strength, resistance of fatigue, stress and infection, pigmentation, hypotension, abnormal electrocardiograms, and electroencephalograms, it results in a return to a normal positive personality and well being. Metabolically, it restores body glycogen stores and blood sugar concentration to normal, and thus minimizes the incidence of hypoglycaemic attacks, which are an adverse feature of therapy limited to DOCA. However, the effect of cortisone on a negative salt balance is only slight and, theoretically at least, a patient so treated would also require salt or DOCA. In actual practice this has been found to be essential only for a minority of patients, cortisone alone proving adequate. When a salt-retaining hormone is required, we now have available a halogen derivative, 9 a-fluorohydrocortisone, which is effective as a tablet by mouth in small doses, e.g. 0.1 mg., or less, once daily. Perhaps, aldosterone, effective in small daily doses of 0.15 mg, will become more generally available as an alternative to fluorohydrocortisone. The latter is not suitable for the treatment of Addisori s disease by itself because its cortisone-like action is very weak compared with its powerful salt-retaining action. In limited trials, aldosterone, 0.15 mg. daily, has also corrected hypoglycaemic tendencies.

The best treatment of Addisonian crisis is its prevention and the oral dose of cortisone should be increased during excessive stress, or infection, or at the first sign of adrenal insufficiency from unknown causes, e.g. malaise, anorexia, increase of pulse rate, lowering of blood pressure, vomiting, diarrhoea, unexplained pyrexia. No harm will result from a temporary increase of cortisone, if in doubt, and many a severe crisis will be thus prevented. If the patient is vomiting, and unable to chew or swallow cortisone, this can be given intramuscularly, its action, however, being slower by this route and not developing effectively until some hours after injection, with a duration effect of sixteen to twenty-four hours. Cortisone is prepared as cortisone acetate, a white powder, only slightly soluble in water, and therefore suspended in saline solution, 25 mg. per ml., in bottles of 20 ml. containing 500 mg. (with benzyl alcohol as preservative). The intramuscular dosage is equivalent to that of cortisone given by mouth. In crisis 100 mg. cortisone should be injected intramuscularly at once and it will provide a depot for steady absorption; but there are now available two preparations suitable for intravenous injection with consequent rapidity of response: (1) a concentrated solution of hydrocortisone, 100 mg. in 20 ml. 50 per cent. alcohol, which is added to 1 litre of physiological saline and 5 per cent glucose, injected at the rate of 25 mg. per hour for the first two hours and 12.5 mg. per hour subsequently; (2) the sodium salt of hydrocortisone-21-hemisuccinate, extremely soluble in water, presented as a powder in a vial, in a dose equivalent to 100 mg. hydrocortisone, to which is added 2 ml. sterile water from a separate vial; the solution of 2 ml. can be injected directly into a vein or added to a saline-glucose drip. Treatment may be reinforced with desoxycortone 10 mg. intramuscularly, or fluorohydrocortisone 0.2 mg. intravenously, but the danger of overdosage with salt-retaining hormones in real. Many patients who look dehydrated and have haemoconcentration recover with cortisone only, without even intravenous saline infusions. Much of the fluid is not lost from the body in crisis but passes from the extracellular spaces to the intracellular spaces of organs, e.g., liver; and DOCA, fluorohydrocortisone, and to a lesser degree also cortisone, reverse this and restore the plasma volume even without the addition of fluid from outside the body, except in the more severe phases of crisis. Intravenous glucose is advisable if severe hypoglycaemia is the predominant feature, but here, too, cortisone by itself has a rectifying action on carbohydrate metabolism. Although a clinician's judgement will influence variations of treatment in each case, cortisone, or hydrocortisone, is now the sheet anchor in the treatment of all phases of adrenal insufficiency. Prednisone and prednisolone, dehydrogenation products of cortisone and hydrocortisone, are four or five times as powerful as cortisone, or hydrocortisone, as judged by their glucocorticoid activity and are sometimes used in Addison's disease as alternative therapy. However, their sodium-retaining action is very much less than that of cortisone and hydrocortisone, and although this makes them more suitable for massive doses in certain non-endocrine states, it is to their disadvantage in the therapy of most patients with Addison's disease.

When cortisone was first introduced, it was feared by some clinicians that the tendency of large doses to cause a spread of infections, especially tuberculosis, as proved by animal experiments would be a danger in Addison's disease due to tuberculous adrenals. In practice this has not proved to be the case, because the relatively small substitution doses used are physiological and not comparable to the large doses employed in non-endocrine conditions. In fact such physiological doses are probably beneficial in tuberculous and other infections, since the adrenalectomized animal is much more sensitive to infections than the normal animal. Where a patient has active tuberculosis, e.g. pulmonary, as well as Addison's disease, it is probably wise to combine cortisone with modern chemotherapy directed to the tuberculosis, e.g., streptomycin &c., until the acute tuberculosis is under control. This may also be wise in the case of severe nontuberculous infection, but it must always be remembered that the onset of infection calls for an increase in the maintenance dose of cortisone, and such an increase should not be withheld.

The advent of cortisone has completely changed the prognosis in Addison's disease, and not only are patients living many more years, but they are doing so with a capacity to follow their work and enjoy their pleasures. Nevertheless undue stress and fatigue, or exposure to infections, should be avoided as far as is practical because a patient with Addison's disease has not the reserve protection or adjustments of a normal individual.

PHAEOCHROMOCYTOMA

Adrenaline was synthesized in 1904 but the existence of the related pressor amine, noradrenaline, was not recognized until comparatively recently, and its release *in vivo* be excitation of adrenergic fibres wass demonstrated in 1949 (Peart). Noradrenaline differs from adrenaline in the absence of an N-methyl group. Both adrenaline and noradrenaline are secreted by the normal adrenal medulla and by phaeochromocytomas. Both produce a rise in systolic and diastolic blood pressure but adrenaline does this mostly by increasing cardiac output and noradrenaline by increasing peripheral resistance; adrenaline produces tachycardia and noradrenaline tends to produce bradycardia.

Incidence

The first complete study of a classical case was made in 1922 by Labbe, Tinel, and Doumer. The condition may be met with at all ages, including childhood and infancy, and in both sexes.

Pathology

The tumours are usually adenomatous but may be malignant, with metastases. Of 103 recorded cases, 13 were bilateral and yet no case due to bilateral medullary hyperplasia has been described. Occasionally the neoplasm arises from para-aortic medullary tissue outside the adrenal gland. The tumours vary in size and may be enormous but, as with other endocrine tumours a tiny tumour may be extremely active in a secretion. The name phaeochromocytoma is based on the fact that adrenaline, in the cytoplasm of the cells, reduces chromium salts to form an insoluble peroxide of chromium, which appears in the cytoplasm as fine brown granules. Most tumours secrete both adrenaline and noradrenaline in varying proportions and contain high concentrations of both substances. An intrathoracic tumour in an infant of five months was described by Mason *et al*..

Clinical Features

Attacks are due to paroxysmal secretory activity of the tumour and may occur at intervals of weeks, or several times a day, and may last from a few minutes to a few hours. In an attack the patient may experience anxiety, palpitations, tremors, perspiration, severe headache, blurred vision, faintness, weakness, dyspnoea, a feeling of suffocation or painful constriction of the chest, or angina-like pain, nausea, vomiting abdominal colic, cramps of the calf muscles, and tingling of the extremities, which may undergo colour changes comparable to those found in Raynaud's disease. The skin is pallid and cold in an attack, with beads of perspiration sometimes visible. Goose-flesh is sometimes present. The blood pressure may be normal in quiescent periods and suddenly rise in attacks, or it may be appreciably raised all the time and rise still further in paroxysms. The pulse rate is often considerably accelerated during the attacks but bradycardia, sometimes associated with a high proportion of noradrenaline, is met with and is characteristic of many cases. The heart beat in an attack may be so violent as to shake the bed, even while the patient sleeps. The systolic pressure is said to rise to a greater extent than the diastolic, but both may be raised considerably, e.g. 280 systolic and 200 diastolic. The heart may be considerably enlarged, and left ventricular failure may ensue. Pulmonary oedema with frothy blood-tinged sputum is also met with. One woman of 66 *was* admitted to hospital three times with attacks of dyspnoea, copious expectoration, sweating, and vomiting. Breathlessness, at rest or on excretion, may be a prominent feature and cardiac asthma is met with, sometimes with left ventricular failure. In one case phases of hypertension (240/150) were followed by phases of hypotension (90/70). The clinical picture may be one of severe progressive hypertension, e.g. 200/110, without any superimposed paroxysms, as in the woman of 29 years of age described by Binger and Craig. The fundi may show papilloedema or hypertensive retinitis, and these changes may be reversible if the tumour is removed early enough. The kidneys may or may not be secondarily involved, but nephrosclerosis has been recorded. In most cases the urea clearance test of kidney function gives values well above normal, e.g. 140 per cent., and this is attributed to the increased blood flow through the kidneys.

The basal metabolic rate is often raised to the extent found in hyperthyroidism, e.g., plus 60 per cent but this is not due to hyperthyroidism since it returns to normal after removal of the adrenal tumour, but is unaffected by thiouracil or thyroidectomy. The thyroid epithelium does not show hyperplasia. An apparently normal thyroid gland may become enlarged and vascular during an attack. The increased basal metabolic rate is often associated with pyrexia, which may be constant or intermittent.

The pyrexia is often associated with leucocytosis, the neutrophil polumorphs being 62 and 75 per cent in two cases.

Diabetes mellitus has often been diagnosed as a complication but here, too, the hyperglycaemia is a result of the hyperadrenalism. The blood sugar concentration is variable and unstable and the patients hypersensitive to insulin. McCullagh and Engel recorded the following blood sugar tolerance curves before and after removal of an adrenal phaeochromocytoma, the values being fasting and 30-minute intervals after 100g. glucose:

Before: 128, 267, 254, 75, 45, 76 mg. per 100 ml.
After: 88, 168, 168, 108, 49, 72 mg. per 100 ml.

Malignant phaeochromocytoma may occur at any age, even in children. The symptoms, apart from metastases, are the same as with adenomas but symptoms of hyperadrenalism are not invariably present.

Diagnosis

The best modern paper on this subject, clinically and pharmacologically, dealing with five cases, is by Hamllton *et al.*. As with other endocrine tumours, the history is sometimes of many years' duration and the condition not recognized until the late stages. Thus benign hypertension, with attacks of apprehension and palpitation have been allowed to proceed to malignant hypertension, with severe retinopathy. It is probable that some cases presenting as persistent hypertension were originally paroxysmal. One man, in whom a phaeochromocytoma was removed at the age of 31, had attacks of pallor and bradycardia at the age of 11, and after a quiescent period of some years had more characteristic attacks, with hypertension, from the age of 23.

The following tests have been used diagnostically and are evaluated by Pearl and co-workers in the paper referred to above.

1. Vasoconstriction measured by heat elimination, by the hand being immersed in a water calorimeter and temperature changes being measured. The heat eliminated measured an average of 35 calories per 100 ml. per minute before operation compared with an average normal of 90. This test is 'simple and useful but not infallible'.

2. The early test of Roth and Kvale was the use of 0-0.25 mg.. of histamine intravenously to produce a release of adrenaline and precipitate an attack. This test is not invariably reliable and such an induced attack in a severe case may prove dangerous.

3. Adrenolytic agents antagonistic to adrenaline, and to a lesser extent to noradrenaline, are added by injection into the tubing to an intravenous infusion of saline. Thus, piperoxane, also called benzodioxane, in a maximum dose of 20 mg. injected in one minute, characteristically produces a fall of blood pressure within a few minutes, but negative results have been obtained in cases proved at operation. The test is not infrequently complicated by headache, nausea, sternal and abdominal pain, palpitations and even pulmonary oedema and hypertensive encephalopathy, especially in patients with essential hypertension, not due to phaeochromocytoma.

Rogitine, or phentolamine, also added to intravenous saline, during one minute a dose of 0.08 mg. per kilogram body-weight, is probably the most satisfactory test, blood pressure falling within a few minutes, and remaining depressed for a few mini or longer. Side effects are rare but induced tachycardia may be troublesome. Thi regarded as a relatively safe and reliable test but false positive and negative findings met with. Phentolamine may be injected directly into a vein, e.g. in a 5 mg. dose, inst of into an intravenous drip. Barbiturates should be omitted for twentyfour hours bee the test. Blood pressure readings are taken at minute intervals for a minimum time ten minutes.

Dibenamine is a powerful adrenolytic substance with a more lengthy act but sometimes give false positive tests in essential hypertension.

4. The measurement of pressor substances in urine and blood is the most die evidence of an adrenaline-secreting phaeochromocytoma. The amines extracted by selective adsorption on alumina and assayed biologically, us. the blood pressure response on the barbitone anaesthetized rat and compar: the results with known solutions of adrenaline and noradrenali: Dihydroergotamine reverses the action of adrenaline but not of noradrenali so that there is a biphasic response, with an initial fall of pressure due adrenaline and a subsequent rise due to noradrenaline. The total excreti with phaeochromocytomas varies between 0.5 and 5 mg. of pressor amines, compared with normals of 0.02 to 00.7 mg. The ratio of noradrenaline adrenaline varies from 0.5 to 4.0. Rarely the values for pressor amines may normal in the presence of a functioning phaeochromocytoma. Burn and Fie have developed a chemical calorimetric method for the assay of press amines. A tumor may be palpable or visible by direct radiography. Episac air insufflation, combined with tomography, may be necessary but m precipitate a severe attack. Since a right-sided tumour is more frequent, so] surgeons prefer an initial right-sided laparotomy when location is not define

Treatment

Atropine is not used before operation as it may cause exacerbation of the hypertensi An intravenous drip is set up and some clinicians give *Rogitine*, or the shorter-act poperoxane, before anaesthesia, in the intravenous drip to minimize the rise of blc pressure that may be considerable and dangerous on handling the tumous, and it sho always be in the operating theatre ready for such emergency. When the tumour removed there is a severe fall of blòod pressure and for this noradrenaline should added to the intravenous drip in a concentration of 10-20 mg. per litre, varying the i of drip according to the blood pressure and keeping the infusion running for twentyfi to thirty hours. Local aecrosis occasionally follows the intravenous infusion noradrenaline and is avoided by choosing a large superficial vein or by using a h polythene tube. The results of operations are excellent and there is usually comp] remission unless permanent changes have occurred in blood vessels, when the bb hypertensive level may persist. Noradrenaline is also useful for the treatment of hypotension which may follow a spontaneous hypertensivc crisis with shock quite apart from operation.

DISEASES DUE TO PANCREATIC HORMONES

The pancreas consists of an exocrine part which secretes enzymes into the gastrointestinal tract via the pancreatic duct, and an endocrine part from which hormones are liberated directly into the blood stream. Autoimmune mechanisms have been incriminated in endocrine failure but not in exocrine failure.

Classification of Diabetes Mellitus

In the past, diabetes mellitus was divided into 'juvenile-onset' and 'maturity-onset' diabetes. The juvenile-onset diabetics usually required insulin while the maturity-onset diabetics did not. In recent years, this classification has been made obsolete by the recognition that many maturity-onset diabetics require insulin for control.

Diabetes is now divided into **insulin-dependent diabetes** ***mellitus*** (IDDM or Type 1) and **non-insulin-dependent diabetes** ***mellitus*** (NIDDM or Type II). Bottazzo and Doniach have recognized two main forms of Type 1 diabetes: the classical, juvenile variant (called Type la), and the type which mainly affects older women and is closely related to other primary autoimmune disorders (Type 1b). Most type la diabetics have islet cell antibodies (1CA) at presentation. However, these are transient and fewer than 10% of this group have ICA some 5 years later. In contrast, ICA tend to persist in Type lb diabetics.

Table 5.1. Types of Diabetes Mellitus

Features	Type I	Type 11
Incidence	1 : 3000 population	1 : 750 population
Age at onset	Usually < 30 years	Usually > 40 years
Speed at onset	Acute	Insidious
Associated with autoimmune disorders	Yes	No
Islet cell antibodies	Yes	No
Other autoantibodies	Sometimes	No
'%, of all cases of diabetes mellitus	20-30%	70-80%
HLA association	Yes-B8/DR3 BW15/DR4	No

Table 5.2. Subdivision of Type 1 Diabetes Mellitus

Features	Type Ia	Type 1b
Possible aetiology	Viral insulitis	Autoimmune polyendocrine disorder
Sex ratio F:M	1:1.2	5:1
Age at onset	< 15 years	Any Age
Associated autoimmune diseases	Occasional	Thyroid, PA, adrenalitis
Islet cell antibodies :		
at onset	90%	Probably
5 years later	<10%	40% persist
Other autoantibodies	Few	Many

Immunopathogenesis of Diabetes Mellitus

Three key factors have been identified in the **pathogenesis** of insulin-dependent diabetes mellitus: heredity, environment, and autoimmunity. In **Type la** diabetes it is believed that an *environmental agent such as a virus infection or chemical poison initiates the destruction of insulin-secreting beta cells* in *the pancreas of* susceptible individuals, and that the resultant autoimmune phenomena (both antibodies and sensitized lymphocytes) perpetuate the damage. Several pieces of evidence support this proposal: (1) there is a seasonal variation in the onset of new cases, with autumn and winter peaks; (2) there is only a 50% concordance in monozygotic twins; and (3) there is minimal difference between the sexes. Some cases in childhood can be directly attributed to viral infections such as mumps, coxsackie B4, rubella and cytomegalovirus. However, in most cases the initiating virus is elusive.

Beta cell damage may precede overt diabetes by many years; the presence of subclinical beta cell destruction is suggested by the presence of circulating ICA before clinical diabetes develops. These **autoantibodies** are not thought to be pathogenic but to be secondary to beta cell destruction. Other autoantibodies, to the surface of beta cells, have recently been shown to block glucose-stimulated insulin release in vitro. Such antibodies are more likely to be pathogenic and they have been detected, prior to ICA, 2 years before overt IDDM.

Diabetes mellitus is an organ specific autoimmune disease and is associated with other organ-specific autoimmune diseases such as thyrotoxicosis. Histologically, there is considerable damage to the pancreas with lymphocytic infiltration and reduction in the number of beta cells. Ninety percent of Type 1 diabetes have serum ICA at presentation and about one-half also have evidence of sensitized T cells when tested with pancreatic extract. The spontaneous development of glycosuria in BB Wistar rats, thought to be an appropriate animal model, can be prevented by prophylactic use of immunosuppressive drugs. This has led to a multicentre trial of cyclosporin A in newly diagnosed diabetic patients with encouraging results.

Type 1 diabetes shows a number of significant associations with the inheritance of certain HLA antigens. Two distinct patterns of HLA inheritance are associated with a high prevalence of diabetes, namely either the HLA-B8, -DR3 or the HLA-B15, -DR4 haplotypes, and this risk is further increased if an individual has inherited both of these 'high-risk' haplotypes. In contrast, possession of the HLA-B7, -DR2 haplotype confers some protection against developing diabetes. These associations suggest that the genes governing susceptibility are located within the major histocompatibility complex on chromosome 6.

Molecular gene probing with DQ-specific probes has shown that the DNA sequences in this area differ between normal DR3/DR4 positive individuals and IDDM DR3/DR4 positive patients. Whether this represents closer linkage to the susceptibility genes or whether the product of this genomic sequence is involved directly in the pathogenesis of IDDM is not clear.

These genes may determine variations in the immune response in those viruses (like coxsackie B4) known to cause beta cell necrosis, or govern the severity of the autoimmune reaction to virus-infected beta cells or the potential for regeneration of islet cells after viral injury. In Type lb diabetes there are probably other genetic factors making the patients prone to autoimmune disease in general.

Type II diabetes is not associated with ICA. This type of diabetes shows a strong a familial tendency, but no association with autoimmunity or with any particular HLA type. However, about 10% of elderly patients initially treated by diet or oral hypoglycaemic drugs do have ICA in their sera at presentation. Often, these patients eventually require insulin therapy to achieve satisfactory diabetic control; therefore, they are latent Type 1 diabetics.

Complications of Diabetes Mellitus

Infection is a major complication of diabetes mellitus. The mechanism of increased susceptibility to infection is not known, although poorly controlled diabetics do have defects in neutrophil function which reverse following adequate insulin therapy.

The long-term complications of diabetes mellitus involve diseases of major arteries (leading to atheroma) or of capillaries (microangiopathy). Microangiopathy is responsible for the retinal and glomerular lesions of diabetes. In developed countries, diab retinopathy accounts for much of the acquired blindness in young and middle al adults. Retinopathy is rarely found within 5 years of diagnosis, but up to 80% of patie are affected 15-20 years after diagnosis. Concern has been expressed that therapy w foreign insulins might induce microangiopathy following deposition of immu complexes of insulin and antibodies to insulin.

Case 4

A 26-year-old pregnant woman attended the Antenatal Clinic regularly. She had i family history of DM. At 24 weeks' gestation she was found to have asynnptomai glycosuria. A glucose tolerance test showed that not only was her fasting blood gluco raised but that she had poor glucose tolerance. *Gestational diabetes* was diagnosed ar the patient was admitted for diabetic control. This was achieved on oral hypoglycaem agents alone and the patient was instructed to check her urine daily. The pregnancy wi uneventful and a normal 3.8 kg baby was born. The patient's glucose tolerance returne to normal in the puerperium; however her serum, which was found to contain antbodi to pancreatic islet cells at the time of diagnosis, remained positive. Nine years later, afte yearly checks, thc patient developed overt *diabetes mellitus*.

Are Immunological Tests Useful?

Immunological tests have no part to play in the diagnosis of diabetes mellitus. However tests for islet cell antibodies may be of **predictive value** in certain circumstances. Ir patients who present with apparent Type II diabetes, the presence of ICA often indicate the eventual need for insulin therapy (and subsequently reclassification as Type I). Ir those pregnant women who have impaired glucose tolerance, the presence of ICA seem to predict those who will develop diabetes mellitus postpartum (as in Case 4). The test i specific for diabetes mellitus; *only 6%* of the patients with other organ-specific autoimmune diseases, 3% of first degree relatives of diabetics, and 0.5% of control patient have these serum antibodies. In patients who have a strong family history of organ specific autoimmune disease, or who have evidence of autoimmune polyendocrinc disease, the presence of ICA indicates the strong likelihood of diabetes mellitus developing later.

HLA typing is not specific for diabetes and not predictive of its subsequen development; many diseases are associated with HLA-DR3 and -DR4. However, evideno from family studies does indicate that where one sibling has already developed diabetes typing of the other siblings is helpful; HLA identical siblings are those at greatest risk o developing diabetes.

The vast majority of diabetics develop detectable antibodies to foreign' insulin within a fez weeks of starting therapy. Although most forms of commercial animal insulins are immunogenic in man, there is considerable individual variation in response, even witl the same type of insulin and 'the same mode of administration. Inheritance of the HLA B15, -DR4 haplotype is associated with the production of high antibody titres to insulin whereas the -B8, -DR3 pattern is associated with lower titres. The advent of human insulin (produced by recombinant DNA technology) avoids this complication in most patients.

Of all insulin-treated diabetics, 15-50% have some adverse reaction to animal insulin and this is clinically significant in 5% of patients. These problems fall into three groups; acute allergic manifestations, lipoatrophy, and insulin resistance. Some patients develop an immediate hypersensitivity reaction with stinging, transient urticarial weals and burning at the site of injection within 30 min. Serious allergic complications are very rare and IgE-class antibodies have usually been implicated. Acute reactions are usually relieved by switching to human insulin. Patients treated exclusively with highly purified insulins rarely develop insulin hypersensitivity.

Lipoatrophy at the injection site occurs in about one-quarter of patients treated with older insulins but is rarely, if ever, seen in patients exclusively given highly purified insulin. Direct immunofluorescent examination of biopsies taken from the edge of lipoatrophic areas shows antibody, complement and insulin within dermal blood vessels.

The daily insulin requirement of a pancreatectomized man is about 50 units. Some diabetics are stabilized on doses below this level and some require more. Patients who need more than 200 units per day are insulin-resistant. This may occur transiently during infection or episodes of ketoacidosis. Alternatively, it may be due to increased metabolism of insulin, to anti-insulin antibodies, or to antibodies directed against insulin receptors. *The commonest cause of persistent insulin resistance is anti-insulin antibodies.* Insulin resistance of this type tends to be self-limiting: In about 60% of cases it remits spontaneously within 6 months. Acanthosis nigrans may be associated with insulin resistance. In one rare form, the condition is due to circulating IgG antibodies which block insulin receptors and cause insulin resistance. These antibodies are like the anti-receptor antibodies found in myasthenia gravis and Graves' disease.

The relationship of insulin to intermediary metabolism is rather more obscure in its details but it possibly acts on hexokinase, which converts glucose to glucose-6-phosphate, or on oxidative phosphorylation by which energy is conserved in the cell, or on some part of the Krebs citric acid cycle. The degree to which insulin affects this intracellular metabolism is dependent on the presence or absence of its antagonists and must also depend on the integrity of the enzyme systems involved.

Discussion of the causes of diabetes mellitus is necessarily complicated by the fact that the disease is not a homogeneous entity but, almost certainly, the end-result of various aetiological processes. The evidence for deficient insulin production as a cause is apparent in some cases, particularly in those who are young, who may rapidly lapse into ketotic coma, but are well controlled by insulin. The histology of the pancreas shows no specific change, but hyaline degeneration and fibrosis of the islet cells are common. However, the insulin content of the pancreas in these cases is extremely low and plasma insulin is not detectable. The optimum dose of insulin, about 50 Units daily, is similar to that required for control of diabetes arising after total pancreatectomy. The reason for this failure of insulin production is obscure but it appears to be an inherited tendency as, taking all diabetics as a single group, there is a strong familial incidence of the disease; diabetes is five times more common in identical as in fraternal twins.

Diet is probably another factor contributing to a breakdown in insulin production. Partially depancreatized animals develop diabetes when fed high fat or even very high; calorie diets; the remaining islet cells undergò 'exhaustion; degeneration after the excessive demands for insulin. Similarly, obesity is a common predisposing factor in human diabetes and Himsworth showed that the incidence of the disease was dependent on the fat intake of the population; a decrease in dietary fat, as in war-time rationing, is followed by a decrease in the incidence of diabetes.

However, absolute failure of insulin production cannot be the prime cause of disease in many of the obese diabetics who exhibit no tendency to ketosis, respond welt to diet and are incentive to insulin; or in those whose insulin requirements are over 100, Units daily. Some extra-pancreatic factor must be incriminated and the pituitary and Adrenal are likely to be responsible. There is an obvious correlation between diabetes and acromegaly, or Cushing's syndrome. About one-third of all acromegalics develop, diabetes at some stage of the disease. In the initial phase, high levels of plasma insulin are found; this may successfully counteract the diabetogenic effect of growth hormone,; or the latter may be present in such a high concentration that diabetes result despite an overactive pancreas. In the later stage, even when excessive growth hormone secretion has ceased, the pancreas may have undergone exhaustion degeneration leading to persistent insulin-deficient diabetes. Cushing's syndrome is commonly associated with, impaired carbohydrate tolerance and sometimes with frank diabetes. Adrenal glucocorticoids increase gluconeogenesis and spare liver glycogen, but antagonize the peripheral action of insulin. Their diabetogenic effect is counteracted by increased insulin production. However, the administration of cortisone will exaggerate a diabetes already present or cause overt diabetes in a subject whose pancreas is incapable of increasing insulin production.

There is no evidence to show that impaired function of cellular enzymes causes diabetes but it is very possible that disorders of fat storage, in the presence of a normal endocrine environment may lead to such a disturbance. Lawrence has studied a rare type of diabetes which he has termed lipotrophic. Patients with this disease exhibit a complete absence of fatty tissue (as compared to abnormal deposition of fat in lipodystrophy) with lipaemia, hyperglycemia, and no ketosis. Hepatomegaly with the later development of cirrhosis is common. He contrasts these cases with the common example of obese non-ketotic diabetes and suggests that the latter may be lipoplethoric diabetes, in which the fat stores are so filled that no further storage of carbohydrate as fat is possible and hyperglycemia results.

Incidence

Diabetes mellitus occur about equally in both sexes and at all ages; it has been reported in infancy. When occurring in successive generations the age of onset may become progressively younger. It is a familial disease, and is said to be a Mendelian recessive. A high incidence occurs in those of Hebrew race.

The peak incidence is in middle age, and the disease is seen far more frequently in fat than in thin people. It is clear that obesity is a predisposing factor to the disease.

Clinical Features

The excess of sugar in the blood produces an osmotic diuresis leading to polyuria and polydipsia; dehydration results with salt depletion so that a dry red tongue, inelastic skin, and muscular cramps are common signs. The inability to use sugar (by combustion or storage) causes a loss of weight without impairment of appetite; indeed, polyphagia may be a prominent symptom.

The associated disturbance of fat metabolism leads to an excess of ketone bodies in blood and urine. The resultant acidosis is followed by coma, which is fatal if untreated. The occurrence of ketosis is not directly related to the height of the blood sugar, and may be exaggerated by vomiting and dehydration. Coma may be the result of a rapidly progressive untreated diabetes, or may be precipitated by failure to continue insulin therapy, or by acute infections. The patient passes from the stage of thirst and polyuria to one of dehydration and vomiting. Consciouness becomes clouded and coma supervenes with peripheral vascular failure.

Complications

Staphylococcal and fungal infections of the skin and vulva frequently complicate uncontrolled diabetes and enhance the disturbance of carbohydrate metabolism. A more sinister complication is the relatively frequent occurrence and rapid spread of pulmonary tuberculosis in younger diabetics. Peripheral neuritis is also associated with uncontrolled diabetes, and in the early stages responds well to adequate control of the carbohydrate disorder by diet and insulin.

The effective long-term control of carbohydrate metabolism by means of insulin has diminished the importance of these complications but it has accentuated the problem of vascular changes accompanying diabetes. In the elderly the frequency and severity of arteriosclerotic peripheral vascular disease is greater in diabetics, but the lesions are not specific to the disease. Now that a generation of young diabetics has survived with adequate insulin therapy, vascular lesions more specific to diabetes have become prominent as a cause of disability and death. The appearance of microaneurysms in the retinal blood vessels herald the onset of a retinopathy which may lead to blindness. Associated with retinopathy is the deposition of hyaline material in the glomeruli of the kidney which causes persistent albuminuria, sometimes complicated by nephrotic episodes; death from uraemia may be the eventual termination. A less specific disorder-but a definite cause of morbidity - is the high incidence of coronary artery disease in women suffering from diabetes. This is of particular significance as women are seldom afflicted in this manner if free from diabetes or mycoedema, both disease associated with abnormal serum cholesterol and lipoprotein values.

Although adequate long-term control of carbohydrate metabolism reduces the incidence and severity of these vascular lesions, it has become obvious that the most effective use of insulin will not prevent their occurrence. Some careless patients whose blood sugar remains elevated for years do not develop any arteriopathy, while others, in whom the disturbance of carbohydrate metabolism has been minimal and easily controlled, may suffer from advanced retinal and renal changes. Moreover, the diabetes of haemochromatosis is not associated with vascular degeneration. It is perhaps significant that we have seen the diabetes of acromegaly end with retinitis proliferans and renal failure, and that hypophysectomy may cure the retinopathy. The classification of such lesions as complications of diabetes mellitus implies a dependence of the arteriopathy on the disorder of carbohydrate metabolism. This doubtful concept is less in keeping with the facts than the hypothesis which suggest that vascular lesions are an integral part of the general metabolic disturbance of diabetes, of which hyperglycaemia is another manifestation. The abnormally high birth weight and liability to foetal death of babies born to diabetics may be present for many years prior to the onset of the typical disturbance of carbohydrate metabolism. This again argues that hyperglycaemia is but one manifestation, and sometimes a late one, of the diabetic state.

Natural History

Diabetics, as judged by the natural history of their disease, constitute a heterogeneous collection not a homogenous group. Bearing in mind the various aetiological factors, diabetes mellitus should be considered as a syndrome rather than as a specific disease entity.

Two main groups may be differentiated from the mass of diabetics. The young diabetic, probably suffering from true failure of insulin production, presents with wasting, thirst, polyuria, and ketosis. The duration of the disease, prior to the onset of coma, is short. Insulin therapy is not only life saving but allows a full and active life. There is a considerable variation in the degree of insulin sensitivity and the diurnal liability of the blood sugar. Some maintain a steady state with a constant dose of insulin, but others show marked, almost hourly, swings in blood sugar despite the most regular regime. These patients are particularly liable both to insulin-induced hypoglycaemia and to the rapid onset of ketosis. The insulin-dependent patient is likely to lapse into ketotic coma if the insulin dose is miscalculated or omitted. Hence it is of vital importance to instruct these patients in the correct administration of insulin with a full explanation of the probable errors, such as syringe leaks or the giving of an inappropriate concentration (i.e. taking the same volume of insulin from a bottle containing 40 units per ml. instead of the prescribed 80 units per ml.) An increased dose of insulin is required in the presence of infection, even when food intake is diminished, and sometimes with an emotional crisis. Pulmonary tuberculosis should always be suspected in a young diabetic whose insulin requirements begin to rise for no obvious reason. Indeed, the prevalence of tuberculosis demands that all younger diabetics should have an X-ray of the chest every year.

The dominant complications of diabetes in the younger individual are related to carbohydrate metabolism, but when the disease has'been present for over fifteen years a few microaneurysms usually appear in the retina. The degree of such retinopathy and the later complications of diabetic nephropathy is mainly dependent on the type of diabetes but can be exaggerated by lack of proper therapy. Rapidly progressive retinopathy can occur with gross loss of vision but luckily the lesions in the majority of cases are not crippling.

The older group of diabetics are usually obese, not liable to ketosis and resistant to insulin. The slow tempo of the disease and mildness of specific symptoms often delays diagnosis. Diabetes is commonly discovered because of an associated vulval moniliasis or balanitis of the same origin in males. Peripheral neuritis, with absent reflexes, glove and stocking anaesthesia, and posterior column sensory loss may be the presenting features. Penetrating trophic ulcers of the foot are a troublesome and not unusual accompaniment. In the majority of these patients the prognosis is good with dietary treatment alone; the glucose tolerance test may become almost normal if obesity is corrected. The response to insulin is poor, large doses being required to bring down the blood sugar. Only a few such patients require insulin; mostly those with peripheral neuritis, which responds quickly to thorough control of the blood sugar. Some of these obese non-ketotic diabetics are prone to retinopathy and renal involvement. It is interesting that the kidneys are more often affected in females.

Diabetes continuing, or arising, in old age accents degenerative changes. Peripheral vascular disease appears to advance more rapidly and uncontrolled hyperglycaemia makes the danger of gangrene ever present. Senile cataract is common and often disabling. Its stellate shape is quite different from the 'snow-storm' appearance of the rare true diabetic cataract which occurs in young diabetics in direct relation to an elevated blood sugar.

Diagnosis

The clinical diagnosis of diabetes mellitus is strongly suggested by a history of loss of weight without anorexia, together with thirst and polyuria, and confirmed by the presence of definite glycosuria. Diagnosis in a comatose patient depends on the association of coma with dehydration, peripheral vascular collapse, and air hunger, with glycosuria and marked ketonuria. Milder cases may present with recurrent staphylococcal skin infections, moniliasis of the vulva, or with peripheral neuritis; cataract, or gangrene of the feet may be the presenting sign of diabetes in the elderly. Patients suffering from these conditions must always have their urine examined for sugar, otherwise a number of diabetics will go undetected.

An oral glucose tolerance test is the necessary confirmatory investigation in cases of suspected diabetes mellitus. If the disease is present, the fasting blood sugar will be raised (above 120 mg. per 100 ml.) and the taking of 50 g. of glucose will be followed by a further rise in blood sugar, which will be maintained over the ensuing two hours. The test is an index of impaired carbohydrate tolerance but has little value as a guide to the severity of the disease. A source of fallacy in the test is the effect of low carbohydrate diets which result in the production of blood sugar curves resembling those of true diabetes. Alleged diabetics, therefore, should not be put on a restricted diet before testing their carbohydrate tolerance.

Renal Glycosuria

Diabetes innocens is a condition in which an abnormally low ren threshold permits glucose to leak into the urine. The blood sugar is, however, norma Transient lowering of the renal threshold is common in normal pregnancy. The ren, threshold in true diabetes mellitus is usually normal (180 mg. per 100 ml.) but may 0 high or low. The pregnant diabetic is likely to develop a low renal threshold whid makes control of the diabetes more difficult to assess.

Diabetes Insipidus

This condition causes intense thirst and polyuria, together wit dehydration and some loss of weight, but is distinguished from diabetes mellitus by thy low specific gravity of the urine and the absence of urinary glucose.

Lactosuria

Lactose in the urine of lactating mother or even during the final wee of pregnancy gives a positive test for sugar when using the standard reagents (Benedict' or Fehling's solution): However, the recent introduction of simple enzyme tests specific for glucose should eliminate confusion in the routine urine testing at antenatal clinics.

Haemochromatosis

Bronzed diabetes is an inborn error of iron metabolism in which' iron is deposited throughout life in the liver, pancreas, gonads, and skin. The disease predominantly affects men, in a ratio of thirty males to one females. Manifestations of the disease seldom appear until middle age because it takes a long time for sufficient iron to accumulate in the tissues and cause fibrosis. The result is cirrhosis of the liver and pancreas with the manifestation of diabetes mellitus. However, clinical evidence of cirrhosis may precede the onset of diabetes. Deposition of iron pigment (haemosidenn in the skin causes a diffuse slaty blue pigmentation (bronze coloration is seldom seen). Haemosiderin deposition in the testes leads to hypogonadism in 12 per cent of cases. More rarely, involvement of the pituitary and adrenals can lead to hypopituitarism or Addison's disease.

The diabetes of haemochromatosis is not accompanied by vascular lesion and ketosis is relatively rare. Insulin requirements vary from case to case but tend to increase as the disease progresses.

Treatment

Restriction of dietary carbohydrate or the subcutaneous injection of insulin (with some dietary modifications) form the basis of therapy. Many middle aged or elderly patients with mild diabetes can be treated successfully by a low carbohydrate diet. Low calorie diets are particularly applicable to obese patients; indeed, a return to a normal weight in, these patients is usually accompanied by a marked gain in carbohydrate tolerance. This group of patients is seldom sensitive to the hypoglycaemic action of injected insulin. It is most probable that their endogenous secretion of insulin is normal and that their diabetic state is due to an agent which either destroys circulating insulin or inhibits its action.

The recent discovery that certain sulphanylureas control some cases with this type of diabetes is of great interest, but of rather limited practical importance. There is as yet no clear understanding of the action of these compounds, but they do not exert any hypoglycaemic effect unless endogenous insulin is present. Hence they cannot be used in young diabetics and they will never control any diabetic who tends to lapse into ketotic coma. The compounds may inhibit the destruction of insulin, or facilitate its action, but most probably their action lies in the control of the hepatic output of glucose. The diabetes of the obese patient will often respond to this type of oral treatment without dietary restrictions. We believe that such patients should be treated first by diet alone to minimize their obesity; hypoglycaemic agents can be added to the dietary regime if full control is not obtained. Carbutamide, the original compound used, had all the toxic effects of sulphonamides-skin rashes, thrombocytopenic purpura, and agranulocytosis-which occurred with some frequency. Tolbutamide has now superseded it because it rarely causes toxic reactions. Its rather rapid rate of destruction demands a routine dose twice daily. An initial regime of *3G.* daily will control a patient whose diabetes is susceptible to the drug. Lack of response to this dose indicates that the drug is unsuitable and larger doses will not alter this. Control of the disease can be followed by a gradual reduction in dose to the minimum level required to prevent hypoglycaemia. The lucky patient who responds to this treatment is spared the monotonous burden of daily self-injection, but the long-term efficiency of the drug is not yet known.

The life-saving properties of insulin are so well known that no further discussion is needed. Over the years many attempts have been made to produce an insulin which will control the blood sugar when given in one injection a day. The following list of insulins indicates the achievements in this field and the variety of insulins available at the discretion of the physician.

Type ofInsulin	*Description*	*Duration of*		*Remarks*
		Maximal	*Total*	
Soluble	Unmodified	3-4	6-7	The only insulin for intravenous use.
Protamine zinc	Complex of protamine with insulin and zinc	12-14	24	Can be mixed with soluble insulin
Globin Zinc	Insulin combined with globin and trace of zinc	6-12	20	May cause midday hypoglycaemia but fail to control diabetesduring night.
Semilente	Suspension of amorp-hous zinc insulin	2-3	8-9	
Ultralente	Suspension of crystalline zinc insulin	6-8	24	
Lente	Mixture of amorphous (*3* parts) and crystalline (*7* parts) zinc insulin	3-4	24	A steady prolonged action.

The Lente insulin are suspended in an acetate buffer and should not be mixed with the other types which are in a phosphate-buffered solution. Lente insulin itself provides an even action throughout twenty-four hours and is the best available insulin for control of diabetes by one morning injection.

This mixture of amorphous and crystalline zinc insulin has constant absorption characteristics as the speed of absorption depends on the size of the particles. Moreover, there is almost complete freedom from allergic reactions because of the absence of any added protein.

However, a few patients respond better to two or three injections per day of soluble insulin to one morning injection of globin insulin, or to a mixture of soluble and protamine zinc insulin.

HYPERINSULINISM

Definition

Hyperinsulinism is a condition of excessive (or uncompensated) secretion of insulin which leads to a fall of blood sugar sufficient to cause symptoms.

History

Spontaneous hyperinsulinism was first observed, by Seale Harris in 1924. The underlying pathological lesion was not demonstrated, but, two years later, Wilder, Allen, Power, Robertson, and Mayo described a case due to carcinoma of the pancreatic islet cells.

Pathology and Aetiology

The causes of hypoglycaemia are as follows: *Spontaneous over-production of insulin:*

(a) Adenoma of pancreatic islet cells.

(b) Carcinoma of pancreatic islet cells.

(c) Diffuse hyperplasia of pancreatic islet cells. This is more common in children than in adults. Children born of diabetic mothers may exhibit this pathological finding, but it is not necessarily associated with hypersecretion of insulin.

(d) Vagus hyperactivity. This is associated with postprandial hypoglycaemia and is commonly seen after gastrectomy.

Disorders of the liver:

(a) Destruction of hepatic glycogen stores by severe liver disease (acute hepatic necrosis or the terminal stages of cirrhosis or severe hepatitis).

(b) Unavailability of hepatic glycogen. Characteristic of von Gierke's disease, a rare familial disorder of childhood in which the hepatic *glycogen* is fixed and

cannot be mobilized by adrenaline. The disease is also characterized by infantilism and marked enlargement of the liver.

Increased sensitivity to normal insulin secretion: (a) Anterior pituitary failure. (b) Adrenal cortex failure.

A lack of insulin antagonists, usually provided by pituitary and adrenocortical hormones, will lead to hypoglycaemia on fasting. Mobilization of glycogen from the liver is controlled largely by hormones of the adrenal, so that a failure of glycogen mobilization contributes to the hypoglycaemia.

Administration of insulin:

An excessive dose of insulin or increased physical activity or starvation will produce hypoglycaemia in a patient whose diabetes is controlled by insulin. Hypoglycaemia deliberately induced by the injection of insulin is a therapy for schizophrenia (insulin shock therapy).

Clinical Features

Many of the symptoms may be explained as due to excessive secretion of adrenaline in fact to nature's attempt to raise the blood sugar. There is, however, an additional direct action on the brain, and fatal cases often show congestion and minute scattered haemorrhages throughout the brain. The symptoms may be differentiated on thebasis, though the division is not necessarily clear cut.

Hyperadrenalism

This result in tremulousness, weakness, tachycardia, sweating, anxiety, apprehension, and sometimes a sense of constriction in the chest. Irritability, anger, and bizarre emotional behaviour may also be due to hyperadrenalism. Pallor of the face may be seen, but often it is suffused and red.

Hypoglycaemia

Disorders of behaviour, often terminating in coma, are very common. Purposeless bizarre behaviour, of which the patient may have no memory, suggest gross neurosis or drunkenness. Sensory disturbances are usual consisting of tingling and paraesthesiae in the limbs and around the mouth. Headaches may be severe and migrainous in nature.

Transient coma is often associated with localized motor disturbances of the nervous system. Motor incoordination of hands and legs, ataxia, temporary hemiplegia or monoplegia can falsely suggest the presence of a local lesion in the brain. Generalized or focal epileptiform convulsions are also common. Dysarthria or aphasia, yawning or purposeless smacking of the lips may precede coma or convulsions. Ocular signs include diplopia, blurred vision, dilated pupils, and, occasionally, nystagmoid movements.

Hunger, often of a ravenous nature, is'an interesting symptom as there is evidence that hypoglycaemia stimulates the vagus to produce gastric hypermotility and hyperacidity, a mechanism that may underlie appetite. Gratification of this hunger in long-standing cases of hypoglycaemia will lead to obesity.

Tumours of teh Islets of Langerhans

Functioning tumours of the islets of Langerhans (insulinomas) may arise at any age, the peak incidence lying between 40 and 50 years. Both sexes are equally affected. The benign adenoma is the most common growth, outnumbering the malignant tumours with hepatic metastases by ten to one. It is important to realize that in about 10 percent of cases more than one adenoma is present in the pancreas. The tumour may be found in any part of the pancreas; there is no truth in the suggestion that they are more frequently found in the tail. However, tumours in the head of the pancreas are less accessible to the surgeon than those in the tail.

Occasionally the pancreas is filled by hyperplastic islets of Langerhans or even a diffuse adenomatosis. Such a pathology is more common in children with hypoglycaemia, but it is apparent from autopsy studies that hyperplastic islets of Langerhans are not necessarily associated with an increased secretion of insulin. Indeed, even modern staining methods for the (3 cells of the islets do not give a good correlation between histological appearance and functional capacity.

There is an extraordinary variability in the time taken for the full development of the syndrome. Some patients are deeply unconscious within two weeks of the first symptom, while others suffer occasional mild attacks over many years before the tempo of the disease quickens and the diagnosis is made. The usual course is one of progression not only in frequency of attacks, but also in severity of the symptoms. Characteristically the symptoms appear before breakfast and later on fasting or exertion. Later still, episodes of coma become prolonged until the terminal attack which leaves the patient in a state of decerebrate rigidity lasting days before death. In this stage the brain has suffered irreversible damage, and consciousness will not return on elevation of the blood sugar; indeed, blood sugar levels are often found to be normal by this time and the correct diagnosis can only be reached from an accurate history of the preceding events.

The transient early episodes of hypoglycaemia may only be noted by relatives, the patient having no memory of his confusion and bizarre behaviour. The absence of abnormal physical signs between such attacks and the vague nature of the fugue-like episode often leads to a diagnosis of hysteria. If the relatives have noted the symptoms of an epileptiform attack, the diagnosis is likely to be idiopathic epilepsy. Such mistakes can only be avoided by considering the possibility of hypoglycaemia followed by estimations of the blood sugar during the attacks.

The latter stages of the disease are more likely to be confused with organic cerebral disease. Signs of hemiparesis are particularly common in the more elderly cases of insulinoma and the patient is seldom able to give a clear history. We have seen two such patients who presented with signs of a hemiparesis and a short history of drowsiness and headache. The initial diagnosis of intracranial tumour was abandoned when a history from the relatives revealed earlier attacks of transient confusion occurring prior to breakfast, and repeated examination disclosed a marked variation in the severity of the neurological abnormality. The correct diagnosis of insulinoma followed the demonstration of blood sugar levels below 50 mg. per 100 ml. in both cases.

Diagnosis

The symptoms of hypoglycaemia are seldom severe in cases of vagal hyperactivity. Characteristically the onset of symptoms follows a meal, particularly if it contains a large proportion of carbohydrate. The diagnosis lies in the clinical interpretation of the symptoms and the proof that they are related to a lowered blood sugar (usually about 50-65 mg. per 100 ml.). Symptoms are not produced by prolonged fasting, and the oral sugar tolerance test (continued for four hours) shows a normal fasting blood sugar with a later drop to hypoglycaemia.

Hypoglycaemia must not be forgotten as a rare cause of convulsions in infancy. It is exceptional to find an organic lesion of the pancreas in these cases, but there is often a strong familial trait. McQuarrie considers that 'the disorder appears to be purely functional in character in that it varies greatly in severity from time to time, is unaccompanied by any demonstrable pathological lesion, and manifests a tendency to undergo spontaneous amelioration with the passage of time.

Hyperinsulinism, due to islet cell tumours of the pancreas, is distinguished by the occurrence of attacks in fasting state with blood sugar values below 50 mg. per 100 ml. and rapid clinical relief from the administration of glucose. The episodic and variable nature of the illness is sometimes confusing; the degree of hypoglycaemia is not constant, symptoms being related to the speed of fall of blood sugar as much as to the absolute degree of hypoglycaemia. An erroneous diagnosis of hysteria, or epilepsy, is often made merely because the possibility of hypoglycaemia is overlooked. When the stage of coma is reached the generalized rigidity of the patient with extensor plantar responses may suggest encephalitis or a mid-brain tumour. In the terminal phase confirmation of the correct diagnosis can be impossible because the blood sugar may be at a normal level despite continued unconsciousness.

Sugar tolerance or insulin sensitivity tests are of very limited use in diagnosis. Functional hypoglycaemia from atomic imbalance is usually accompanied by an oral sugar tolerance test which shows a rapid drop in blood sugar to subnormal levels after the initial rise following the ingestion of glucose. Starvation does not induce hypoglycaemia. In hyperinsulinism of organic origin, starvation induces hypoglycaemia but sugar tolerance tests give no consistent pattern. Moreover, hypoglycaemic unresponsiveness is usually seen after the injection of insulin.

Treatment

The immediate treatment of hypoglycaemia is the administration of sugar by mouth, stomach tube, or intravenously. If the condition is not due to an hepatic lesion, the injection of 1 ml. of adrenaline may restore consciousness.

The prevention of functional hypoglycaemia should be by dietetic means. carbohydrate exaggerates the symptoms, treatment consists of a high protein and I carbohydrate diet, taken in frequent small meals. The patient should avoid all sugar his diet. Of course, sugar will relieve the symptoms if they occur, but prevention symptoms can be achieved only by cutting sugar from the diet.

If a diagnosis of hyperinsulinism due to an islet cell tumour is made, Burg removal of the tumour is essential. The operation may be dramatically successful eve the patient has been comatose for three or four days and exhibits decerebrate rigid However, such prolonged hypoglycaemia is likely to have caused irreversible damage the brain leading to intellectual impairment.

On occasion the presence of a tumour may be in doubt despite clinical evidencE severe hypoglycaemia. An exploratory laparotomy should be undertaken, with a par resection of the pancreas if no tumour can be found. This situation usually arises children, their illness being successfully terminated by subtotal pancreatectomy desF the absence of demonstrable islet cell tumour or hyperplasia.

Prior to operation it is not difficult to maintain a normal blood sugar concentrat by the infusion of glucose. After operation transient hyperglycaemia is common, l does not require insulin therapy. The maintenance of the blood sugar in the presence functioning metastases is a serious problem. Malignant islet cell tumours are seldh fatal from their invasive properties but kill by hypoglycaemia which cannot be treat surgically. The use of alloxan has proved disappointing and dangerous. Administrati of very large amounts of carbohydrate is seldom successful for any length of time. 7 most promising form of therapy is cortisone, which promotes gluconeogenesis a inhibits the action of insulin. Obviously one is fighting a losing battle with a malign tumour but cortisone may so moderate the attacks of hypoglycaemia that the patier life is extended for several months. The administration of cortisone or ACTH is a invaluable for those patients, without islet cell tumours, who continue to have disabli hypoglycaemia despite a high protein diet.

6

DISEASES DUE TO GONADAL HORMONES

HYPOGONADISM

Since the two functions of the gonads are to produce hormones and to produce gametes, it would be logical to include, under the heading "Hypogonadism", insufficiency of either of these functions. In general, however, the term is confined to insufficiency of endocrine activity and in what follows attention will be restricted mainly to this aspect of the subject.

Two main forms of hypogonadism may be recognized, namely, *primary* where the main lesion resides in the gonad itself; and *secondary,* where gonadal changes are due to deficiency of pituitary gonadotrophic stimulation. Before puberty a condition of physiological hypogonadism exists because there is little or no production of gonadotrophins by the pituitary gland. When, at puberty, the pituitary gland becomes functionally effective, oversecretion of gonadotrophin arises if the gonad is unable to respond, so that in primary hypogonadal states an excessive urinary excretion of gonadotrophin is a diagnostic feature. In secondary hypogonadism, however, the excretion of gonadotrophin is very low or non-existent. It follows, therefore, that determination of the urinary gonadotrophin level is a key diagnostic test in differentiating these kinds of hypogonadism, but, since the existing methods of gonadotrophin assay are crude, it is not surprising that doubtful cases are sometimes. encountered.

Hypogonadism in Males

Hypogonadal males are called eunuchs when their hypogonadism is due to castration before puberty, and eunuchoids when they possess the physical and psychological characteristics of eunuchs, but have gonads which, however, remain infantile. These terms are less commonly applied to hypogonadal females.

PRIMARY HYPOGONADISM

This can be either congenital or acquired. A convenient grouping of congenital primary male hypogonadism, due to Sohval and Soffer, is as follows:

anorchism (testicular agenesis);

prenatal testicular atrophy;

germinal aplasia (testicular dysgenesis);

failure of normal differentiation of Leydig cells (testicular dysgenesis) due to:

(a) long-standing cryptorchidism,

(b) unknown causes;

as part of syndromes or diseases characterized by multiple congenital anoma including;

(a) Laurence-Moon-Biedi syndrome (certain cases),

(b) dystrophia myotonica,

(c) the male counterpart of Turner's syndrome;

non-classifiable because of inadequate clinical, histologoical, or hormonal data.

Bilateral anorchism is exceedingly rare, though the unilateral variety is probably less uncommon. It is of considerable interest that the first authentic case of bilateral anorchism was recorded as long ago as 1564 in a soldier who was hanged for rape; post-mortem examination failed to disclose testes either in the scrotum or in the abdomen. It may be very difficult, or impossible, to differentiate prenatal testicular atrophy from true testicular agenesis.

Attention was first drawn to the form of testicular dysgenesis called germinal aplasia in 1947 by Engle and later in the same year by del Castillo, Trabucco, and de la Baize. In this condition, which is not an uncommon cause of azopermia, there is complete absence of cells of the spermatogenic series, though Sertoli and Leydig cells appear to be intact. The suggested cause of this condition is a failure of migration of the primordial germ-cells during embryonic life from the yolk-sac endoderm to the median-cell ridge. The gonadotrophin excretion in these patients may be entirely normal, though in some instances it appears to be elevated. The normal gonadotrophin excretion suggests that there is no deficiency of testicular hormones, particularly of that moiety which inhibits the overactivity of the pituitary gland. Since the Sertoli cells are intact in these patients, it has been argued that these cells are the source of the pituitary inhibiting X hormone. A condition in which the testicular biopsy is indistinguishable from the described above may arise where normal testes have been expected to irradiation of a degree sufficiently intense to destroy the germinal epithelium, but not so intense as to destroy the Sertoli or Leydig cells.

The other form of testicular dysgenesis is that in which the Leydig cells are not normally differentiated. McCullagh, Beck and Schaffenburg drew attention to "A syndrome of eunuchoidism with spermatogenesis, normal urinary FSH, and low or normal ICSH ("fertile eunuchs"). In two of their five patients the ICSH (or LH) excretion was normal, yet Leydig cells were apparently absent. In the other three patients of ICSH excretion appeared to be low, so that these patients should therefore be regarded as special examples of secondary hypogonadism. It is interesting to note that sperm counts in these patients ranged from very low figure (though not azoospermia) to 102 millions per ml. Landau has described a similar case of hypogonadism with spermatogenesis; this man had mind hypogonadism and unusually low seminal fructose. Androgen treatment led to a rise in the seminal fructose, the completion of masculinization and a temporary increase in the output of spermatozoa.

The hypogonadism of the Laurence-Moon-Biedi syndrome has generally been assumed to be secondary to pituitary gonadotrophic deficiency and Roth was the first to prove this by urinary gonadotrophin assays. More recently Francke has shown that in some of these patients gonadotrophin production is probably not deficient. In a 45-year-old patient who came to necropsy the testicular condition was indistinguishable from that found in the Klinefelter syndrome (a primary hypogonadal syndrome to be discussed later). It is therefore probable that, in some at least of the cases of Laurence-Moon-Biedl syndrome the hypogonadism is primary, the gonadal defect being just one more of the multiple congenital anomalies.

The association of gonadal deficiency with dystrophia myotonica has been known for a long time and several recent reports have described the testicular lesions in this condition. These consist of complete tubular sclerosis with normal Leydig cells and no interstitial fibrosis. The urinary 17-ketosteroids are usually low and the gonadotrophins usually, though not always, elevated.

It would seem that Turner's syndrome in the male forms a less well-defined entity than when found in the female. The combination of deficient stature, congenital anomalies of various kinds, testicular hypoplasia with androgen deficiency, and increased urinary gonadotrophins would qualify a male for inclusion in this category. Of the various cases described in the literature, no uniformity of testicular pathology has been found. This is in contrast to the condition in the female where the gonads consist merely of stromal elements with associated structures such as rete and medullary canals, but with total absence of the follicle apparatus. As will be seen later in the section on Turner's syndrome in the female, some of these so-called females appear to be of male chromosomal sex, their apparently female morphology being considered to arise as the result of the failure of development of a male-type gonad in early intrauterine life.

The above remarks on the heterogeneity of male Turner's syndrome apply also to a variety of miscellaneous cases of congenital primary hypogonadism in which mixed testicular lesions are found. Two such cases occurring in brothers were reported by Sohval and Soffer. These men had a moderate degree of androgen deficiency, small testes, aspermatogenesis, gynaecomastia, and increased urinary gonadotrophins. The testicular lesions differed from those of the Klinefelter syndrome; there was germinal aplasia together with a varying extent of completely hyalinized tubules. A further example of male hypogonadism with a mixed testicular lesion was described by Swyer and' Hughesdon. This patient also showed hypogonadism, slight gynaecomastia, azoospermia, and moderately increased gonadotrophins, but the testicular histology showed not only areas of germinal aplasia and of complete hyalinization but also some tubules with apparently normal spermatogenesis.

Acquired primary hypogonadism includes the following main conditions:

surgical castration;

functional prepuberal castration (some cases);

Klinefelter—Reinfenstein-Albright syndrome (sclerosing tubular degeneration);

Mumps orchitis and less commonly, tuberculous, syphilitic, or other infective conditions of the testes; Male climacteric.

The first of the above conditions will be considered further in the clinical section.. Functional prepuberal castration was first described by Heller, Nelson, and Roth. Some of their cases probably fell into the congenital group, but in others the lesion was very likely an acquired one. In this condition the testes are absent or completely atrophic, though characteristically the Wolffian duct derivatives descend into the scrotum. It is probable that many of these patients are mistakenly lebelled as cryptorchid. *Gynaecomastia* is common.

The syndrome of sclerosing tubular degeneration was first described by Klinefelter, Reinfenstein, and Albright in 1942 as "A syndrome characterized by gynecomastia, aspermatogenesis without aleydigism, and increased excretion of *follicle-stimulating hormone*'. It has since been the subject of numerous further reports. The condition has its onset at about the time of puberty, either earlier or later, and involves fibrosis and hyalinization of the basement membrane of the seminervous tubules, thereby leading to the cutting off of the blood supply to the tubular contents. There is in consequence a greater or lesser degree of destruction of the entire tubular contents-germinal epithelium and Sertoli cells. In addition the *Leydig cells* may be affected in varying degrees; in many cases they appear to be increased in numbers and, by the use of special staining techniques, it can be shown that they are morphologically abnormal. Although Albright and his colleagues consider that the elevated gonadotrophin output in patients with the *Klinefelter syndrome* provides evidence that the Sertoli cells are the source of the pituitary-inhibiting X hormone, it is possible that an alternative hypothesis might more adequately explain the aberrant findings in this condition. According to this the primary lesion would lie in the inability of the Leydig cells adequately to convert the precursor substances into their normal hormonal products (that is, both testosterone and X hormone). Because of this the pituitary is uninhibited and secretes excessive gonadotrophin which in turn causes hyperplasia of the Leydig cells. The lack of normal Leydig-cell hormones is then held to be responsible for the tubular lesions and for the other clinical defects. This hypothesis, it will be noticed, corresponds with that explaining the nature of the adrenogenital syndrome due to adrenal hyperplasia.

According to Heller and Nelson, patients with the Klinefelter syndrome can be subdivided into three groups: (1) eunuchoidal,.(2) moderately eunuchoidal, and (3) non-eunuchoidal. This grouping depends upon the degree of failure of Leydig cell function. In general, the extent of gynaecomastia appears to be related inversely to the degree of Leydig cell failure, so that it is greatest in the least eunuchoidal types. There are, however, exceptions to this general rule.

Bradbury, Bunge, and Boccabella have reported the finding of female-type sex chromatin in the nuclei of buccal mucosal cells in all of five cases of the *Klinefelter syndrome.* (There have been several subsequent confirmatory reports). This indicates that some of these patients may represent a hitherto unrecognized form of female pseudohermaphroditism. Nelson has put forward reasons for supposing that there are two varieties of Klinefelter's syndrome, which he calls "true" and "false". The former are genetic females in whom the autosomal genetic male influence overrides the feminizing effect of the pair of X chromosomes so as to produce a male-type gonad and, in consequence, secondary sex characters. Mostly, the germ cells are sufficiently resistant to the male influence to prevent their functioning, but Segal and Nelson have described complete spermatogenesis in some tubules in a testicular biopsy taken from a case of "true" Klinefelter's syndrome with sex chromatin of female type, and Bunge and Bradbury had encountered similar findings in three of their patients. The "false" cases of Klinefelter's syndrome, according to Nelson, are genetic males in whom the sclerosing tubular degeneration is an acquired attribute. On this basis of differentiation, "true" Klinefelter's syndrome should be grouped with female pseudohermaphroditism.

SECONDARY HYPOGONADISM

As previously mentioned, the normal prepuberal child displays secondary *hypogonadism,* but requires no further notice here. In pituitary dwarfism there is presumably a failure of all the trophic functions of the anterior lobe of the pituitary gland; the testes along with the other target endocrine glands, remain in an unstimulated condition. The commonest variety of eunuchoidism is that due to idiopathic deficiency of follicle-stimulating hormone production by the pituitary gland. The 17-ketosteroid excretion ranges between levels such as would be found in prepuberal boys and low adult figures. The FSH excretion is, of course, low. The testicular histology is virtually indistinguishable from that found in the prepuberal state.

The presence of an organic lesion in or near the pituitary gland may lead to insufficiency of gonadotrophin production and so to secondary hypogonadism. The testicular lesion appears then to depend on the stage of testicular development attained prior to the onset of gonadotrophin suppression. When this happens before the completion of testicular maturity the general appearance is similar to that in idiopathic eunuchoidism, except that the tunica propria of the tubules is found to be thickened. When the lesion is of later onset more extensive degenerative change is usually found. Again, thickening of the tunica propria occurs but in these cases it is very marked, and is accompanied by peritubular fibrous tissue proliferation and Leydig cell degeneration. There is extensive impairment of germ-cell activity and the Sertoli cells contain lipoid-filled vacuoles.

Hypogonadism Without Endocrine Disturbance

In this group the main complaint is usually of infertility which may range from azoospermia to varying degrees of oligospermia. Azoospermia due to duct obstruction is, of course, excluded. The three main varieties are: (1) germinal aplasia, which has been mentioned already; (2) arrest of maturation; and (3) hypospermatogenesis. Little or nothing is known of the causes of these two conditions which, by the definition of this group, would appear not to be of endocrine origin.

Clinical Features of Hypogonadism in the Male

Genital Organs

In eunuchoids the testes are always smaller than normal and frequently minute pea-like bodies such as might be found in an infant. However, in some of the hypogonadal syndromes mentioned in the previous action (e.g. germinal aplasia), the testes may be of apparently normal size. The penis is usually smaller than normal and may be infantile in size. The size of the penis is much more variable than that of the testes. The scrotum is usually, but not invariably, smaller than normal. In some patients the testes are undescended. The prostate is small and rarely palpable per rectum.

Hair

Pubic and axillary hair is nearly always scanty and the pubic hair does not ascend in triangular fashion to the umbilicus, but is limited horizontally as is typically the case in the female. This distribution probably merely reflects only the decreased extent of body hair generally. There is little or no facial hair and that on the rest of the body is usually very scanty, though axillary hair may sometimes be present in normal amounts. The scalp hair is typically luxuriant and baldness is most unusual.

Skin

The skin generally is thinner than that in normal adult males, and the skin of the face is soft in texture as in the female. Although the haemoglobin and red cells are normal, the face usually has a pallid appearance in strong contrast to the plethora which may be seen in Cushing's syndrome. The face and body are usually free from acne, although this may make its appearance in the course of treatment with testosterone.

Sexual Behaviour

Libido is typicallly absent in the eunuchoidal patient and erections and emissions may never occur. In those hypogonadal syndromes where Leydig cell function is unimpaired, normal sexual behaviour may be found. Some eunuchoids may experience relatively infrequent erections and may be able to effect coitus, but their *sexual potency is usually of a low order and may frequently prove* unsatisfactory to their wives, should they marry. It is said that a high incidence of gonorrhoea has been found among Eastern eunuchs and it may therefore be concluded that some, at least, of these individuals are able to undertake sexual play. Postpuberal castrates, who have previously had normal libido and potency, may retain these in spite of the loss of their testes.

There is no evidence that homosexuality, either active or passive, is more frequently. encountered among eunuchoids than among other males.

Skeletal Changes

Many, though by no means all, eunuchoids are tall, and some indeed (e.g. male cases of Turner's syndrome) may be below the average height. The tall eunuchoids may have been above average in height throughout life, or their tallness may have been due to continued growth after the age of 18 when it stops in normal people. This continued growth may proceed until the age of *26* or later, as a result of delayed apiphyseal union which is invariable among eunuchoids. The bone age in childhood or adolescence is younger than the chronological age. The younger bone age and delayed union of the epiphyses are also found in infantilism and is almost certainly due to lack of androgenic secretion by the testes. In contrast sexual precocity is associated with advanced bone age, premature union of the epiphyses, and an ultimate height less than average. Because of the delayed epiphyseal union there is a relative overgrowth of the long bones, leading to the typical eunuchoidal proportions in which the span of the outstretched arms exceeds the height and the lower measurement (from the soles of the feet to the symphysis pubis) exceeds the upper measurement (from the symphysis pubis to the vertex).

The fingers are usually long and thin, but not invariably so. The general bodily build of eunuchoids varies in much the same way as does that of normal men, some being slender with rather thin bones, and others being more sturdy.

The pelvis tends to be gynaecoid, and is of greater breadth than the shoulders, which is the reverse of normal males, and similar to the skeletal proportions of females; or it may be intermediate between the male and female dimensions. The discrepancy between shoulders and pelvis is more marked in some than in others.

Not uncommonly eunuchoids show poor dentition, and the pattern of large central and small lateral incisors with blunt canines is said to be typical, though it is far from invariable. Unerupted permanent teeth may often be seen in X-ray films of the skull.

Gynaecomastia

Enlargement of the breasts, due to the development of mammary tissue, as opposed to the mere localized accumulation of fat, is encountered in certain groups of hypogonadal males. It is seen particularly in the *Klinefelter-Reifenstein-Albright syndrome*, though, as mentioned previously, it is then more likely to occur in the less eunuchoidal subjects. It is frequent in patients with functional prepuberal castration and has also been reported in miscellaneous cases, some of them having mixed testicular lesions.

No satisfactory explanation for the *gynaecomastia* of these patients is forthcoming, nor inded, is there any for the benign gynaecomastia not uncommonly encountered at the time of puberty in otherwise perfectly normal males. In particular there is no evidence that it is due to excessive oestrogen secretion. The possibility that it is due to excessive pituitary "*mammotrophic hormones*"-still uncertain in nature, perhaps prolactin and growth hormone-remain open.

Adiposity or Leanness

Contrary to general belief, many eunuchoids are not fat, and, indeed, there may be a conspicuous absence of fat. In some of these patients, however, although their general appearance is not that of a fat person, there may be localized deposits of fat, for example, on the pubis, breast, abdomen, and buttocks. Thin eunuchoids may become obese in later life. One patient, for example, was tall and thin as a child; at the age of 21 he was still very thin and weighed only 112 lb., although his height was 70 in. In the next five years he grew 4 in. in height and put on 56 lb. in weight, becoming obese. In this particular instance a phase of pituitary activity manifested by growth was also apparently associated with the deposition of fat.

Cardiovascular System

The blood pressure is normal, or moderate hypotension may be found. The pulse rate tends to be slow. Radiographic studies may show subnormal heart measurements, findings which are consonant with the experimental fact that testosterone produces hypertrophy of cardiac muscle.

Muscular System

It is typical that eunuchoids have poorly developed and flabby muscles, so that they are unable to do heavy muscular work or to play games requiring skill or stamina. This state of affairs is directly due to the deficient secretion of androgens, since the muscular development and increased strength normally associated with puberty fail to occur. In contrast, sexual precocity is often associated with abnormal muscular development and strength.

Larynx

The larynx tends to remain small, and the voice highpitched. This may not always be obvious, except in emotional states, or on the telephone. On the other hand, it is important to realize that some otherwise entirely normal males retain a high-pitched voice. The possession of such a voice, in the absence of other stigmata of eunuchoidism, cannot therefore be used to diagnose testicular insufficiency.

Emotion and Intellect

Intelligence is normal, and in some patients may be well above normal. The behaviour pattern, however, shows many interesting features. On the whole, eunuchoids are passive and accommodating. They are not necessarily afraid, but they have little pugnacity or external aggressiveness in their make-up. Their inertia may sometimes pass into somnolence. In contrast to their general placidity, they may exhibit phases of obstinacy, contrariness, sensitivity, or irritability; and may flare up like *a prima donna*. Such outbursts or tantrums are usually short-lived. Eunuchoids are sometimes introspective and secretive and may be given to intrigue. They may be depressed and have a sense of inferiority about their subnormal genital development. Commonly, though by no means invariably, they have little interest in the opposite sex. The range of variation in emotion and intellect among these cases is wide, and not a few eunuchoids have achieved outstanding intellectual and social success.

Familial Incidence

There have been several reports of eunuchoidism among many members of different families. An excellent summary of familial hypogonadism has been given by Ferriman.

Incomplete Eunuchoidism

This is probably more frequent than is generally recognized, the patient showing some undoubted stigmata of eunuchoidism, but being normal in other respects. One may also encounter examples of dissociation of androgenic effects. Thus, the genital, and libido may be normal, but the facial hair almost non-existent, or, as previously mentioned, the voice may remain high-pitched. It must be presumed in these cases that there is a failure of target-organ response rather than any insufficiency of male hormone production.

Diagnosis

The diagnosis of hypogonadism requires the demonstration of insufficiency of either androgen production of gametogenesis, or both. The most important criteria of androgen deficiency are the clinical features described in the previous section. The determination of androgen excretion in the urine is not a practical procedure for routine use and the measurement of 17-ketosteroid excretion is not always helpful because only a fraction of the urinary 17-ketosteroid in the normal male arise from the testes, the remainder being of output is usually low in eunuchoids, there may often be overlap with normal figures.

Insufficiency of gametogenic function can be determined by seminal analysis or by testicular biopsy. The latter is becoming increasingly used as a diagnostic measure, and although the evidence obtained from it seldom influences one's choice of therapy, there is no question that it greatly increases the precision both of diagnosis and of prognosis.

Testicular biopsy is essentially a simple procedure which can be carried out either under general anaesthesia or under local analgesia.

It entails little or no discomfort for the patient and should not incapacitate him in any way. It is sometimes none too easy to perform when the testes are very small and soft, and occasionally it may be complicated by the development of a haematocele if unusually free bleeding occurs.

The important differentiation into primary and secondary hypogonadism can be made on the basis of urinary gonadotrophin estimation. In the first of these conditions, the output is increased for reasons which have already been explained, and in the second it is reduced or absent. Differentiation can also be made on the basis of the clinical response of the patient to treatment with chorionic gonadotrophin. The intramuscular injection of 1,000-3,000 I.U. of chorionic gonadotrophin twice weekly for six to ten weeks will be followed by distinct enlargement of the penis and increase in the growth of pubic hair in patients with secondary hypogonadism, but in primary hypogonadism this treatment will have no effect.

Treatment

The theoretically correct treatment for secondary hypogonadism is pituitary gonadotrophic hormone. Since commercial preparations of this are not available, recourse may be had to chorionic gonadotrophin and there have now been numerous reports that it may be wholly effective, not only in dealing with the eunuchoidal physical feature but also in promoting normal spermatogenesis. For this purpose large doses are necessary. For example, Maddock, Epstein, and Nelson used 5,000 I.U. of chorionic gonadotrophin thrice weekly for three months or more.

The great drawback of gonadotrophin therapy is the need for indefinitely prolonged and oft-repeated intramuscular injections. Since testosterone is fully effective in dealing with the eunuchoidal physical features and is the only available treatment for patients with primary hypogonadism, and since it can be administered far more conveniently than gonadotrophins, it is the treatment of choice in most cases. Moreover, it seems possible that in some patients with secondary hypogonadism, testosterone may also lead to spermatogenesis as well as to the development of normal secondary sex characters; Hurxthal, Bruns, and Musulin described four patients who showed such a response; one of these subsequently had two children and another also had a child (the other two patients were unmarried). A similar response to testosterone with the development of full spermatogenesis which persisted long after the last implantation was reported by Swyer. This was in a man who at the age of 27 still had genital development only of a degree to be expected in a boy of about 14. It is very doubtful if the argument sometimes raised, that the alleged results of treatment in these patients are, in fact, no more than the spontaneous development of late puberty, which occurred-or would have occurred-in spite of treatment; can apply to all the patients reported. For example, one of the patients of Hurxthal *et al.* was still eunuchoidal at the age of 43, only to become fertile after testosterone treatment.

Testosterone may be given by intramuscular injection of the propionate (50 mg. three times a week), the phenylpropionate (100 mg. weekly), or the oenanthate (125-250 mg. weekly or fortnightly); orally as methyltestosterone, effective when swallowed (25-50 mg. daily); or as testosterone linguets absorbed sublingually (25-50 mg. daily), the latter being a more cumbersome method; or by the subcutaneous implantation of pellets. Methyltestosterone has very rarely appeared to produce jaundice in adults but not in children, although the proof of the relationship is still *sub judice*. The implantation method is simple, and the implantation of six or eight 100 mg. pellets usually provides effective therapy for some six months.

The effect of treatment is usually dramatic. Libido and potency develop and may become supernormal. Orgasm occurs but detumescence may be delayed. Fluid emission is usually slight and sometimes absent. The penis and prostate grow in size but the testes remain unchanged. There is a remarkable increase in strength, muscular development, and weight. The latter is largely due to muscular development, since there is marked nitrogen retention. The appetite usually increases remarkably and, strangely enough, though fat eunuchoids may lose some weight through increased muscular activity, the thin ones usually gain some fat.

Clear changes in psychology and personality usually follow treatment. The shyness and diffidence are lost and the patient may become extroverted, creative, energetic, and, occasionally, aggressive. Depression and apathy disappear, being replaced by initiative and the capability of assuming responsibility. Naturally these changes are more marked in some patients than in others.

Marked growth of hair on the pubis and in the axillae occurs, and to a lesser extent, hair growth on the rest of the body is also stimulated. It is, however, rare for the facial hair ever to grow at the normal rate, perhaps because of some initial failure of development of the hair follicles. The voice deepens.

The disadvantages of treatment which may be encountered are the development of acne in some patients, the occasional development of gynaecomastia, and the occurrence of penile erections at unwanted times. However, the advantages far more than outweigh the disadvantages.

If treatment ceases, some residual physical benefits usually remain, although libido and potency may disappear completely.

Post-Puberty Castration

Because of the varied accounts in textbooks, often based on other textbooks or literature, what follows is based on personal experiences. A series of representative case reports is followed by a summary of the clinical picture, males and females being treated separately. . It will be seen that the lack of uniformity of response to castration after puberty and, in some cases, a glaring contrast or anomaly, are striking; at the same time, other features will be found to occur as a sequel with some consistency.

Post-Puberty Castration in Males

Case S. I, aged 21. This patient was said to have had a normal puberty at the age of 13, and during adolescence had indulged in some masturbation and experienced nocturnal seminal emissions. In April 1945, at the age of 21, he was wounded in battle in the left groin, and both testicles had to be removed surgically. He commenced intermittent treatment with methyltestosterone by mouth in December 1945; but before this, between April and December, he experienced nocturnal dreams with slight fluid emission, and he masturbated once weekly with resulting erection and emission. Frequent hot flushed, followed by cold perspiration, started in September 1945, and were partly controlled by 30 mg. methyltestosterone by mouth daily, and completely by double this dosage. His voice broke at the age of 14, and not changed following the accident. He stated that he did not require to shave until he was 18 years old, and the accident had no effect on his daily shaving. He had a rather scanty moustache, and did not appear to have a hairy face that would require daily shaving. His height was 6 ft. [1]h in. and growth had ceased at the age of 18. His span was equal to his height. His weight was 13 st. and he had put on 1 st. since the accident. He attributed the increased weight to lack of exercise through a stiff knee, and his surgical wound.

On examination he was seen to be a tall, slim type, with narrow shoulders and only slightly wider pelvis. The fingers, however, were not long and slender, but rather average. His penis was quite large.

No testicular tissue could be felt in the scrotum. The pubic hair was normal in amount, and of male type ascending along the linea alba. Axillary hair was moderate. He also had some hair on the chest.

CRYPTORCHIDISM

Cryptorchidism, or undescended testes, is the term applied to failure of descent of one or both testes into the scrotum.

Incidence

Since the incidence of maldescent is much greater in children than in adults, it is clear that spontaneous descent before or during puberty must take place in a large number of cases. At birth the incidence is about 10 per cent; at puberty about 2 per cent; and in manhood about 0.2 per cent.

Mechanism of Descent

The precise mechanism responsible for descent of the testes into the scrotum is uncertain. In normal development the processus vaginalis, an evagination of the posterior parietal peritoneum, grows downwards along with the gubernaculum, and the testis follows so that by the seventh month of intrauterine life, it lies at the lower end of the inguinal canal. Although it has often been asserted that the gubernaculum is responsible for the descent of the testis, from anatomical considerations this cannot possibly be true.

It has long been known that chorionic gonadotrophin will induce testicular descent in man and since it is only in the human that fully descended testes are normally found at birth, while the human female is the only organism in which chorionic gonadotrophin circulates throughout pregnancy, it seems possible that this hormone plays an important role in bringing about normal testicular descent. Presumably chorionic gonadotrophin stimulates the interstitial cells of the foetal testis to secrete testosterone and this promotes elongation of the structures of the spermatic cord and development of the scrotum. It is doubtful, however, if this can be the whole explanation.

Causes of Maldescent

Although a number of anatomical abnormalities responsible for maldescent have been described, in the majority of cases such abnormalities are not in fact present, since descent eventually occurs spontaneously or can be induced by gonadotrophin therapy. In these cases, therefore, the cause of maldescent is obscure. Thus, it could scarcely be due to lack of hormonal stimulation-and could certainly not be due to such a cause when the maldescent is unilateral. The possibility of failure of the foetal testis to respond to maternal gonadotrophin seems more reasonable, as also that spontaneous descent at or near to puberty may be the consequence of a responsiveness to gonadotrophin acquired later on. Examples of familial maldescent are not uncommon.

Effects of Maldescent on the Testis

There is little doubt that a testis which is not in the scrotum by the time of puberty may suffer irreparable damage to its germinal epithelium with consequent defect or failure of spermatogenesis. The effect on the interstitial cells is much less serious, though testes retained within the abdomen may fail to secrete testosterone under gonadotrophic stimulation. Although it may be true that some ectopic testes have an inherent defect of spermatogenesis, regardless of environmental temperature, the ectopic position is itself harmful, the deleterious effects of cryptorchidism on the seminiferous tubules being due to the temperature of the retained testis remaining similar to that of the body generally. For reasons which are quite unknown, spermatogenesis will occur only at a temperature a few degrees lower, such as obtains in a scrotal testis.

Up until the time of puberty, the seminiferous tubules retain a normal prepuberal appearance, even though the testis be undescended; but at puberty differentiation of the undescended testes fails to occur and degenerative changes appear, consisting in fibrosis and eventual disappearance of the tubules.

Opinions are divided on whether testes suffer damage even before puberty through maldescent. Some authorities believe that irreversible damage may occur in a retained testis before the age of 6; other writers have taken the view that a testis descending or being brought into the scrotum at the time of puberty will be none the worse for its extra-scrotal sojourn until then. Since the fate of the undescended testis clearly influences one's decision on treatment, it is obviously unfortunate, to say the least, that this uncertainty should prevail. It is also necessary to realize that cryptorchidism may represent one aspect of more extensive testicular dysplasia by reason of which normal spermatogenesis fails to occur even in testes effectively brought into the scrotum. This situation is most clearly exemplified by the not uncommon infertility of men with unilateral maldescent, the scrotal testis being relatively small and soft. Of course, many men with unilateral cryptorchidism are fully fertile.

Types of Maldescent

There are two main types of maldescent: (1) retractile testes and (2) retained testes. Retractile testes do not come under the heading of cryptorchidism. They consist of testes which are easily withdrawn from the scrotum into the inguinal region by the cremaster muscle (low retractile), or alternatively of testes which are at times situated in the inguinal region but can be manipulated into the scrotum (high retractile). Many patients referred because of alleged cryptorchidism in fact fall into one or other of these groups. Examination of the patient only in the supine position, and especially if done with cold hands, greatly increases the incidence of this misdiagnosis. For this reason a boy suspected of cryptorchidism should always be examined standing and the examiner's hands should be warmed.

An undescended testis may be *(a)* intra-abdominal and not palpable, (b) inguinal, not palpable when in the inguinal canal but palpable if it has passed through the canal and reached the superficial inguinal 'pouch', which lies between the external abdominal ring and the upper scrotum, and (c) ectopic, when the testis is found in a position never occupied during normal descent. A testis lying inside the inguinal canal may be palpable in a very thin subject but, with this rare exception, it is correct to state that a testis in this position is not normally palpable. A testis that is clearly palpable, or visible, in the line of the inguinal canal, or to one or other side of it, is usually ectopic. An ectopic testis cannot be made to disappear into the inguinal canla or to pass into the scrotum.

Ectopic testes lie outside the inguinal canal; they may be situated superficial to the aponeurosis of the external oblique muscle (superficial inguinal ectopic testes), in the perineum or in the femoral region. The superficial inguinal ectopic testis is by far the commonest variety of ectopia. Its differentiation from an inguinal non-ectopic testis is important, since surgery is the only treatment for the ectopic testis. In this differentiation, Spence and Scowen have pointed out that the ectopic testis lies more superficially than one which is in the superficial inguinal pouch or within the inguinal canal; that it becomes more obvious when moved upwards and outwards and that it cannot be moved into the canal or into the scrotum.

Course and Complications

Spontaneous Descent

This occurs frequently before or during puberty but only rarely after puberty. The retractile testis always descends more completely at puberty but may remain retractile even in adult life. Cases are in fact known in which the inguinal canal remains sufficiently patent for the testis to pass right through it back into the abdomen but nevertheless to descent again spontaneously.

When maldescent is the result of an anatomical abnormality or ectopia, spontaneous descent can never occur. It is very rare that abdominal testes descend spontaneously Testes within the superficial inguinal pouch or actually within the inguinal canal may or may not descend spontaneously. Normal function can generally be expected in a testis descending before or during puberty, but, as previously mentioned, this is not invariably the case.

Hypogonadism

Failure of spermatogenesis is to be expected in the case of persistent bilateral cryptorchidism and such patients are ordinarily sterile. As previously mentioned, this also occurs in some cases of unilateral cryptorchidism. With bilateral abdominal testes eunuchoidism may or may not occur.

Hydrocele and Torsion

The undescended testis is more prone to injury than the scrotal testis and hydrocele formation is not an uncommon complication. Torsion of an undescended testis is a rarity.

Psychological Disturbances

Boys (and their parents) vary enormously in their emotional reaction to cryptorchidism. Some are compeletely oblivious to the condition. Others may be disturbed because they differ from other boys or because they become the objects of sarcasm or ridicule when seen undressed by other boys. Persistence of cryptorchidism after puberty is more likely to result in emotional disturbance, particularly when bilateral. The realization of sterility adds yet further to the psychological burden of cryptorchidism.

Malignancy

There is no doubt that malignancy occurs more frequently in a cryptorchid than in a scrotal testis, though the precise incidence is a matter of uncertainty. Hinman quotes the frequency as being twenty times more than in scrotal testes—but malignancy is still a rarity.

Treatment

The first decision is clearly as to whether treatment of any kind is necessary. Retractile testes require no attention. There is no uniformity of opinion on the best treatment for retained testes. Ectopic testes can only be brought into the scrotum by surgery, but there is no certainty that such surgical treatment will produce a normal testis, fully functional from the endocrine and spermatogenic points of view. The real difficulty arises when the diagnosis of ectopia cannot be made with certainty, or when the testes are not palpable.

While it is true that the majority of undescended testes reach the scrotum spontaneously by adolescence, the dilemma facing the physician is that no one can say for certain which retained testes will descend spontaneously and which will not, while, on the other hand, the probability of infertility resulting from failure of descent by the time of puberty seriously challenges an attitude of mere watchful expectancy.

It has frequently been asserted that treatment with chorionic gonadotrophin will cause descent only of those testes which would have entered the scrotum spontaneously during puberty; from this it is argued that such treatment is unnecessary. If it were possible to diagnose with certainty cases where spontaneous descent by the time of puberty would occur, and if it were certain that retention of the testis until the time of puberty caused no harm, then the case for never using chorionic gonadotrophin in cryptorchidism would be firm. The situation, however, is otherwise. It is impossible to predict which retained testes will descend spontaneously at puberty, and it is uncertain that retention of the testis until puberty leaves it unharmed. Therefore, a therapeutic trial of chorionic gonadotrophin in young boys with cryptorchidism not definitely diagnosed as ectopic seems thoroughly justified. One cannot be dogmatic on the age at which such therapy should be started. The likelihood of response is greater the nearer to puberty, but, on the other hand, the risk of testicular damage increases with age. Perhaps, therefore, the right time to start is somewhere between *8* aand 11 years of age. The course should consist of 500 or 1,000 I.U. of chorionic gonadotrophin intramuscularly twice a week for about ten weeks. In the vast majority of cases, descent of some degree, if it is going to occur at all, will be seen within this time. If no descent is discernible, a further similar course of treatment, perhaps with an increase of dose to 1,500 I.U., may be given a few months later. Under no circumstances should *continued* therapy-going on for months on end-be permitted. It seems probable that all the cases of precocious puberty resulting from chorionic gonadotrophin therapy have been brought about by excessively prolonged treatment. The writer has never seen any untoward genital development resulting from a single ten-weeks' course of treatment as outlined above. The use of testosterone as an alternative to chorionic gonadotrophin is not recommended.

The real problem arises in the cases of undescended testes which have failed to respond to an adequate course of gonadotrophin. Most surgeons are agreed that the results of orchidopexy are largely very disappointing and this has led some to take the view that:

The boy with unilateral cryptorchidism has a much better chance of having two testes normal in size, consistency, and position if nature is allowed to take its course and surgical treatment is avoided until his 16th year. The question of the best treatment for bilateral non-descent is vital. The boy with this condition also has a much better chance of eventually having normally functioning testes if late spontaneous descent is allowed to take place and surgical interference is deferred until the 16th or 17th year. There is no question in my mind but that the results of most operations that have been performed to correct bilateral non-descent of the testes actually have unintentionally produced what they have been performed to prevent-that is, sterility.

If one could be certain that this view is correct, the course to follow would be clear. Unfortunately, in the writer's opinion, it is not possible to accept this view unequivocally and no doubt each surgeon undertaking the surgical treatment of cryptorchidism will base his opinion whether to operate or to leave alone on his own experience.

When one is confronted with a post-puberal patient with bilateral cryptorchidism, the is no doubt that surgery ought to be undertaken, even though the chance of bringing the testes into the scrotum may be small (especially if they are not palpable) and the chance of fertility even smaller (though not zero). With unilateral cryptorchidisn the necessity for treatment is far less clear. Obviously, gonadotrophin therapy is useless the patient having undergone puberty, his testes will already have been subjected ti effective gonadotrophic stimulation. Since the likelihood is high that a retained testis brought into the scrotum after puberty will fail to produce spermatozoa, there is little point in carrying out such surgery. The risk of malignancy may counsel removal of *the* undescended testis, but it seems to the writer that this should only be undertaken if the patient, having been fully appraised of the situation, specifically requests it.

GYNAECOMASTIA

Although its Greek derivation indicates a woman's breast, the term gynaecomastia is applied to the development, either bilateral or unilateral, of true breast tissue in the male. The accumulation of pectoral fat in men, unassociated with actual breast tissue, should not be called gynaecomastia and has sometimes been referred to as "pseudo-gynaecomastia".

Incidence

Gynaecomastia, usually mild and transient, is said to occur in about 80 per cent of boys at the time of puberty. Apart from this, gynaecomastia is relatively rare. In a general way, it may be said that when the onset is before the age of 25 it is essentially a manifestation of puberty and of no special consequence (though it may be of sufficient extent to cause embarrassment requiring plastic surgery for its alleviation); but when the onset is after the age of about 25, the likelihood of there being a sinister underlying disease is strong and requires full investigation. Exceptions to this rule certainly occurs: Wilkins described gynaecomastia due to a feminizing adrenocortical carcinoma in a boy of 5, and Holl in a boy of 15.

Aetiology

Oestrogenic stimulation in the male may lead to gynaecomastia and undoubtedly in some cases the condition arises from this cause. But it is far from certain that oestrogenic stimulation alone-or even at all-is responsible for all cases. It is well known, for example, that androgens, as employed in the treatment of eunuchoidism, may sometimes cause gynaecomastia, and so may both deoxycortone and cortical extracts. It is possible that pituitary hormones, particularly prolactin associated with growth hormone, may be of aetiological importance in other cases (for example, the gynaecomastia sometimes seen in acromegaly). Very often the cause of the condition is quite obscure and it may be that in some of these cases an undue sensitivity of the rudimentary breast tissue to normal hormone levels is responsible. Clearly this must be the case in unilateral gynaecomastia; and since the unilateral condition is relatively common, it rather suggests that target-organ sensitivity is one of the more important aetiological factors.

Pathology

The histological picture is identical with that of the gland in normal women, but adenoma formation and fibrosis are occasionally seen. Sometimes the picture is similar to that of fibrocystic mastopathy in women.

Clinical Aspects

Puberty

As already mentioned, puberty gynaecomastia is so common that it may almost be considered as physiological. The condition may be trivial, representing merely a sub-areolar swelling which disappears within a few months to a year, or it may consist of substantial breast development which causes great embarrassment to the boy and may interfere with physical activities. The major variety shows no tendency to regress spontaneously. The condition is often unilateral. In the minor varieties, first one breast and then the other may be affected. Puberty gynaecomastia may sometimes persist.

Exogenous Oestrogens

Gynaecomastia is an unfortunate side effect of the treatment of carcinoma of the prostate with oestrogens. It also arises as a result of exposure to oestrogens during their manufacture and has occasionally been reported as arising through the contamination of other drugs, such as certain batches of amphetamine with oestrogenic impurities. The use of digitalis in heart failure has sometimes resulted in gynaecomastia; digitalis contains cardiac aglucones which possess the cyclopentenophenanthrene structure of the steroids.

Male Intersexuality

Breast enlargement is found in certain forms of male pseudohermaphroditism.

Hypogonadism

Adrenal Cortical Tumours and hyperfunction. Adipose gynandrism.

Testicular Tumours

Gynaecomastia has been reported as an accompaniment of most of the varieties of testicular tumours, such as interstitial cell tumour, chorioepithelioma, teratoma, seminoma, and the one case of so-called Sertoli cell tumour reported in a human male. It is generally supposed that an increased secretion of oestrogens by the tumour cells of the testis, or by hyperplastic Leydig cells stimulated by the chorionic gonadotrophin produced by the tumour cells, is responsible for the breast enlargement in these circumstances.

Hepatic Disease

Gynaecomastia may be found in association with severe hepatic disease and is believed to be due to failure of the liver to conjugate oestrogens with the result that relatively high concentrations of free hormone remain in the circulation. The proof that this is true is still lacking. Testicular atrophy is another accompaniment of this condition.

Re-Feeding Gynaecomastis

Kark, Morey, and Paynter reported the occurrence of gynaecomastia in severely under nourished cirr'hotics during treatment with high-protein, high-calorie diets and suggested that it might be due to the introduction of arginine in adequate quantities in the diet. Re-feeding gynaecomastia was frequently observed among repatriated prisoners of war during the period in which their nutritional status was undergoing rapid improvement. In these cases, the gynaecomastia was transient and consisted of firm sub-areolar *plaques*. *In* some individuals it was accompanied by *mild orchitis* and return of libido.

Miscellaneous Conditions

Tender breast enlargement in men with hypothyroidism has been reported by Berson and Schreiber. In a review by Wheeler *et al.*, attention is drawn to a previously unrecognized or unstressed relationship found between gynaecomastia and the following conditions: chronic generalized dermatitis, rheumatoid arthritis, angiodermatomyositis, lymphoblastoma, diabetes mellitus, chronic pyelonephritis, chronic glomerulonephritis, and essential hypertension. Gynaecomastia, they point out, may occasionally be the initial manifestation or presenting complaint of serious underlying disease.

Diagnosis

The differentiation from pseudo-gynaecomastia is usually easily made on palpation. A typical granular consistency is found in true gynaecomastia, whereas, where fat alone is present, the tissues have a uniform feel. At puberty, examination of the testes will reveal whether normal enlargement, is occurring or testicular hypoplasia, associated with hypogonadism, is the aetiological factor. Search for other possible endocrine causes or some of the more obscure miscellaneous causes mentioned above should be made.

Treatment

There is no effective endocrine treatment for gynaecomastia which does not regress by itself. Appropriate plastic surgery is required where the condition is extensive and is causing psychological or physical embarrassment.

THE MALE CLIMACTERIC

Whereas, for reasons which have been fully discussed in the preceding chapter, every woman who lives long enough must undergo a climacteric, the same is by no means true for men. Gametogenesis in the male, as has already been pointed out, is a function of sexually mature individuals and does not involve the continual loss of primordial germ cells. As a consequence, spermatogenesis may continue until very old age and there are authentic examples of the retention of fertility into the ninth decade. Based on these considerations, and because a syndrome in males corresponding to that of the climacteric in females is relatively rare and its features somewhat vague, it has been widely held that there is no such entity as the male climacteric. This view, however, is untenable, as was argued in the second edition of this book; and a restatement of the case leading to this conclusion has been given by Spence. The fact, which is accepted by all endocrinologists of experience, is that a small proportion of males flo undergo a phase of waning testicular function and may in consequence experience symptoms of the same general character, and no doubt arising in the same way, as are experienced by a far greater proportion of women. It is also generally agreed that when it occurs, the male climacteric appears later in life than the female, usually between the ages of 55 and 65.

The first to produce scientific evidence indicating the existence of a male climacteric were Heller and Myers who found that whereas in 15 men with psychoneuroses or psychogenic impotence, the urinary gonadotrophin excretion was normal, in 23 men whom they considered to be suffering from the male climacteric, the titre was unequivocally higher. Moreover, having performed testicular biopsy on 8 of these 23 man, they found in 5 a reduction in the size and activity of the seminiferous tubules, together with a reduction in the size and number of the Leydig cells; and, in the remaining 3, hyaline degeneration of the tubules. Later observers have reported normal testicular histology, in spite of the presence of increased urinary gonadotrophins, or normal tubules but decreased numbers of Leydig cells with abnormal histological characteristics.

According to Howard *et al.*, the climacteric can be divided into a compensated and a decompensated stage. In the former there is a tendency to decreased production of gonadal hormones, which is met by. overproduction of pituitary gonadotrophin so that gonadal function remains essentially intact. In the decompensated stage this tendency to gonadal failure is not counterbalanced, in spite of increased gonadotrophin production, and so gonadal failure becomes clinically demonstrable. In the female, the compensated stage lasts only a very short time, but in the male, on the other hand, it is the decompensated stage which is seldom encountered. They therefore considered their patients with the male climacteric whose testicular biopsies appeared normal, in spite of increased urinary gonadotrophin titres, still to be in the compensated stage.

Clinical Features

Decrease in both potency and libido is suggestive of declining testicular function, whereas impotence in the presence of normal libido is more likely to be of psychogenic origin. Nevertheless, in some cases of the male climacteric, the libido may remain essentially unchanged even though potency has decreased considerably. In yet other cases, neither potency nor libido undergo a change, yet nervous and vasomotor changes, so characteristic of the female climacteric, may be found. Among the psychic symptoms are anxiety, irritability, impairment of memory, loss of power of concentration, indecision, and insomnia. The principal vasomotor disturbances are not flushes and sweats, palpitation and tachycardia, shortness of breath on exertion and precordial pain. Other symptoms may include easy fatigability, tinnitus, vertigo paraesthesiae, and urinary difficulties-though these latter are more likely to be the direct result of prostatic enlargement. Involutional melancholia and suicidal tendencies are occasionally encountered. Symptoms may persist for several months to several years.

Diagnosis

Differentiation of true male climacteric syndrome from an anxiety state can be made on the basis of the gonadotrophin excretion, though it is seldom necessary to resort to this rather tedious investigation for clinical guidance. A prompt symptomatic response to injections of testosterone propionate would certainly be suggestive of the male climacteric, though the psychological effect of the injections must also be considered. In authentic examples of the climacteric syndrome, the substitution of an inert oil for testosterone propionate leads to relapse, wheras this is not the case when improvement in an authentic cases, testicular biopsy may reveal normal histology, it is clear that resort to this procedure is of no value in the diagnosis of the male climacteric.

Treatment

Testosterone in one form or another is the obvious treatment for the male climacteric. It is difficult to be dogmatic about the dose to be used, since marked individual variation to responsiveness may be encountered. There is something to be said for commencing treatment with relatively large doses, for example, testosterone propionate, 50 mg. thrice weekly, or testosterone phenylpropionate,100 mg., weekly. If with such doses no clinical improvement occurs, the diagnosis of male climacteric can promptly be discarded. On the other hand, a small fraction of these doses may be quite sufficient to maintain the patient in a comfortable state; and occasionally large doses may precipitate prostatic emergencies or cardiac insufficiency, so considerable circumspection should be used. Once a clear response to injection treatment has been obtained, it may prove advantageous to continue treatment by means of implants of testosterone, the appropriate quantity being two to six 100 mg. pellets, renewed as often as the patient feels necessary. These patients usually have no difficulty whatever in deciding when the beneficial effects of the implant have disappeared. Reimplantation becomes necessary every six to eight months, as a rule.

The more serious psychological disturbances are seldom materially affected by testosterone therapy, and for these psychological treatment may be necessary.

SEXUAL ABNORMALITIES

HERMAPHRODITISM

The term 'hermaphrodite' is derived from Greek mythology, being the composite name given to the bisexual child resulting from the celestial union of Hermes and Aphrodite. Hermaphrodite is frequently depicted in Greek sculpture either as a beautiful youth with well-developed breasts or as an aphrodite with male genitalia.

It is perhaps unfortunate that this subject, like that of sexual precocity, had become bedevilled with the use of 'true' and 'pseudo-descriptive' terms. The terms 'gonadal' and 'genital' hermaphrodites have been advocated for what are more generally referred to as true and pseudohermaphrodites, but these, too, are unsatisfactory. In the former group, both male and female gonads or a combined ovo-testis are present, whereas the latter are intersexes in whom the external characters do not conform with the genetic or gonadal sex.

True Hermaphroditism Aetiology

The cause of true hermaphroditism is unknown, and the adrenocortical hyperplasia sometimes met with is concomitant and not aetiological. The condition is by no means uncommon in the animal and plant kingdoms; it is, for example, normal for many species, such as the earthworm, and it is not infrequently met with in pigs and goats. The hen is potentially hermaphrodite, as the right gonad is rudimentary, and will become fully functioning testis if the left ovary is removed. The change of sex in the hen may be so complete that the mother of chicks may become the father of chicks. This remarkable transformation is perhaps less difficult to appreciate if it is remembered that the medulla of the ovary is the homologue of the testis. In man the cells of the genital ridge which are destined to become either ovary or testis cannot be differentiated before the embryo has reached the seventh week of development. Whether the central portion (the medulla) of the genital mass of cells develops into a testis, or whether the outer area (the cortex) becomes an ovary, depends normally upon the genetic or chromosomal influence, but what goes wrong with this normal process so as to permit the development of an ovary on one side and a testis on the other, or of an ovo-testis (either unilateral or bilateral) is quite unknown. That the genetic factor may be unilateral is well illustrated by the very rare occurrence in the bullfinch of a testis on the right and on ovary on the left, associated with masculine plumage on the right half of the body and feminine plumage on the left half. This must mean that one half of the body is genetically determined to have a responsiveness to androgenic hormone and not to oestrogenic hormone, and vice versa, since the secretions of both gonads are circulating throughout the body. Similar responsiveness and refractoriness, although not unilateral, may be seen in human hermaphrodites. The importance of these conceptions is thrown still further into relief when it is remembered that both testis and ovary can secrete androgenic and oestrogenic substances.

Clinical Features

True hermaphroditism is rare, there having been only some forty cases reported in the literature. The diagnosis can only be made after microscopical examination of gonadal biopsies. Owing to the unpredictable responsiveness, or refractoriness, of tissues to circulating hormones, the external appearances may be predominantly male or female, or obviously mixed. This is also true of the sexual and secondary sexual organs; as well as of the emotional and psychological attitudes, which do not necessarily correspond to the predominantly genital or physical characteristics.

Young described a 'man' of 20, an excellent athlete, 6 ft. tall and weighing 144 lb., with normal male hair on the body and face, and with a well-developed penis, who was operated upon at the age of 20 for a tender mass in the left groin, clinically believed to be an undescended testis. The contents of hernial sac, however, presented a small uterus, and a normal ovary and Fallopian tube, all of which were removed. A biopsy of the right scrotal testis showed interstitial cells of Lyedig and seminiferous tubules, which, however, did not contain any spermatozoa. The patient had normal masculine sexual feelings and potency, and passed through a normal boy's puberty. The only abnormality of the external genitalia, apart from an 'undescended testis', was the presence of hypospadias, a condition which can actually be produced experimentally in male rats by injecting the pregnant mother with oestrogens.

The combination of unilaterally undescended testis and hyposp-adias, especially if associated with *gynaecomastia*, should always raise the suspicion of true hermaphroditism. A case described by Greene *et al.*, a 'boy' of 15, displayed this triad. In this patient, biopsy of the testis actually showed normal spermatogenesis; while there was a uterus opening into the urethra, a single uterine tube, and an ovary in which the presence of fresh corpus luteum showed that ovulation had recently taken place.

A different type of *true hermaphroditism*, predominantly female, was described by Seligman, Kraushar, and Byron. At birth the genitalia consisted of an apparently, normal vulva, and protruding therefrom an organ resembling a penis, about 2.5 cm long. There was no urethral opening in this organ. The child was brought up as a girl. From the age of 13 she experienced abdominal cramps and nausea each month, but apart from one slight bleeding in her thirteenth year and again in her fifteenth year, there was no menstruation. At the age of 17 she sought advice because of a large penis like organ of male dimensions which erected frequently and pleasurably. The urethral opening lay in the vestibule. The labia were normal and the vaginal orifice admitted two fingers. Her psychology remained essentially female and she had a male friend. However, she was tall, thin, and flat-chested, with male-type breasts and skeletal form. She had a little hair on her upper lip and hair on the pubis, axillae, and legs. Laparotomy revealed an infantile uterus and Fallopian tubes. Two small gonads were seen, and a wedge resection from each revealed an ovo-testis showing on histological section: (1) ovarian tissue with degenerating primordial follicles; (2) testicular tissue with well-defined interstitial cells and seminiferous tubules without spermatozoa; and (3) cords and strands of large mononuclear cells which resembled adrenal cortex tissue. The gonads were removed and the penis was amputated. The administration of oestrogens was followed by gain in weight, fat deposition, the development of feminine contours and breast, while the essentially feminine outlook and habits remained.

Diagnosis

As mentioned above, this can only be made with certainty on the basis of histological examination of gonadal biopsies.

Treatment

This depends essentially upon the external configuration and the emotional-psychological attitude. The gonad corresponding to the latter is usually retained, and the other gonad removed. Appropriate reconstruction of the external genitalia, such as removal of the penis or hypertrophied clitoris, and dilatation of the vagina, or, on the other hand, repair of the hypospadias, are carried out. Where both gonads are ovo-testes it might be advisable to remove them both and to administer either oestrogens or androgens, depending upon the above considerations. Each patient has to be evaluated and the appropriate treatment carefully planned.

PSEUDOHERMAPHRODITISM

Pseudo- or *genital hermaphroditism* is a condition in which there is only one type of gonad—testis, or ovary—but in which the external genitalia either present a mixture of male and female characteristics, or are appropriate to the sex opposite to that of the gonads. The term should be applied only to those cases in which the condition is present from birth, and not to those instances of virilism or feminization which may develop in later life.

The recent development of simple techniques for the determination of the chromosomal (and presumed genetic) sex has helped greatly in the diagnosis of the kinds of intersex which fall into this group. This is particularly true of the so-called male pseudohermaphrodites, in which the genetic sex is male but the external appearances are, to a greater or lesser extent, female.

Two sharply contrasted types of *pseudohermaphroditism* are found. Most female pseudohermaphrodites arise as a result of the excessive production of androgens by adrenal cortex, commencing during foetal life. This is nearly always due to adrenal hyperplasia of the kind already met with in the previous chapter, and which becoming manifest in post-natal life, may cause adrenal sexual precocity or adrenal virilism. Very rarely the condition may be due to an androgen-secreting adrenal tumour arising in foetal life. No such simple overall description can be given in the case of male pseudohermaphrodites. These are individuals of male genetic sex, in whom, for reasons which are not understood, either the medulla of the undifferentiated embryonic gonad has failed to develop into a testis; or apparently normal testes have developed but have descended incompletely and the external genitalia have, to a greater or lesser extent, failed to develop as those typical of the male having, on the contrary, assumed a disposition more or less characteristic of the female. On the basis of this overall description it would seem that male pseudohermaphrodites fall roughly into two groups: first, those in which failure of gonadal differentiation is responsible for the intersexualization (this group would therefore include the gonadal agenesis or Turner's syndrome); and second, those in which apparently normal gonadal embryogenesis has occurred, but the somatic tissues have failed to respond to the foetal testicular hormone which, it would appear, is normally responsible for the foetal development of male genitalia.

In both male and female pseudohermaphroditism the external genitalia are partly male and partly female, and the predominance of male or female external characteristics does not necessarily indicate the nature of the gonads. If the latter are palpable in the perineum, scrotal sac, 'labial folds', or in the region of the inguinal canal, they are more likely to be testes than ovaries; but this cannot be assumed. Ovaries are usually, but by no means invariably, intra-abdominal, though many surprises have been encountered on laparotomy.

In both types the general habits and skeletal development tends to be male, but a gynaecoid pelvis and female pseudohermaphrodites are usually stronger than normal females and male pseudohermaphrodites are usually weaker than normal males. Male pseudohermaphrodites commonly have less hair on the face than do female pseudohermaphrodites. Mistake in the sex of the child is common in the adolescent or adult phase female pseudohermaphrodites tend to have a female libido and sexual behaviour, and rarely function as males. Male pseudohermaphrodites may function as male or female, or as active or passive homosexuals, according to genetic tendencies, upbringing, or anatomical genital configuration.

In both types fat deposition is unusual, the patients tending to be on the lean and muscular side. However, female or eunuchoidal fat deposition is occasionally encountered.

FEMALE PSEUDOHERMAPHRODITISM

Genitalia

The external genitalia may not be distinguishable from those of male pseudohermaphrodites. The clitoris is greatly enlarged, resembling a penis, and the phallus may be used successfully as a penis in intercourse with females. The clitoris has a gland and a section of its body show corpora spongiosa as in the males. The urethra, however, opens at its base, or in the preneum *or* vestibule; very occasionally, as in the case reported by Bentinck, Lisser, and Reilly, it may be penile (only five similar cases have previously been reported).

The labia major may be completely fused, giving the appearance of a bifid scrotum, or incompletely fused with a minute vaginal orifice, or well formed with underlying labia minora surrounding a normal vaginal opening and hymen.

When no vaginal orifice is present, urethroscopy will reveal a vaginal orifice opening into the urethra. Such a vagina may be of considerable size and depth and the cervix uteri may be visualized. Injection of radio-opaque medium through a catheter permits the radiographic demonstration of the shape and size of the vagina. A male type of prostate is sometimes present around the urethra and may be palpable per rectum.

Ovaries and Uterus

The ovaries are usually intra-abdominal and are found on laparotomy. They are most commonly infantile, or in an adult may be found to correspond to normal ovaries of a child of about 10 years of age. They may, however, be involuted and fibrotic with multiple cysts. Normal adult ovaries with well-developed Graafian follicles and corpora lutea are not usually found. In fact, the ovaries are similar to those found in cases of the adrenogenital syndrome, or experimentally when a female animal is injected with testosterone. Failure of ovarian development must be attributed to lack of gonadotrophic stimulation and to the excess of adrenal androgens. The uterus and Fallopian tubes are also poorly developed in most patients. Amenorrhoea is the rule, but slight bleeding or vaginal discharge, or vicarious nasal menstruation, are sometimes found.

Urination

This is carried out as by the normal female, but in some patients incontinence of urine or urgency of micturition is met with. The vagina may open into the urethra, or the urethra may open into the vestibule as in the normal female.

Intermediate positions of the urithra on the perineum are sometimes found.

Hair

Some patients have a feminine distribution of hair and none on the face; but the majority have a male distribution and may have a moustache and beard. This, of course, is attributable to the adrenal androgens. Hair on the face may be present in childhood or may not develop until puberty. This would indicate the adrenals take on an even greater activity at this time.

Breasts

The breasts are usually flat and of male type, but sometimes they appear more feminine in structure.

Somatic Development

In childhood, as in cases of sexual precocity due to an adrenal tumour or hyperplasia, development is precocious and a child of 4 may have the muscular and skeletal development of a child of 8 or 10. The voice may be deep. The bone age and epiphyseal development is advanced. The relative proportion of shoulders to pelvis is usually of male type, but a gynaecoid pelvis may be encountered.

Metabolic disturbances

Defective secretion of glucocorticoids (and perhaps of aldosterone) by the hyperplastic adrenals of these patient may, in some cases, lead to Addisonian symptoms due to excessive salt loss or to hypoglycaemia.

Libido and Sexual Behaviour

This depends to a considerable extent upon the upbringing. However, in the majority of patients the libido is directed towards the male, even when the patient is hirsute and the clitoris enormous. If the vagina is patent, or made patient, sexual intercourse with the male may be quite satisfactory. Rarely the adult pseudohermaphrodite may function as a male in coitus with a female.

Diagnosis

Diagnosis of adrenal pseudohermaphroditism depends upon the detection of a marked increase in 17-ketosteroid excretion. The differentiation between the much commoner adrenal hyperplasia and the rare adrenal tumour can be made by the presence or absence of a response to cortisone or prednisone administration. With hyperplasia a prompt fall in 17-ketosteroid output follows such treatment, whereas when a tumour is present, the output, usually much greater, remains essentially unchanged.

Chromosomal sex determination, by the skin biopsy, leucocyte or buccal scraping technique, reveals the genetic sex to be female. Very rarely it may be necessary to biopsy the gonads in order to make certain of the diagnosis.

The birth of pseudohermaphrodites to mothers given androgens or progestens during pregnancy has been reported.

Treatment

The treatment of female pseudohermaphroditism is essentially the treatment of the underlying adrenal hyperplasia, which has already been discussed.

Wilkins *et al.* have pointed out how important it is to regulate the dose of cortisone according to the individual needs of the patient. In the older patients the best result were obtained by using the minimal amount of cortisone necessary to keep the 17-ketosteroid excretion below 8 mg. per day. Six patients, between the ages of 8½ and 18½ years, when treated with cortisone showed prompt development of the breasts, and the vaginal smears indicated oestrogenic stimulation. Three of the patients began menstruating regularly and hirsutism decreased in all. On the other hand, when an infant was treated with 25 mg. of cortisone per day intramuscularly, growth and osseous development were inhibited, though 5 mg. per day proved sufficient and allows normal growth. They therefore advise that during childhood the 17-ketosteroid excretion should be followed closely and the rates of growth and osseous development should be used as guides to treatment. As further effects of cortisone treatment they observed disappearance of an Addisonian type of pigmentation in two cases, and in three others the undesirable development of marked hypertension. It is probable that for some-if not for all-patients, prednisone or prednisolone by mouth, in a dose about one-fifth that of an effective cortisone dose is the treatment of choice.

The treatment of those patients who show salt-losing tendencies can be far more difficult. In these, cortisone alone is usually insufficient to prevent the excessive loss of sodium and the undue elevation of the plasma potassium. The addition of DOCA may be sufficient to maintain a normal electrolyte balance though the amounts which have to be injected may be large, for example, 10 mg. per day, or more. Clearly, for such patients aldosterone would be the ideal therapeutic agent. There is some evidence that cortisol (hydrocortisone) is more effective than cortisone and that 9 a-fluorohydrocorticsone (fludrocortisone) is a great deal more effective than cortisone in maintaining electrolyte balance. In the case of a patient of one of the authors (G. I. M. S.)-a child of 2-cortisone, 25 mg., and DOCA, 10 mg., daily as well as large salt supplements, were necessary in order to obtain electrolyte balance. It was found, however, that 0.25 mg. of 9 a-fluorohydrocortisone daily was more effective than the large dose of DOCA and maintained effective electrolyte balance with much smaller salt supplements, or even without salt.

An excellent account of the surgical reconstruction of the external genitalia in patients with severe anomalies has been given by Jones and Jones.

MALE PSEUDOHERMAPHRODITISM

There would appear to be three main types of male pseudohermaphroditism: the first and most well known of these resembles the female pseudohermaphrodite in many particulars and may in some cases be distinguishable therefrom only by hormone studies, chromosomal sex determination or gonadal biopsy; the second and third types which will be considered in more detail later, bear a strong resemblance to more or less normal *females.* These types would appear to represent increasing degrees of intersexualization.

Type One

External Genitalia

The penis may be small or of normal size but it is frequently held down to the perineum by congenital fibrous bands, and the resulting concave bending of the penis towards the perineum (chordee) tends to prevent erection and make the organ less prominent. When it is small it is often mistaken for a large clitoris. Hypospadias is nearly always present and the urethra may open under the gland at the base of the penis or several centimeters behind in the perineum, or in the vestibule between the pseudo-labial folds as in the female. The scrotum is bifid and where the two halves fail to meet a vaginal or pseudo-vaginal orifice presents itself with a varying degree of labium formation. This opening may have no depth or may have the dimensions and histological structure of a true vagina. According to the relative size of the penis (or assumed clitoris) and degree of failure of union of the scrotal folds (pseudo-or real vagina), the child is brought up initially as a girl or as a boy.

Testes

The testes are usually undescended, but if the scrotal folds are well developed the testes may have descended partially and be palpable. Their macroscopic appearance is usually testicular and they may be normal in size or small. Microscopically they show apparently normal interstitial cells but although the seminiferous tubules are frequently well formed, spermatogenesis is not found. Sterility is the rule, even when coitus and seminal emissions are possible.

Uterus and Fallopian tubes

In some of these patients there are no female organs apart from a pseudo-vagina, but in others there may be found, usually in a hernial sac, an infantile uterus and Fallopian tubes. In one such case the gonad was in the position in which the ovary is usually found and its consistency and appearance were ovarian in character, but subsequent section showed it to be a testis.

Urination

Owing to the hypospadias, especially when the urethral opening is perennial or vestibular, most patients claim that they are unable to urinate except in a sitting position, as assumed by the female.

Hair

Pubic hair is abundant and may be either of the so-called female type, which is horizontal in its upper boundary, or it may extend upwards to the umbilicus, as is more characteristic of the male. It is rare, however, that much hair is present on the body. The facial hair is of the male type, usually rather sparse and slow growing so that shaving is not a daily necessity. This would appear to indicate that inspite of normal interstitial cell tissue, the secretion of androgens is subnormal, or, alternatively, that there is reduced responsiveness of the hair follicles or a scarcity of their distribution on the face. The fact that the prostate is usually small in size supports the probability that androgen production is at a somewhat reduced level.

Breasts

The breasts are usually flat and of male type but may respond to oestrogenic therapy when such attempted.

Somatic development

The general habitus is of male type, with the shoulders broader than pelvis. The muscular development, however, is usually poor and only rarely excessive. Tall, thin eunuchoid types, as well as adipose eunuchoid types have also been recorded, but are not the rule.

Libido and sexual behaviour

This depends to some extent on whether the patient is assumed to be a boy or girl in childhood, but even so the predominant type of behaviour appears to be masculine. Thus, after freeing the penis from adhesions to the perineum, satisfactory vaginal penetration and coitus, with orgasm and emission are usual, and happy married life may be achieved. The fluid emission comes from urethral and prostatic glands and contains no spermatozoa. *Masturbation* is frequent with younger patients, and in adults if coitus is not possible.

Some patients have been brought up as girls, perhaps in convents, and then on the finding of testicular tissue in the gonads have adopted-with success - male clothing and habits. Others have had the clitoris removed and, both before and, more so, after surgical enlargement of the vagina, have 'married' their male lovers and lived sexually and socially as women, although both gonads were testes and no uterus or Fallopian tubes were present.

Diagnosis

Differentiation from female pseudohermaphrodites can be made on the absence of elevated 17-ketosteroid excretion and on the finding of chromosomal sex patterns of the male type in skin biopsies or polymorphonuclear leucocytes. The most conclusive differentiation would of course depend upon the histological examination of gonadal biopsy material.

Treatment

This consists of freeing the penis from adhesions, plastic operation on the hypospadias, and closure of the vaginal orifice. In some patients the external genital structure and the psychological attitude justifies removal of the penis and enlargement of the vagina.

Type Two

Attention was originally drawn to this type by Goldberg and Maxwell who collected seven cases in a search of the literature up to that date and to which they added a description of their own case.

Schneider, van Ommen, and Hoerr found six more cases which had been reported since 1948 and added six cases of their own, all of which were distributed among three generations of one family. Williams described briefly another case and referred to the condition as 'intersex males with purely feminine external genitalia and bodily habitus'. Morris described two cases as examples of *'testicular feminisation'*. Two other cases have been described by Beatty, Champ, and Swyer described two cases as examples of 'testicular feminisatiori . Two other cases have been described by Beatty, Champ, and Swayer and by Armstrong.

These patients have an apparently normal female appearance, and a normal feminine mentality and libido. Breast development is normal, though the areolae and nipples tend to be small. The external genitalia are normal but the labia are small. The clitoris is not enlarged. Axillary hair is absent and the pubic hair very scanty or absent. There is a short vaginal pouch which ends blindly, the cervix is absent and the uterus is absent or rudimentary. The gonad is usually intra-abdominal, most often in the position of the ovary, but not infrequently it is in the inguinal canal where it may be associated with a hernia. A moderate degree of vaginal cornification is present, and the 17-ketosteroid output is at the normal feminine level. The diagnostic criteria laid down by Schneider *et al.* are; feminine habitus, primary amenorrhoea, absence or almost complete absence of pubic or axillary hair, blind vaginal pouch with absence of cervix, and intra-abdominal or inguinal testes.

Hormone Studies

There are a few reports of hormone studies in these patients. There is general agreement that the 17-ketosteroid output is within the normal range; in the case of Beatty *et al.* it was 9.2 mg. and in that of Armstrong 8.8 mg. per twenty four hours. In the case of Goldberg and Maxwell urinary gonadotrophin output was high (at least 96 mouse units per twenty-four hours), but in that of Beatty *et al.* It was less than 10 units per twenty-four hours. The urinary oestrogen excretion of this patient was found to be as follows: oestrone, 1.5 pg.; oestradiol, 2.5 pg.; oestradiol, 2.0 pg., per twenty-four hours. The urinary oestrogen secretion by Armstrong's patient was as follows: oestrone, 2.4 and 3.1 pg.; oestradiol, 0.5 and 1.4 pg.; oestriol, 2.0 and 1.6 pg.; per twenty-four hours. These figures are strikingly similar to those of the other patient; they are rather lower than those found in normal women and the fact that vaginal cornification of significant degree is found in these patients suggests the possibility of some enhancement of target-organ response to oestrogens.

The gonads are characteristically found in the abdomen, lying in the position of the ovaries and indeed resembling them so strongly that patients with this syndrome have probably submitted to laparotomy without a biopsy of the goands having been performed, the assumptions having been made that they were ovaries, not testes. Sometimes the gonad is partially descended and involved in an inguinal hernia; this was the case in the patient of Beatty *et al.*, who had a left inguinal hernia repaired at the age of 5, at which time the partially descended testis on that side was removed. Occasionally cysts have been found within the substance of the gonads. Histological examination show them to be completely devoid of ovarian elements. They usually consist of numerous small tubules, surrounded by a thin basement membrane containing either wholly undifferentiated cells or,' in some cases, ***Sertoli cells*** only. ***Leydig cells*** are found in abundance, sometimes in excess, in the interstitial-cell tissue. The gonads, therefore, typically resemble immature sterile cryptorchid testes.

Cytological studies by Danon and Sachs have shown that there is an excess of nuclei with three chromocentres in skin cells. They believe this means that there is a whole X chromosome in excess, the sex chromosome constitution therefore being XXY.

Type Three

The application of chromosomal sexing techniques led to the diagnosis of male *pseudohermaphroditism* in the case of two patients presenting with primary amenorrhoea but showing features differing from those of Type 2 described above.·The case reports of these patients are as follows

Case 1. This patient, aged 19, was referred on account of primary amenorrhoea. The mother and father were normal and there was a normal sister, aged *161h,* whose menarche had occurred at about 15 and whose menstruation had remained regular. The patient was about 6 in. taller than her sister, a little taller than her mother, and the same height as her father. Her height was normal until about the age of 11 or 12, when she began to grow rapidly, so that she became then one of the tallest in the family, which included no other known examples of sexual abnormality. She had always been thin. The past history·and social history were not remarkable. The patient worked as a typist and was happy in her occupation. Her interests were entirely feminine and appropriate to her age, though socially she was rather retiring, had no boy friends, and did not dance.

On physical examination her height was found to be 69. in., span 71 in., lower measurements 36 in., and upper measurement 33 in.; these are definitely eunuchoid proportions. Her weight was 116 lb. and her leanness was quite noticeable. Her voice was that of a girl. The breasts were undeveloped, the nipples and areolae small. The scalp hair was normal and there was a little hair on the upper lip. Hair was present in moderate amount in the axillae and more extensively on the pubis. There was also some hair on the arms and legs.The skin and musculature were normal. The pulse was 80 a minute and the blood pressure 130/180. There was nothing remarkable in the chest or abdomen and there were no inguinal herniae. The external genitalia were of female type, apparently normal except for marked enlargement of the clitoris, and the labia minora were prominent. A vaginal smear was markedly *hypo-oestrogenic*.

Examination under anaesthesia showed the clitoris to measure 4.5 by 1.25 cm. The hymen was small and intact, the vagina about normal in size but with poorly developed rugae. A normal cervix was present, but the uterus was extremely small-about 1 in. long. No adnexus could be felt. A skin biopsy was taken from the medial aspect of the thigh.

Laboratory Investigations

Blood picture and plasma electrolytes normal. Urinary neutral 17-ketosteroids, 6.6 mg. per twenty four hours. Urinary oestrogens; oestrone, 5.3; oestradiol, nil; oestriol, 40 pg, per twenty-four hours. Urinary gonadotrophins, nearly 20 mouse units per twenty-four hours. The chromosomal sex, as judged by the polymorphonuclear leucocytes and skin biopsy, was male.

She has had treatment with stilboestrol, 2 mg. daily, in twenty-day courses, and regular oestrogen withdrawal bleeding, as well as some mammary enlargement has resulted.

Case 2. This patient, aged 24, was also referred on account of primary amenorrhoea. At the age of 17 she had been seen by a gynaecologist, who stated that the ovaries had not developed and that she would never menstruate. She had four sisters, all older than the patient and all with normal menstruation; three were married with children. There was also a married brother with children, and an unmarried brother. Her past history and social history were unimportant. She had a normal feminine outlook and libido, and worked as a machine operator.

Her general appearance was that of a tall, eunuchoidal female. The height was 70½ in., span 75 in., upper measurement 34 in., lower measurement 36½ in., weight 149 lb. Her voice was noticeably deep. The breasts were poorly developed, containing a small amount of mammary tissue. The skin was normal, except for the presence of a few pigmented moles, and .a spider telangiectasis on the neck. The scalp hair was normal; axillary and pubic hair was present, though rather scanty. The musculature was normal, as were the pulse (76 a minute) and blood pressure (120/170). There was nothing remarkable in the chest or abdomen, and there were no inguinal herniae. The external genitalia were of female type and apparently normal, with no enlargement of the clitoris. The vagina was of normal length, but a vaginal smear was markedly *hypooestrogenic*.

Tabnle 7.1. Differential Diagnosis of Primary Amenorrhoea (Excluding Imperforate Hymen, Uterine Agenesis, and other Purely Anatomical Causes)

Clinical type	*Stature*	*Congential anomalies*	*Breasts*	*Body Hair*	*Vagina*	*Cervix*	*Chromosal sex*	*Gonado-trophins*	*Oestrogens*
Classical male pseudoherma-phroditism	Normal or tall	"	Developed	Absent or very scanty	Short, oestrogenized at least in some	Minute or absent	Male	Normal	Low
New type of male pseudoherma-phroditism	" " "	"	Little or no develop-ment	Within nor-mal limits	Normal, unoestro-genized	Normal	"	"	Apparently normal
Gonadal agenesis syndrome	Short	Frequent	Undeveloped	Absent or scanty	Infantile	Infantile	Male or female	High	Low
Primary female gonadism	Tall	"	"	"	"	"	Female	"	"
Secondary female hypogonadism	Tall, normal,	"	"	"	"	"	"	Low	"

Examination under anaesthesia confirmed the normality of the vulva, clitoris, and vagina, except for the poor rugose development of the latter. The cervix was small, but not minute; the uterus was rudimentary, not exceeding 1 in. in length. No adnexus could be felt. A skin biopsy was taken from the medial aspect of the thigh.

Laboratory Investigations

Normal blood picture. Plasma cholesterol, 153 mg. per 100 ml; B.M.R. minus 6 per cent. Urinary neutral 17-ketosteroids, 8.3 mg. per twenty-four hours. Urinary oestrogens: oestrone, 4.2; oestradiol, 2.8; oestriol, 17 pg. per twenty-four hours. The chromosomal sex, as judged by the polymorphonuclear leucocytes and the skin biopsy, was male. X-ray films of the pelvis revealed a masculine configuration, and the radiological bone age was estimated at 18-20 years, 4-6 years retarded.

She has been under treatment with ethinyloestradiol, 0.1 mg, daily, in twenty-day courses, and there have been oestrogen withdrawal bleedings, as well as some enlargement of the breasts.

These patients had the following features in common; they presented as 'females' complaining of primary amenorrhoea; they were tall, with eunuchoidal proportions; there was little or no mammary development, and pubic and axillary hair was present in essentially normal amounts; the vagina was of normal length, though with evidence from the mucosa of marked oestrogen deficiency; the cervix was almost normal but the uterus was very small; no adnexus could be palpated; the 17-ketosteroids were in the normal range and the urinary oestrogens definitely higher than is usually found in primary amenorrhoea; the chromosomal sex was male. The only important differences between the patients were the presence of a definitely enlarged clitoris in one, who had a significant (normal) output of urinary gonadotrophins, and of a rather deep voice in the other. It is unfortunate that the histological status of the gonads has not yet been determined.

The differentiation of this type of male pseudohermaphroditism from the more generally recognized form of 'intersex males with purely feminine external genitalia and bodily habitus' depends upon the presence of body hair and normal vagina and cervix in the former and their deficiency in the latter, together with the deficiency of mammary development in the former and its relative normality in the latter. It is also of interest that, whereas in the two cases described here the oestrogen excretion was not unlike that found in normal females, while the vaginal smears appeared to be very hypo-oestrogenic, in the male pseudohermaphrodites reported by Beatty *et al.* and Armstrong the very similar oestrogen excretion was at a definitely lower level, though the vaginal smears showed unmistakable evidence of oestrogenic stimulation. It is therefore, tempting to postulate an enhanced tissue responsiveness to oestrogens in Type 2 male pseudohermaphrodites and a decreased responsiveness in those Type *3*, though without doubt there is sufficient endometrial responsiveness in these latter patients to permit the occurrence of oestrogen withdrawal bleedings.

The other conditions from which this new type of male pseudohermaphroditism must be differentiated are the gonadal agenesis syndrome (Turner's syndrome) and primary and secondary female hypogonadism. In the gonadal agenesis syndrome the patient is short and stocky, often showing various congenital abnormalities; there is no mammary development, and body hair is scanty or absent; the vagina and uterus are infantile; the urinary gonadotrophins are usually high and the oestrogen excretion is low; the chromosomal sex may be male or female. In primary (excluding the above) and secondary hypogonadism the chromosomal sex is female; mammary development is absent and the genitalia are infantile; the height may be increased in primary, and normal, increased or decreased in secondary hypogonadism; body hair is scanty or absent; the urinary gonadotrophins are increased in primary and decreased in secondary hypogonadism, while the oestrogen excretion is low in both.

Treatment

It should be emphasized that under no circumstances should patients of this kind or that represented by Type 2 male pseudohermaphroditism be given any indication of their chromosomal-that is, presumably genetic-sex, but should merely be told that through a congenital abnormality of the development of the reproductive tract, they will be unable to bear children. Apart from this, they should be given to understand that they are essentially normal females. Since the two patients described have shown themselves responsive to oestrogens, there seems to be good justification for continuing interrupted courses of oestrogens so as to bring about the occurrence of regular 'periods', the psychological value of which is undoubted, as well as to stimulate breast development with its equally undoubted psychological advantages.

8

Diseases due to Gonadal Hormone

Oophoritis

Primary *amenorrhoea* or a premature menopause are often described in women with autoimmune disease, particularly 'idiopathic' *Addison's disease*, *myxoedema* or *hypoparathyroidism*. Histologically, the ovaries show lymphocytic infiltration, as do the other target organs in autoimmune endocrinopathies. These women sometimes have steroidal cell antibodies which react with Leydig cells, ovarian granulosa and theca interna cells. The presence of such antibodies predicts ovarian failure, especially in patients who have Addison's or other autoimmune diseases, yot who still have normal menstrual function. The pathogenic significance of ovarian antibodies in autoimmune oophoritis remains to be determined.

Infertility

Case

A 29-year-old builder had been married for 6 years but had no children. His wife had been extensively investigated; she ovulated regularly with a normal menstrual cycle, and had patent fallopian tubes and normal endocrine function. He had normal levels of luteinizing and follicle stimulating hormones and testosterone. He had no past history of orchitis or testicular trauma. On examination, he was a well-virilized, healthy-looking man with normal sized testes. A semen sample showed a low sperm count with sluggishly motile sperm and sperm-associated immunoglobulin (IgA and IgG). The sperm-cervical mucus contact test was abnormal and the use of normal donor sperm and normal cervical mucus confirmed that only the husband had antisperm antibodies. Antibodies to fresh donor sperm were detectable in the serum to a titre of over 1/1000, and in the seminal plasma to a titre of 1/32. The patient was treated with high dose steroids on days 1-10 of his wife's menstrual cycle. His wife became pregnant in the cycle following the fourth course of treatment and subsequently gave birth to a healthy baby girl.

Immunology of Infertility

Human spermatozoa and seminal plasma contain strongly imonunogenic material: some of these antigens are unique to sperm or seminal plasma (semen-specific antigens), but others are shared with other fluids, secretions and organs. Five to 14% of infertile couples show evidence of spermantibodies. ***These antibodies may be produced by the man, the woman, or both.***

Experimental male animals can be made sterile by active or passive immunization against testicular or seminal antigens. In man, damage to the seminal tract by surgery, *accidental trauma*, occlusion or infection may trigger autoimmunity to testicular and seminal antigens. For example, antisperm antibodies appear in the serum in 50% of vasectomized men within 6-12 months of surgery. Antisperm antibodies seldom appear in seminal plasma following vasectomy as local antibody production occurs proximal to the operation site. High titres of antisperm antibodies may appear in the semen after reversal by vasovasostomy and *modify the success of the reversal.*

Autoantibodies to sperm antigens may cause infertility in otherwise normal men by: (1) immobilization and agglutination of spermatozoa; and (2) inhibition of mucus and/or egg penetration by sperm, possibly by blocking specific receptors on the sperm surface.

Investigations of possible *autoimmune infertility* include a postcoital test. Poor mobility of sperm in this test suggests the existence of antisperm antibodies. Serum from both partners, cervical mucus and seminal plasma are tested for sperm antibodies using normal donor sperm and cervical mucus. When semen is mixed with cervical mucus, spermatozoa normally move rapidly and unidirectionally; IgA antibodies to spermatozoa prevent this type of movement.

Before considering treatment, it is important to make sure that there is no additional cause of infertility. Prostatitis has been found in about one-third of men with antisperm antibodies, and prolonged antibiotic treatment may be accompanied by a significant fall in antibody titres and pregnancy in a proportion of the wives. Manipulative techniques such as in vitro fertilization (IVF) or gamete intrafallopian transfer (GIFT) have been used with limited success but are not widely available. High dose intermittent steroid therapy has many side-effects and its use is therefore debatable but it can be successful.

The harmful effects of antisperm antibodies in women is unclear. Since the female genital tract is well endowed with immunocompetent cells, local isoimmunity is probably important in infertility. Where antibodies are found only in the female partner, treatment has been disappointing though controlled studies are lacking. *Immunosuppressive therapy with steroids is contraindicated* as exposure of the zygote and early embryo to high dose steroids may result in congenital abnormalities.

HYPOGONADISM IN FEMALES

Primary Hypogonadism

As in the male this can be either congenital or acquired. Congenital primary *hypogonadism* is sometimes called ovarian infantilism. Two main groups can be distinguished:

(1) developmental inadequacy of the ovaries; (2) ovarian agenesis.

Albright, Smith, and Fraser were the first to describe patients with sexual infantilism accompanied by an increased excretion of gonadotrophins and not associated with significantly decreased stature. They suggested that the condition could be explained on the basis of a 'premenarchal menopause praecox', the process of follicle atresia which normally commences at birth having proceeded to such a degree that no further responsive follicles were left by the time pituitary gonadotrophin secretion commenced.

Ovarian agenesis is a fascinating form of congenital primary hypogonadism which is usually associated with a group of other congenital anomalies giving rise to a fairly clear-cut syndrome. Decreased statural growth associated with a rather typical stocky habitus is almost invariably found. Webbing of the neck is another typical feature, but is not uncommonly absent. Cubitus valgus, giving rise to an increased carrying angle of the arms, is seen to some extent in nearly all cases. Other anomalies include cardiovascular abnorm-alities- in particular, coarctation of the aortadigital deformities, squints, and so on.

The urinary gonadotrophin output is elevated once the age of normal puberty has been passed. Laparotomy reveals the uterus and tubes to be of infantile dimensions, and the ovaries to be represented merely by a fibrous cord, the continuation of the ovarian ligament. Histological examination of this ovarian remnant reveals a normal stroma with rete ovarii and medullary canals, but no trace of follicles in any stage of development. Clumps of hilus cells (large pale staining polygonal cells disposed along the course of nerves and strongly resembling the *Leydig cells* of the testis) are sometimes prominent.

The growth failure in these patients may conform with one or other of two distinctive patterns. In the first, there is a conspicuous smallness from early infancy, and in the second, growth continues apparently normally until the age of about 9 or 10 years, whereafter it remains at a level appropriate to this age. It is probable that it is in this group of cases alone that the absence of the normal prepuberal and puberal growth spurt is contributory to the growth failure. The fact that some of these patients begin to grow again when treated with oestrogens conforms to this view. Since primary hypogonadism is not always associated with growth failure, it seems clear that the growth failure in this syndrome is an associated defect, either genetically determined, or induced as a result of a mutually injurious influence operating in the 5- to 17-mm. phase of embryogenesis. It is at this stage that the cortex of the primitive genital ridge undergoes organization for the process of penetration by the primordial germcells, the sex of which is already determined genetically, which migrate from the endoderm of the yolk-sac. Upon this penetration further sexual differentiation of the gonads would seem to depend, so that with failure of this process the cortical elements specific to the sex of the gonads would not emerge, whereas medullary rudiments would remain relatively unaffected.

This hypothesis of the pathogenesis of ovarian agenesis would seem to receive considerable support from two different sources. The first relates to experimental work in which it has been shown that removal or destruction of the gonads of embryos in mice and rabbits in the sexually indeterminate stage leads to the development of foetuses all of which are apparently female, the males having undergone intersexualization. The .second is the demonstration, by means of the skin biopsy technique for differentiating the chromosomal sex, that some, at least, of the patients with Turner's syndrome are of the male chromosomal sex. It is of interest that Polani *et al.* were led to suspect this possibility from the consideration that male examples of Turner's syndrome are very rare; that coarction of the aorta is common in the 'female' cases of *Turner's syndrome* but is otherwise decidedly commoner in males than in females; and from these facts they suspected that some of the apparent female cases of Turner's syndrome might actually be completely intersexualized genetic males. The three 'female' patients with Turner's syndrome associated with coarctation of the aorta on whom they determined the chromosomal sex by skin biopsies all proved to be genetic males. Wilkins *et al.* reported eight patients with the ovarian agenesis syndrome; six of these had male-type epidermal nuclei and two had the female type.

Acquired primary hypogonadism is rare and due either to surgical trauma or removal, or to local pelvic diseases which is itself rare in prepuberal girls. It is possible that long-standing and debilitating diseases can also lead to intrinsic ovarian failure and so to acquired primary hypogonadism.

Clinical Features of Primary Hypogonadism in Females

Genital Organs

The presenting complaint on account of which girls with primary hypogonadism are brought to the physician is usually either failure of the onset of menstruation or failure of sexual development. The external genitalia remain of infantile character and proportions and the vaginal epithelium fails to undergo the changes normally seen in postpuberal girls as a result of endogenous oestrogenic stimulation. The vaginal smear, therefore, consists almost exclusively of small, rounded basal cells with relatively large vesicular nuclei, and it may contain numerous leucocytes. The breasts, including the nipples and areolae, are either completely undeveloped, or at most show no more than trivial enlargement. The uterus remains of the infantile size, and the passage of a sound demonstrates that the cervical canal is considerably longer than the uterine cavity proper (infantile proportions; in the adult uterus these proportions are reversed).

Hair

There is considerable variation in the amount of pubic and axillary hair. This may be quite absent or represented only by scanty hairs on the labia majora, whereas in other patients the growth is more abundant. Yet a further pattern is for the pudendal hair to be very scanty, while the axillary hair of normal amount. This latter arrangement depends upon the fact that growth of the axillary hair is more largely due to adrenal androgens which may be produced in normal quantity in these patients, whereas the pudendal hair is more oestrogen dependent.

Skeletal changes

These resemble those of eunuchoidism in the male, and typically eunuchoidal proportions (span exceeding height and lower measurement exceeding upper) are commonly found even when there is decreased overall stature as in Turner's syndrome. The fingers and toes may be long and slender, though this is less commonly so in Turner's syndrome. The shape of the pelvis approximates to that of the male. Dentition may be delayed. The radiological bone age is less than the chronological age and there is delay in epiphyseal union. Osseous retardation is less marked in Turner's syndrome than in those patients with primary hypogonadism without decreased stature.

Sexual Behaviour

These patients are normally completely lacking in libido and have no attraction towards the opposite sex. They usually remain somewhat infantile in outlook and present an immature mentality. They may also feel a sense of inferiority as a result of the knowledge of their physical shortcomings.

Special features in Turner's Syndrome

Several of these have already been mentioned. Shortness of stature and associated congenital anomalies distinguish this condition from primary hypogonadism without decreased stature. Generalized osteoporosis of the skeleton has been reported in some patients with this condition. It may give rise to *scoliosis* and *lordosis*. *Chondrodystrophia* of the dorsal vertebrae has also been described.

The commonest congenital deformities are webbing or apparent shortening of the neck, and cubitus valgus, giving rise to an increased carrying angle of the arm. A characteristic shield-shaped chest has also been described; the thorax being prominent anteriorly and broader than normal with an increased antero-posterior diameter. Other defects which have been reported include per cavus, increased pronation of the feet, syndactylism, spina bifida, congenital deafness, and ocular disturbances, such as bilateral ptosis, slight exophthalmos, internal and external squint, cataract, tubular vision, and lack of retinal pigment. Some patients have shown mental deficiency. The occurrence of coarctation of the aorta has already been the subject of comment. Hypertension with a systolic blood pressure between 130 and 150 and a diastolic pressure between 90 and 112 has been noted in many patients with *Turner's syndrome*, independently of the existence of coarctation of the aorta.

Hormone Excretion

Typically, patients with primary *hypoovarianism* have an increased excretion of pituitary gonadotrophins. The extent, however, of this increase is very variable, and in not a few patients the excretion has been found to be within the normal range. It seems clear, moreover, that day-to-day fluctuations of considerable magnitude may be encountered. The excretion of 17-ketosteroids is usually somewhat diminished but figures within the normal range have been encountered. Only a few measurements of oestrogen excretion have been made in these patients; the expected low values have been found, but oestrogen are not entirely absent from the urine. The microgram or two presumably arise from the adrenal cortex and not from the gonads.

Diagnosis

The differentiation of primary *hypogonadism* without decreased stature from secondary hypogonadism due to idiopathic deficiency of pituitary gonadotrophin can be made only on the basis of the urinary gonadotrophin excretion, and this is not always reliable. The two forms of primary hypogonadism are distinguished by the shortness of stature and congenital anomalies found in Turner's syndrome but not in the other variety. The differentiation of Turner's syndrome form pituitary infantilism is summarized in the following comparative table, adapted from del Castillo, de la Balze, and Argonz:

Rudimentary Ovaries	*Hypophyseal Dwarfism*
Women of short Stature.	Dwarfs.
Infantile mammary glands and genital organs.	The same.
Development of pubic and axillary hair.	Lack of pubic and axillary hair.
Well-nourished and strong.	Weak and easilyu tired.
Bone age some years retarded.	Very marked delay in bone age.
Late closure of teh epiphyses.	Lack of closure of the epiphyses.
Very frequently vertebral chondrodystrophia.	The same.

Follicle-stimulating hormones increased in the urine.	Lack of follicle-stimulating hormones
17-ketosteroids some what diminished.	17-ketosteroids consideratbly dimished.
Normal insulin curve.	Persistent hypoglycaemia after intravenous insulin.
Congenital abnormalities.	Not observed.
Diffuse osteoporosis and early senility.	Not observed.
Normal sella turcica.	Pathological modifications may be observed.
Visual fields : some functional alterations.	Abnormalities in teh presence of a neoplastic lesion.

Secondary Hypogonadism

Pituitary dwarfism is one cause of *primary amenorrhoea*, the failure of sexual maturation corresponding with that seen in the same condition in the male. Perhaps the commonest cause of primary amenorrhoea is idiopathic deficiency of pituitary gonadotrophin secretion, without evidence of failure of production of the other pituitary trophic hormones. Girls with this condition are usually of normal or slightly increased stature and may be either thin or adipose. In spite of the rudimentary state of the genital organs and absence of mammary development, pubic and axillary hair may be present in relatively normal amounts. In a few of these patients the clitoris is enlarged, perhaps as a result of relative adrenocortical hyperfunction. Secondary hypogonadism may also be the result of cretinism, juvenile myxoedema, and milder forms of hypothyroidism, toxic goitre, and diabetes mellitus. When primary amenorrhoea is the result of adrenocortical hyperfunction, virilizing changes are also found. Secondary hypogonadism may result from severe and long-standing disease in other systems, such as anaemia, chronic nephritis, sepsis, and malnutrition.

Diagnosis

The differentiation of secondary from primary hypogonadism can only be made on the basis or urinary gonadotrophin excretion. In secondary hypogonadism the excretory level is too low to be measured by the available clinical tests.

Treatment of Hypogonadism in Females

The treatment of primary *hypo-ovarianism* can clearly only be substitutive, since it is impossible to replace the functionless or missing ovarian endocrine tissue. Theoretically the ideal treatment of secondary hypo-ovarianism would be the administration of the appropriate pituitary gonadotrophins. In practice, however, this cannot be achieved, and in general it may be said that treatment with the gonadotrophin preparations available for clinical use is mainly disappointing. Consequently the treatment of both primary and secondary hypogonadism in the female resolves itself into the administration of oestrogens so as to bring about growth of the oestrogen-sensitive tissues-principally the genitalia and breasts - and to produce cycles of uterine bleeding. The necessity, or even desirability, of achieving either of these ends is sometimes questioned, but there can be little doubt that most patients afflicted with hypogonadism are very grateful for the changes which can be brought about by oestrogen therapy, and experience great satisfaction in having regular bleeding even though they understand these are essentially artificial and do not indicate their normality from the reproductive standpoint.

Under physiological conditions oestrogens would appear always to be secreted in cyclically fluctuating fashion. It is therefore reasonable to assume that oestrogen substitution therapy ought also to be cyclic. Once a responsive endometrium has been built up, it is imperative that oestrogen administration be discontinuous, since otherwise endometrial hyperplasia with resultant prolonged and excessive irregular bleeding will be the consequence. Some authors consider that continuous oestrogen administration may be employed in the initial stages of treatment so as to produce quicker results. It is doubtful, however, whether there is any advantage or even justification for this.

The simplest form of oestrogen therapy is oral; stilboestrol 2 mg., or ethinyloestradiol 01 mg., daily, is a reasonable average dose and may be given for courses of twenty days. Ten days should elapse between each successive course, unless an oestrogen-withdrawal bleeding occurs in the meantime. When this happens, the succeeding course may begin on the fifth day of the 'cycle' so established, counting the day of commencement of uterine bleeding as day number one of the new cycle. Once begun, these courses of treatment must be continued indefinitely-or at least until the age at which a climacteric might have been expected has been attained. This certainly is true for patients with primary hypogonadism, and is probably true for most of those with secondary hypogonadism also. For some of the latter, however-that is, those patients wherein the defect appears to be an idiopathic deficiency of pituitary gonadotrophin secretion-the hope may be entertained that eventually normal menstrual function might occur, just as in some male eunuchoids of the same type normal testicular function appears to be able to continue after initial treatment. In these cases, therefore, it is reasonable to stop treatment after several months in order to see whether spontaneous *menstruation* might occur thereafter. On theoretical grounds there is something to be said for combining progesterone of ethisterone with the second half of the oestrogen course in the hope that these hormones will together influence the anterior pituitary in such a way as to evoke gonadotrophin secretion. A method which has sometimes proved successful is as follows:

After several cycles of treatment with oestrogen alone, a daily dose of 40 mg. of ethisterone is given for the last ten days of the twenty-day course of oestrogen (stilboestrol 2 mg., or ethinyloestradiol 0.1 mg., daily). On the fifth day of the next cycle another twenty-day oestrogen course is started, this time at half the previous dose, and on the fifteenth day of that cycle it is combined with 60 mg. daily of ethisterone for ten days. On the fifth day of the next cycle a final oestrogen course is started, the daily dose again being halved (stilboestrol 0.5 mg., or ethinyloestradiol 0.025 mg.), and on the fifteenth day of that cycle a daily dose of 80 mg. of ethisterone is started for ten days. All treatment is then stopped and the patient is observed to see whether spontaneous menstruation will occur.

No useful purpose is served by giving progesterone or ethisterone to patients with primary hypogonadism.

Some girls are unable to tolerate oral oestrogens, complaining of nausea and vomiting; ,for these, and for these alone, oestrogens must be given by intramuscular injection. Oestradol benzoate or oestradiol dipropionate, 5 mg. twice weekly for three weeks out of every four, is a convenient regime; a further possible alternative is oestradiol monobenzoate in microcrystalline suspension, in a dose of 10 mg. every four weeks. It is claimed that oestrodiol valerianate provides prolonged oestrogenic stimulation when administered intramuscularly, in oily solution, 10-20 mg. every three or four weeks being an appropriate dose. Being in solution, this long-acting ester preparation does not suffer from the disadvantages of microcrystalline suspensions.

In addition to.stimulating growth of the genitalia and breasts, oestrogen therapy for hypogonadal females may be expected to have important psychological effects. The patient loses her childlike mannerisms and psyche, becoming more adult in mentality and outlook. Whether this is a direct effect of oestrogens on the psyche, or whether it be a psychological response to the morphological maturation, is unknown. Oestrogens appear to stimulate growth in some patients with primary hypogonadism and decreased stature. This is expecially true of those cases where growth was relatively normal until what should have been the age of puberty, but then ceased. It is less likely to be true for those cases where growth was always deficient. As part of the growth-promoting picture, however, oestrogen therapy leads to epiphyseal closure, whereupon, of course, growth ceases. The maximum growth increment is therefore strictly limited and unlikely to exceed 3 or 4 inches. Even this however, is much welcomed by these patients.

THE CLIMACTERIC

The *climacteric* or '*critical period*' or '*change of life*' covers the phase of waning ovarian function which is a consequence of the continual loss or degeneration of potential ova and the absence of any provision for their replacement. When no more primordial follicles remain in the ovaries reproductive ability obviously comes to an end, but, on the other hand, the endocrine activity of the ovary undergoes a more gradual phase of diminution. This phase begins before the menstrual periods cease and continues for some time afterwards. The *menopause*, or cessation of menstruation, is merely a single incident of this climateric period.

Physiology of the Climateric

In contrast to spermatogenesis, which is essentially a function of sexually mature males, oogenesis-the actual production of oocytes-is probably purely a foetal activity. Though the more or less classical view as put forward by Swezy and Evans was that the production of new oocytes from the germinal epithelium continued throughout life, the idea was opposed by Simpkins and the accurate observations of Zuckerman and his colleagues have failed to substantiate it. At birth the two ovaries contain some 400,000 (more or less) primordial oocytes, but of these, only a small proportion, perhaps 400, are destined to take part in ovulation. The remainder 'disappear through the process of atresia. Loss of bocytes by atresia begins at least as early as birth, and is indeed most active before puberty, for the ovary of the new-born has many thousands more primary follicles than that of the adolescent girl. During the proliferative phase of each menstrual cycle several follicles commence to grow but only one reaches the stage of ovulation. The remainder, outstripped by the 'chosen' follicle, regress and become atretic. In this way, during each cycle some *30* or 40 follicles are lost by atresia for each one by ovulation. Since the ovarian hormones are secreted by the follicles or their derivatives, it is clear that when few or no follicles remain, ovarian hormone production must fall to a low level or cease altogether.

The age at which the climacteric commences varies in different women in much the same way as does that at which the menarche occurs; it is in fact more or less normally distributed. Various factors-racial, hereditary (other than racial) general health, sociological and so on-no doubt do determine it, and diseases of various kinds directly affecting ovarian physiology can accelerate it.

It has often been supposed that there is a relationship between the age of the menarche and that the earlier the occurrence of the former, the later is that of the latter. This is probably not true: in an investigation of the menopause of 1,000 women it was found that the average age at the menopause for women whose menarche occurred at 13 years was 47.3 years; while that for women whose menarche occurred at 18 years was 47.5 years. Occasionally, the menopause occurs at a very early age-even before 20 years; in these cases there is nearly always an underlying endocrine abnormality. There have also been reports of the continuation of menstruation until very advanced years-up to the age of 104 in one instance. In general, however, prolongation of the menopause after the age of 55 calls for gynaecological examination to exclude the possibility of genital malignancy. There is good reason to suppose that many of the patients with delayed menopause reported in ancient literature had oestrogen-producing tumours of the ovary (such as granulosacell tumours). It is, of course, equally important, or even more so, to make a gynaecological examination if, after the menopause has definitely occurred, genital bleeding should reappear. Although this is frequently of benign cause (particularly if injudicious oestrogen treatment for menopausal symptoms has been given) all too commonly malignant disease of the cervix or body of the uterus if found to be responsible.

When the number of ovarian follicles has become significantly reduced, ovulation ceases to occur in every cycle although more or less regular cyclic activity may continue for some time. Later, ovulation ceases altogether and by this time some irregularity of the cycles has usually become apparent. Anovular cycles may continue for some time-interspersed with an occasional ovular cycle perhaps-the bleeding becoming more infrequent and scantier, eventually to cease altogether. In other women, the *menopause* may take the form of an abrupt cessation of previously regular periods. Yet a further variant is that in which the alterations in ovarian hormone production lead to the development of irregular, prolonged and often heavy *bleeding-climacteric menorrhagia*. It is sometimes considered that in these circumstances a phase of increased oestrogen production precedes the termination of ovarian endocrine activity. It is doubtful, however, if this is true and more probable that the menorrhagia is the result of continuous, as opposed to discontinuous, oestrogen production, albeit on a decreasing scale.

The gradual lessening of ovarian endocrine activity during the climacteric leads to many secondary changes. Foremost among these are regression of the genital organs-uterus, vagina, vulva, and breasts. But in many women the changes are almost imperceptibly slow and long after the menopause, little evidence of genital regression may be seen. In particular, the vaginal smear in post-menopausal women often reveals little evidence of significant oestrogenic deficiency. However, atrophy of the vaginal epithelium may be the cause of post-menopausal bleeding, or pruritus. The tendency to gain weight, which is commonly seen at this stage of life, leading to so-called 'middle-age spread' has been thought to result from failing ovarian function, but this is not likely. As seen in the previous chapter, bilateral ovariectomy by no means invariably leads to the development of adiposity. A more probable explanation is that, as part of the general ageing process, less energy is expended; however, because the appetite remains unchanged, a previous balance between energy intake (in the food) and that expended in the day's activities becomes converted into an excess of energy intake, thereby leading to deposition of fat. It is said that this fat has a peculiar distribution, accumulating mainly around the abdomen, hips, and thighs. The possibility must not be overlooked that the distribution is the same as would have occurred, given a comparable weight gain, in earlier years. A suggested explanation for the alleged special distribution (assuming that it is in fact special to this time of life) is that the normal ageing process is accompanied by a relatively greater loss of adipose tissue cells in other parts of the body and that, when new fat is laid down, most appears where the adipose cells remain in greater abundance.

Further secondary effects of ovarian failure are changes in the activity of the endocrine glands. These are most important for a complete understanding of the physiology of the climacteric. Because of the progressive failure of ovarian response to pituitary gonadotrophic stimulation, the modifying effect of the ovarian hormones on the activity of the pituitary gland becomes less and less. With the reduced inhibitory effect of oestrogen, the production of pituitary gonadotrophin (mostly of follicle-stimulating type) increases, so that in post-menopausal women a great excess can usually be detected in the urine. Sometimes this gives rise to false pregnancy-diagnosis tests, thus confusing an already delicate issue if the woman fears (or hopes) that the delayed period caused by the climacteric is due to pregnancy. Along with this increase in pituitary gonadotrophin production, there is probably also an increase in the output of thyrotrophic and adrenocorticotrophic hormones. These find responsive target organs, and so hyperactivity of the thyroid and adrenal cortex may ensue. It is probably the combination of falling oestrogen level and increased output of thyroid and adrenal hormones which is responsible for most of the untoward effects which may be experienced by women at this stage. An alternative view has supposed that the pituitary overactivity itself is responsible for the climacteric symptoms; but since these are often suppressed by very small dosses of oestrogen which have no detectable effect on the pituitary hyperactivity, it seems far more probable that the falling oestrogen level is the more important factor.

The increased activity of the adrenal cortex tends to restore the endocrine balance by taking over some of the functions of the ovary. Thus, there is little doubt that most of the oestrogen which circulates in post-menopausal women, when the ovaries have become quite functionless, is secreted by the adrenal cortex. This oestrogen, and the other adrenal cortical hormones produced in increased amounts, serve to depress the excessive pituitary activity and so reduce the thyroid overactivity. With still further advance in age, it is likely that some degree of refractoriness occurs in both the adrenal and the thyroid gland, so that in these older women the clinical picture may suggest deficiency, rather than excess, of function of both of these glands.

Clinical Features

Certain special features relating to the altered endocrine function of the climacteric will now be considered.

Virilism

Because of the increased adrenal output of androgens, the male characteristics, represented to a slight degree in all females, may become accentuated. Thus, the down on the upper lip and chin tends to become thicker and sometimes the hair is sufficiently coarse and luxuriant to form a moustache and beard, causing great mental anguish. Hair may also increase at the sides of the face, and the pubic hair may extend upwards along the linea nigra towards the umbilicus. It is rare, however, that hirsutism assumes the proportions and distribution of pathological virilism. Nevertheless, in one young woman with a pre-existing tendency to virilism, bilateral ovariectomy, for a gynaecological condition, produced severe hirsutism. The pubic hair tends to become uncurled at the climateric and the development of facial hirsutism may be accompanied by loss of scalp hair. The voice may become deeper and more powerful, so that singers sometimes find themselves able to reach notes lower than any previously possible, the upper notes, on the other hand, becoming more difficult to obtain.

A change in mental outlook with an approximation to 'male' characteristics may take place, greater resolution, command, initiative, originality, and administrative capacity being shown with the attainment perhaps of considerable commercial or public success in later life. These changes are more likely to develop in the later part of the climacteric, after the menopause itself has occurred. As further evidence of increased adrenocortical activity, it may be noted that patients with Addison's disease may show considerable amelioration, or even cure, at the climacteric, although this is preceded by an earlier phase in which the disease appears to be aggravated. The occurrence of pigmentation in some women at the menopause may well be directly due to the increased pituitary production of melanocyte stimulating hormone, along with adrenocorticotrophic hormone.

Hypertension

This is a common accompaniment of the climacteric and may be of a labile type, disappearing spontaneously after a year or two. In such circumstances it is presumably the direct consequence of vasomotor lability. When, however, it progresses to a more severe and permanent *type,* with secondary changes in the vessels, it seems doubtful if the climacteric itself can be held responsible and more probable that the hypertension is a consequence of general ageing processes. This conclusion follows from the fact, already pointed out in the preceding chapter, that ovariectomy or radium castration does not necessarily lead to hypertension.

Impaired Carbohydrate Tolerance

Although only a small percentage of women develop clinical

diabetes mellitus at the climacteric, it can be shown by investigation of the carbohydrate tolerance that an impairment to some degree occurs in a considerable proportion. It is likely that this is due to pituitary overactivity, since suppression by sufficient doses of oestrogen, so as to cause disappearance of urinary gonadotrophin, may lead to a normal carbohydrate tolerance curve, while cessation of oestrogen treatment is followed by a return to the original condition. Presumably, both pituitary growth hormone and the increased production of adrenal glucocorticoids must be held responsible for the impaired carbohydrate tolerance shown by many climacteric women.

Thyroid Changes

The excessive production of thyrotrophic hormone by the pituitary gland may initiate *exophthalmic goitre* at the climacteric, or lead to an exacerbation of pre-existing mild or latent hyperthyroidism. Sometimes a symptomless and long-standing goitre or small adenoma is driven into activity, with the development of symptoms of toxic goitre (*secondary thyrotoxicosis*). Climacteric hyperthyroidism may be progressive or there may be a gradual return to normal in mild cases. Sometimes this involution is excessive and goes on to myxoedema, but the latter, however, may appear without an obvious preceding hyperthyroid phase.

Breasts

At the climacteric, the mammary glands tend to undergo atrophy but this may not be evident owing to the deposition of fat which indeed, can produce an actual enlargement. As a result of loss of cyclic oestrogen production during the climacteric, there may be changes in the ducts. These may undergo lengthening and tortuosity, associated occasionally with epithelial proliferation; and various symptoms, such as tenseness, paraesthesiae, hyperaesthesia (sometimes erotic.) and pain may develop. Occasionally, the breast secrete a thin fluid, probably as the result of the superimposed activity of the pituitary lactogenic hormone (*prolactin*), which in turn is a consequence of the general hyperactivity of the pituitary; as also may be the prolonged lactation which is sometimes observed in women who become pregnant towards the end, of the reproductive period.

Acromegaly

Mild, or fugitive *acromegaly* sometimes occurs at the climacteric and can be explained by an increased output of pituitary growth hormone.

Hypopituitarism

Occasionally, following the climacteric, and particularly when there is a history of multiple pregnancies, an indefinite syndrome, with some features of *Simmonds' disease*, may be encountered. Presumably, in these patients, the pituitary gland enters upon a phase of exhaustion, following the phase of hyperactivity, in much the same way as hyperthyroidism may be replaced spontaneously by hypothyroidism.

The Climacteric Syndrome

The precise frequency with which climacteric symptoms of more than minor degree are experienced is uncertain. Hamblen quotes one authority who estimated 75 per cent. of all women as suffering from distressing symptoms at the climacteric, and other authorities who held that 70 to 90 per cent of climacteric women experience no symptoms materially interfering with general health, or with domestic or social activities.

The symptoms of the climacteric syndrome consist mainly of psychological disturbances and vasomotor instability. There is no doubt that the former are the more important, for it is just those women who have, or through force of circumstances develop psychological inadequacy, who are most liable to suffer from climacteric symptoms and who do so most severely. Two classes of women provide the majority of climacteric sufferers. At one end of the social scale is the woman of wealth and social standing, for whom the menopause is a remainder which cannot be ignored of advancing years with their attendant loss of good looks, sex appeal, and consequent dominance in her social circle. At the other end if the woman who has led a frustrated existence, deprived of good looks and the activities open to the more fortunate, who has been unwanted and unloved; for her the expectation and realization of the approaching end of reproductive function mean the abandonment of all hope of fulfilling her natural childbearing destiny. It is not surprising, therefore, that she should show evidence of despair or, instead, a protest reaction. The least susceptible women are those who have had a healthy, happy life, who have made a successful marriage and have raised a healthy family. For them the menopause is merely another milestone in life passed, with every reason to expect the next phase to be no less worth living than those which had gone before.

The psychic symptoms are largely conditioned by the circumstances which have evoked them. In all instances, however, irritability and depression and predominant. The former makes the woman short-tempered and intolerant; any slight deviation from the expected course of affairs provokes an exaggerated protest. There may be associated anxiety with vague forebodings of ill health or economic disaster in the future. Depression may be associated with tearfulness or with sadness, indifference, and apathy. The woman may lose all ambition, ceasing to care for her husband, her home, and her appearance. As part of the climacteric syndrome, changes in libido may occur. There may be an increase as a compensatory reaction to waning reproductive ability, or as a 'last fling' effect; or it may disappear abruptly as in the case, for example, of an unhappily married woman for whom the menopause can serve as an excuse for avoiding distasteful sexual activity. In the well-balanced woman the climacteric need cause no change in libido and many women continue to have normal and satisfying sexual relations long after menstruation has ceased.

The commonest manifestations of vasomotor instability in the climacteric are hot flushes (*vasodilatation*) often starting in the face and travelling all over the body. They occur spontaneously, or may be induced by emotion. They may be infrequent, or may be repeated many times during the day and, typically, even more frequently at night. The flushes are often followed by a wave of chilliness (vasoconstriction) and profuse perspiration. The blood pressure may fall during the flushes and rise with the chilliness. Paraesthesiae, cold extremities, tremors, palpirations, colonic spasm, cardiospasm, angioneurotic oedema, and pseudo-angina are other features of vasomotor instability.

Migraine is sometimes very troublesome at the climacteric. It appears to be influenced by endocrine factors, as witness its association with puberty, menstruation, and the climacteric, together with a tendency to disappear during pregnancy, lactation, and postclimacteric life. Though often aggravated in the earlier phase of the climacteric many women lose their migrainous symptoms after this period. Its exacerbation at the climacteric might be explained by vasomotor spasm of the cerebral vessels, since cervico-thoracic sympathectomy relieves the condition. An alternative explanation is that it is due to enlargement of the pituitary gland, since migraine is a feature of pituitary syndromes, with or without neoplasm. It has beenthought that migraine occurs more commonly in those women whose suprasellar diaphragm is calcified, so preventing pituitary expansion. The pituitary theory is supported by the beneficial effects of doses of oestrogen which are sufficient to suppress pituitary activity to the extent of causing the disappearance of urinary gonadotrophin. Since benefit may also result from injections of gonadotrophin, which would itself depress pituitary hyperfunction, it is clear that the migraine cannot be due to the excessive production of that hormone. About half the cases of idiopathic migraine obtain relief-from an artificial menopause but in the remainder the condition is made worse.

General or local pruritus may be very troublesome and various forms of dermatitis and impetigo occur. Pruritus, leucoplakia, kraurosis, and even superimposed carcinoma may affect the vulvar skin and cause much suffering. These abnormalities are aggravated by glycosuria, but also occur in its absence. It is uncertain to what degree the endocrine changes of the climacteric themselves should be held responsible for those various dermatoses, and to what extent they should be attributed to general ageing processes.

Treatment

The first point to be stressed is that the climacteric itself requires no treatment, being a physiological condition. It is only when symptoms supervene, of a degree sufficient to interfere with general health, or with domestic or social activities, that treatment is required. The second point to be stressed is that the successful treatment of the climacteric syndrome demands common sense and delicacy. The routine administration of oestrogen, often for long periods and in excessively high dosage, is strongly to be condemned; just as is the unhekpful, nihilistic approach which taking its stande on teh physiological nature of the climacteric, refuses any form of treatment. It is perfectly true that mild cases can be treated effectively merely by reassurance and perhaps moderate sedation, such as is provided by phenobarbitone, ½ gr. twice a day; but it is equally certain that the more severe cases will require oestrogen therapy and, is occasional instances, psychotherapy as well.

The basic principles of intelligent oestrogen therapy for the climacteric are as follows: first oestrogen is never produced continuously under physiological conditions, so that oestrogen treatment should always be in interrupted courses; second, the object of the treatment is to convert an abrupt fall in oestrogen level into a more slowly declining one. It follows, therefore, that if comparatively large doses are given, so that the total oestrogen level is restored to the previously normal value, symptoms will be certain to reappear every time treatment is stopped. Ignorance of this situation is responsible for most of the so-called 'difficult cases' who have been on oestrogen therapy for long periods at a time, but who relapse miserably each time the treatment is stopped. The view is held by some that large doses of oestrogen are required in order to suppress the pituitary hyperactivity-doses which, in fact, are sufficient to bring about the disappearance of *urinary gonadotrophin*. It is, however, a matter of clinical experience that relief of climacteric symptoms may be obtained with oestrogen doses which are a small fraction of those necessary to produce tangible pituitary depression; and since the drawbacks to the use of large oestrogen doses are serious and numerous, their exhibition in the climacteric seems to be indefensible. Chief among these drawbacks are: nausea; gastro-intestinal disturbance; backache and pelvic congestion; uterine bleeding, which may be prolonged, excessive, and extremely difficult to control, except by surgery; mastopathy; and, possibly, carcinogenesis.

In general it is convenient to start treatment with stilboestrol, 0.2 mg. daily. The treatment should be continued for twenty-eight days and then should be stopped for a fortnight, when it can be resumed at the same dose level. With this dose, most, if not all, of the symptoms will be relieved. Indeed, it is best if an occasional hot flush still occurs while the patient is under oestrogen treatment. Generally some return of symptoms will be experienced during the fortnight off treatment. However, as these monthly courses of treatment proceed, the stage will be reached when symptoms no longer return on omitting treatment. This is the time to reduce the dose of stilboestrol to 0.1 mg daily. Two or three further interrupted courses of treatment at this level will often be sufficient to see the end of all significant symptoms. Occasionally, 0.2 mg. will prove inadequate for controlling the symptoms; if this be so, the dose may be increased to 0.5 mg. daily but it is seldom necessary to exceed this figure.

Ethinyloestradiol may be used instead of stilboestrol; the corresponding dose is about one-twentieth that of stilboestrol so that *0.2* mg. of the latter would be represented by 0.01 mg. of ethinyloestradiol.

It has been claimed that natural *oestrogens* (oestradiol, oestrone sulphate, oestriol) are superior to synthetic oestrogens in controlling climacteric symptoms since they 'promote a sense of well-being' which the synthetic oestrogens do not. There is no truth whatever in this contention.

In recent years, a vogue has developed for the use of mixed hormone preparations, usually containing ethinyloestradiol and methyltestosterone. The rationale for such treatment is a little dubious but the general idea is that the two hormones are synergistic in many of their desirable characteristics, while being mutually antagonistic as far as some of the undesirable side effects are concerned. By the use of such a mixture, one is often able to control climacteric symptoms with far smaller oestrogen doses than would be possible without the admixture of the androgen. Generally speaking, there is little need to use these mixed preparations in the average case. It does appear, however, that for the more difficult patient who is responding poorly to oestrogen alone, the mixture may be of real value. The general principles mentioned above apply equally to the use of mixed hormone preparations, the starting dose for which should be about two tablets per day. Some patients prove unduly sensitive to the androgen moiety of these mixed preparations, developing troublesome hirsuties.

Recently, a synthetic oestrogen of the allenolic acid series called methallenoestril *(Vallestril),* for which certain special properties have been claimed, has been advocated for the control of climacteric symptoms. It is claimed for this oestrogen that, whereas in a dose of 3-9 mg. per day climacteric symptoms may be fully controlled and an atrophic vaginal mucosa restored to normal, remarkably little effect is produced on the endometrium. The consequent advantage is that the risk of inducing uterine bleeding is minimized. Although this is of no importance in the majority of cases, if treated with stilboestrol in the manner described above, it is on the other hand true that occasionally women are found to have withdrawal bleedings following treatment even with as little as *0.2* mg. of stilboestrol daily. For these patients, *Vallestril* may be the drug of choice. Another recently introduced oestrogenic substance, chlorotrianisene (tri-p-anisylchloroethylene, marketed under the name *TACE)* has interesting properties by reason of which, it is claimed, it has particular advantages in the treatment of the climacteric symdrome. It is stored in the body fat, from which there is slow prolonged release. *TACE* itself is a pro-estrogen, without direct oestrogenic activity, but is converted in the liver into a true oestrogen, the nature of which is unknown. The recommended course of treatment is two capsules (each of 12 mg. of chlorotrianisene dissolved in oil) by mouth daily for thirty or sixty days. This is stated to ensure complete relief in 50 percent of patients. A second course can be given; not more than 1 per cent. of patients are said to require a third course.

Some physicians feel the need for elaborate laboratory investigations, such as repeated vaginal smear studies or even urinary gonadotrophin determinations, as indices to progress in the treatment of the climacteric syndrome: Common sense alone shows that these studies are totally unnecessary, since the treatment is purely a symptomatic one, the climacteric itself being a physiological state, as already stressed. The clinical state of the patient is the only guide needed in the treatment of this syndrome. The uselessness of vaginal smear studies is underlined first by the fact that many post-menopausal women, even though suffering from climacteric symptoms, may still show a relatively well-oestrogenized smear and second vaginal that the production of a fully oestrogenized smear by oestrogen therapy is suggestive not of correct treatment but of over dosage.

Where marked psychological aberrations are present, it is obviously necessary to adopt psychiatric measures in addition to such hormonal therapy as may be required. Since the syndrome is a self-limited one, the prognosis is usually fairly good and it is not often that elaborate psychotherapy is needed.

CIMACTERIC MENORRHAGIA

Except in mild and transient cases, it is a wise rule to subject every patient with *cimacteric menorrhagia* to a diagnostic dilatation and curettage. This procedure appears to be curative in a fair proportion of patients; estimates vary between *30* and 60 per cent. If the curettage fails to reveal any endometrial pathology, but severe haemorrhage nevertheless persists, a complete menopause, with cessation of bleeding, can be produced by external radiation, insertion of radium into the cervix, or by hysterectomy. Both external radiation and radium are relatively simple measures but may precipitate cimacteric symptoms and adiposity in some patients. A carcinoma of the body of the uterus may also be overlooked. Hysterectomy does not involve the ovaries and does not therefore disturb the endocrine system. It is, however, a major surgical procedure not entirely free from risk, or from anxiety on the part of the patient, but it is probably the method of choice in severe menorrhagia not responding to hormone therapy.

After a diagnostic curettage it is reasonable to try medical treatment before deciding on surgery or radiation. Androgens, progesterone, and oestrogens are used for their local action on the uterine endometrium, as well as for their inhibition of pituitary gonadotrophic activity. Nevertheless, treatment remains empirical. Ethisterone, 15 mg., together with methyltestosterone, 5 mg., as two tablets or in a combined tablet *(Androgeston)* may be given twice daily sublingually, commencing a week before the period is expected and continuing until the third day of bleeding. This treatment will often restore the heavy period to more normal proportions. When the bleeding is prolonged and irregular, the choice lies mainly between treatment with progesterone to produce 'medical curettages' or with oestrogens.

A daily intramuscular injection of progesterone, 25 mg., and testosterone, 50 mg., for four days will usually terminate a prolonged bout of bleeding. A few days later a self-limited progesterone withdrawal bleeding will occur. Repetition of the progestrone injections (without the testosterone) at approximately monthly intervals will usually produce regular and normal 'periods'. Oestrogen therapy depends upon the fact that a sufficient dose of oestrogen will usually terminate a bout of bleeding. It may be given conveniently as stilboestrol, 2 mg., or ethinyloestradiol, 0.1 mg., daily, continued for a total of twenty days. If there has been no noticeable effect on the extent of the bleeding within forty-eight hours, the dose should be doubled and continued at this higher level for the remainder of the twenty days. Within a week or ten days after stopping the oestrogen treatment, a withdrawal bleeding will occur and on the fifth day another course of oestrogen therapy should be begun. In this way the regular bleeding is converted into regular cycles and the dose can gradually be reduced in succeeding months. Eventually a stage will be reached when the dose will be too small to provoke oestrogen withdrawal bleeding and the menopause will have been established. If during the course of oestrogen administration the bleeding stops but begins again before the course is completed, further oestrogen should be withheld for five days and then a new course commenced as before.

Fears have been entertained that administration of oestrogens to women at the menopause may lead to carcinogenesis. There is no acceptable evidence to substantiate such a fear, and in any case, provided the oestrogen is given discontinuously and in minimal effective doses as recommended above, the likelihood, even on theoretical grounds, of its exerting a carcinogenic action seems to be remote.

Failure to respond to hormonal treatment is not uncommon in cases of cimacteric menorrhagia; it is obviously unwise to persist in such treatment if it is proving ineffective, and recourse should then be had to surgical measures without undue delay.

Abnormalities of Menstruation

In a textbook of major endocrine disorders, only limited aspects of abnormalities of menstruation call for attention. The gynaecological implications have always to be borne in mind, and the information on these should be sought in textbooks of gynaecology. Moreover, abnormal uterine bleeding or amenorrhoea may be part of obvious clinical disorders of the endocrine glands (e.g. adrenogenital syndrome, hyperthyroidism, myxoedema) and as such are considered elsewhere in the present work. This chapter will deal only with certain conditions in which the disorder of menstruation appears to be the only evidence of endocrine dysfunction.

AMENORRHOEA

Absence of menstruation for long intervals of months or years is termed *amenorrhoea*. It is said to be primary when the patient has never menstruated, or secondary if it supervenes after some years of more or less normal menstruation. Physiological amenorrhoea occurs during pregnancy.

Primary Amenorrhoea

Apart from purely gynaecological causes, such as imperforate hymen or uterine aplasia, *primary amenorrhoea* is of two main types: the first, due to primary hypogonadism, consists in failure of response of the ovaries to adequate gonadotrophic stimulation and has already been discussed; in the second there is secondary hypogonadism, that is, a lack of gonadal function due to absence of gonadotrophic stimulation. This may be the result of a hypothalamic lesion or ill-understood functional disturbance. It may result from a lesion of the anterior pituitary gland, such as *craniopharyngioma* or *chromophobe adenoma*. It is also a characteristic feature of pituitary infantilism, or may be the result of an apparent selective deficiency of gonadotrophin secretion. In hyperpituitarism due to an acidophil tumour resulting in giantism, primary amenorrhoea is caused by destruction of the basophil cells which are considered to be the source of the pituitary gonadotrophins.

Other endocrine conditions in which primary amenorrhoea may occur are cretinism, juvenile myxoedema, and milder forms of hypothyroidism, toxic goitre, diabetes mellitus, and adrenocortical tumours. It may also result from severe organic disease of other systems, such as anaemias, chronic nephritis, chronic sepsis, and malnutrition.

It may be very difficult clinically to differentiate between delayed puberty and primary amenorrhoea. Consequently the continuation of normal menstruation after the exhibition of therapy for primary amenorrhoea cannot necessarily be regarded as *prima facie* evidence of cure of the primary amenorrhoea, since one may have been dealing merely with delayed puberty. Reference has already been made to male pseudohermaphroditism as a possible cause of apparent primary amenorrhoea.

Secondary Amenorrhoea

Without doubt, the commonest cause of cessation of the periods more or less normal menstruation has been established, apart from the occurrence of pregnancy, is psychological. Sometimes such a cause is of major proportions and obvious in its implications, but in many instances the precise psychological factors may be obscure and difficult to elicit.

As in the case of primary amenorrhoea, *secondary amenorrhoea* may be caused by severe general diseases, such as anaemias, advanced tuberculosis, chronic nephritis, malignant disease, chronic infections, and malnutrition. It is uncertain by what mechanism these conditions bring about the cessation of normal pituitary-ovarian activity.

Secondary amenorrhoea also arises in a large variety of endocrine disorders. These include hypothalamic disease affecting anterior pituitary function; *Simmonds' disease* and other forms of hypopituitarism; ecromegaly, as a result of destruction of basophils by the eosinophil adenoma and Cushing's syndrome. Amenorrhoea may occur in both hyper- and hypothyroidism, in diabetes mellitus, and in Addison's disease. It is present in the adrenogenital syndrome and is also a symptom of virilism due to other causes, such as arrhenoblastoma and adrenal rest tumours of the ovary. It arises when destructive lesions, of whatever kind, of both ovaries destroy, a sufficient amount of oestrogen-producing tissue.

The normal cimacteric is a natural form of secondary amenorrhoea, resulting from the loss by ovulation and atresia of Graafian follicles. If this happens at an unusually early age, and is not accompanied by typical cimacteric symptoms, the secondary amenorrhoea which results may be clinically indistinguishable from that which may occur from other causes; in such cases the finding of a raised gonadotrophin excretion would indicate the climacteric nature of the condition. Other possible causes of amenorrhoea are a functional failure of the pituitary gland to secrete adequate amounts of gonadotrophins, or a loss of the ability of the ovaries to respond to stimulation by gonadotrophins (for reasons other than those which apply at the climacteric), or of the endometrium to respond to the action of ovarian hormones.

Treatment of Amenorrhoea

The treatment of *amenorrhoea* is largely unsatisfactory and a long digression on the methods which have been employed is not warranted. Suffice it to say that the use of gonadotrophin preparations and of steroid hormones, though occasionally apparently successful, is essentially unreliable and good results cannot be predicted. In primary amenorrhoea the principal indication for long-continued cyclic oestrogen therapy is the effect that this has on the development of secondary sex characters and the psychological advantages to the patient of having apparently normal menstrual bleedings. In secondary amenorrhoea the value is again mainly psychological, except in those instances where, on cessation of a fairly prolonged course of such interrupted therapy, normal menstruation is re-established. For many intelligent women for whom sterility is not a complaint, reassurance that secondary amenorrhoea is not due to underlying disease is often sufficient, and for these hormone therapy is apparently quite unnecessary.

ABNORMAL UTERINE BLEEDING

Regular menstruation which is nevertheless excessive in the amount of blood loss, and often at the same time in the duration of the bleeding, is usually referred to as *menorrhagia* or *hypermenorrhoea*. Irregular uterine bleeding is usually called metrorrhagia, and when it is associated with hyperplastic changes in the endometrium, the condition is described as metropathia haemorrhagica. The too frequent occurrence of menstrual periods is called polymenorrhoea and their too infrequent occurrence, oligomenorrhoea. Unusually scanty menstrual periods constitute hypomenorrhoea.

In the elucidation of the causes of abnormal menstrual bleeding, proper gynaecological examination, including, in most cases, diagnostic curettage, is an essential preliminary.

Menorrhagia

In the absence of organic cause, such as fibroids, or pelvic inflammatory disease, this condition most commonly has a psychological basis and would seem to consist essentially in an abnormality of neurovascular control in the endometrium. Biopsy of the endometrium usually reveals an entirely normal secretory pattern in the immediately premenstrual phase, and may show no abnormalities if taken during bleeding itself. In such circumstances it is difficult to imagine any possible endocrine basis for the disturbance and it is not surprising that hormone treatment often has little success.

In some cases, however, an endometrial biopsy taken about the fifth day of bleeding shows the pattern of incomplete shedding of the endometrium, in which mixed proliferative and secretory changes are found alongside each other. It is possible that in these cases there is a delay in the involution of the corpus luteum, with a corresponding prolongation of the secretion of progesterone, though in sub-optimal amounts; the continued elimination of pregnanediol during part of the bleeding episode (it usually disappears from the urine, except for traces, before the onset of bleeding) supports this supposition. Unfortunately no treatment based on such an hypothesis has succeeded in dealing effectively with the condition.

Polymenorrhoea

This is often combined with menorrhagia, and when not due to organic cause is again most commonly of emotional origin. It may also arise as a result of early ovulation, and in some cases ovulation may occur even before the menstruation has ceased, thus leading to involuntary sterility. Occasionally it may arise as a result of premature degeneration of the corpus luteum with a corresponding reduction in the post-ovular phase of the cycle. The fundamental disturbance may then be one of anterior pituitary function.

Metrorrhagia

Irregular uterine bleeding, which may also be prolonged and heavy, can result from organic pelvic lesions, but commonly occurs in the absence of any such obvious causes. Diagnostic curettage may reveal a normal proliferative endometrium, a hypoplastic one or a hyperplastic one, showing typical cystic glandular hyperplasia (the '*Swiss cheese*' hyperplasia of Novak). Occasionally mixed hyperplastic and secretory patterns have been described.

This abnormality of menstruation may arise at any age between the menarche and menopause being relatively rather common close to both of these epochs. The essential feature appears to be absence of ovulation, with a consequent lack of cyclic production of oestrogen and progesterone by the ovary. There is no certainty that the typical picture of metropathia haemorrhagica, in which cystic ovaries are found, in association with cystic glandular hyperplasia, is due to an excessive oestrogen production, and the precise hormonal derangements are not known. Some women appear to have an essentially unstable menstrual rhythm, so that they may alternate between phases of regular menstrual function. and of irregular metrorrhagia. A wholly endocrine cause of metrorrhagia is the occurrence of an oestrogen-secreting tumour of the ovary, such as the granulosa-cell tumour. These tumours occur most frequently in the climacteric phase and later.

Treatment of Abnormal Uterine Bleeding

The diagnostic curettage itself provides effective treatment in. a proportion of patients with abnormal uterine bleeding. This proportion, however, seems to vary with different observers. Menorrhagia of emotional origin is unlikely to respond to any kind of hormonal treatment and logically should be dealt with on psychiatric lines. Unfortunately this approach too is often fruitless, and in severe cases hysterectomy has seriously to be considered. In other cases of regular menorrhagia not due to organic disease, the results of any kind of treatment are unpredictable. However, in the writer's experience, a regime worth trying consists of methyltestosterone, 5 mg., and ethisterone, 15 mg., twice daily sublingually, beginning a week before the period is expected and continuing until the third day of bleeding. A combined tablet containing these steroids in the above proportions is marketed as *Androgeston*. The methyltesterone can be replaced by *Androstalone,* 25 mg., daily, and for some patients this regime is more effective.

Hormone treatment is most likely to succeed in cases of metrorrhagia without orgainc cause and may take various forms. For the arrest of prolonged and excessive uterine bleeding, the injection of progesterone and testosterone propionate for a few days is often the most effective procedure. If the endometrium is known or suspected to be atrophic the injection should also include oestradiol benzoate or di-propionate. The doses of these steroids are not very critical and something like progesterone 50 mg., testosterone propionate 25 mg., and oestradiol benzoate 2 mg., daily for three or four days is usually sufficient to bring about a complete arrest of bleeding or a very marked amelioration. A few days later a progesterone withdrawal bleeding, which may be likened to a normal period, begins and is self-limited, ending after five or six days. It is of course necessary to inform the patient that this will happen, as otherwise she will fear that the treatment has been ineffective.

It is usually a wise plan to follow this treatment with oestrogen therapy, beginning on about the fifth day of the withdrawal bleeding referred to above. Stilboestrol, 2 mg., or ethinyloestradiol, 0.1 mg., daily should be given orally for a total of twenty days, when an oestrogen withdrawal bleeding will begin some days later.

An alternative method for securing haemostasis, where the bleeding is not severe, is to begin with oestrogen. The dose may be similar to that mentioned above and if there is no reduction in the bleeding within forty-eight hours the dose should be doubled and maintained at that level for the rest of the twenty-day course. Difficulties are sometimes encountered because the dose of oestrogen necessary to secure haemostasis leads to nausea or vomiting as a side reaction. A further possibility is that of the bleeding, having ceased, beginning again before the twenty-day course is completed. If this happens treatment should be stopped for five days and then begun again when effective control will usually be obtained.

Haemostasis having been secured, it is then necessary to re-establish cyclic bleeding, and this is conveniently done by repeating the courses of oestrogen, commencing on the fifth day of each withdrawal bleeding and continuing as before for twenty days. After three such courses there seems to be an advantage in combining the oestrogen with progesterone or ethisterone, since by this means the chances of including ovulation seem to be increased. A method which has been found effective in a fair proportion of patients is as follows: after three controlled cycles with oestrogen alone a fourth cycle is started as before with oestrogen on the fifth day of the cycle (stilboestrol, 2 mg., or ethinyloestradiol, 0.1 mg., daily for twenty days). On the fifteenth day of the cycle, that is, after oestrogene alone has been given for ten days, ethisterone 40 mg. daily, is given for ten days. In this way the ethisterone course, overlaps the second half of the oestrogen course. On the fifth day of the next cycle the dose of oestrogen is reduced to half its previous value, and on the fifteenth day of the cycle ethisterone is begun again, this time at a dose of 60 mg., daily for ten days. In the next and final cycle the dose of oestrogens is again halved (stilboestrol, 0.5 mg., or ethinyloestradiol, 0.25 mg., daily) and on the fifteenth day of the cycle ethisterone is again started, this time at a dose of 80 mg., for ten days. Evolation has been known to occur during the final cycle of treatment and pregnancy to ensue. Satisfactory results can be expected in some 80 or 90 per cent. of patients with irregular, prolonged, and excessive uterine bleeding after treatment in this way, though some of these may later relapse. In about 40 per cent. of the patients ovulation will be re-established following this regime.

An alternative form of treatment for this kind of menstrual disorder is with progesterone, as originally described by Scowen. Once haemostasis has been secured, a few injections of progesterone (the precise dose seems to be relatively unimportant: 20 mg. on alternate days for three injections, or even 50 mg. in a single injection seems to be satisfactory) will be followed by a withdrawal bleeding. These injections are repeated monthly so as to bring about regular progesterone withdrawal bleedings, which, accompanied as they are by endometrial shedding, prevent the building up of a thick vascular proliferative endometrium from which future irregular bleeding could occur. In some patients it is possible, after a few courses of such injections, to substitute ethisterone (e.g., 50 or 60 mg. daily for about five days, repeated monthly) and to obtain equally satisfactory results.

Other forms of treatment, using androgens and gonadotrophins have often been advocated. The use of androgen combined with progesterone has been mentioned already and is very effective for initial haemostasis. Androgen alone, however, is, in the writer's opinion, much less satisfactory, the dose required to produce a satisfactory effect often being such that, when given for even moderately prolonged periods of time, it tends to cause undesirable virilizing effects. The use of chorionic gonadotrophin has little to recommend it, but it is possible that *Synapoidin,* which is a combination of chorionic and pituitary gonadotrophin, may sometimes prove effective where other measures have failed.

STEIN-LEVENTHAL SYNDROME

Although it was as long ago as 1929 when Stein performed his first wedge resection of bilateral '*polycystic ovaries*' for the relief of the accompanying amenorrhoea, it is only within comparatively recent years that general interest has been aroused in what has now come to be known as the '*Stein-Leventhal syndrome*', the literature on which, up to 1954, has been summarized by Bishop. The fact that some abnormality of menstruation is usually (though not invariably) a part of the syndrome is the justification for considering it in this chapter.

Bilateral ovarian enlargement is the only invariably finding in this syndrome; however, there is usually amenorrhoea or oligomenorrhoea, and there is commonly also hirutism of varying degree. Though some patients are obese, many are not and there is no justification for including obesity as part of the syndrome.

The Ovaries

As mentioned above, bilateral enlargement is invariable and is usually palpable on pelvic examination, if necessary under an anaesthetic. However, cases have been reported in which the ovaries, though found to be enlarged on laparotomy, were not palpably enlarged on pelvic examination. Indeed, Stein, Cohen, and Elson stated that in only about half of their series of 75 patients could the ovarian enlargement be detected on pelvic examination and they therefore felt that radiological investigation, following the induction of a pneumoperitoneum, which outlines the shape and size of the ovaries, should be an essential procedure in attempting to establish the diagnosis. Other procedures which have been advocated for this purpose are culdoscopy and peritoneoscopy, and combined *pneumoperitoneum* and *hysterosalpingography* (*'gynaecography'*).

Although the condition has been referred to as 'polycystic ovaries', the cysts, which are not always present, are in fact no more than slight or moderate enlargements of multiple follicles. Sometimes the ovaries are quite solid, there being no cystic change at all. On microscopical examination, the most striking feature is marked overgrowth of the ovarian stroma. Numerous follicles may be found in all stages of maturation, and in general, there is evidence of increased atresia also. In some cases masses of luteinized cells are found, but these are rather unusual. Hyperplasia of the hilus cells is a feature of some of these ovaries, but again others fail to show it. Although some authors have stressed hyperplasia of the theca interna cells and Fraenkel coined the term *'hyperthecosis ovarii'*, such hyperthecosis is by no means invariably and it seems doubtful if the term is at all justifiable.

Menstrual Disturbance

Most commonly this is *secondary amenorrhoea*, though one case associated with primary amenorrhoea has been described. Some patients have oligomenorrhoea, in which the interval between menstruation may be anything from a matter of several weeks to several months. In yet others, occasional or more frequent irregular heavy bleeding occurs, the clinical picture resembling that of metropathia haemorrhagica. Most often there is absence of ovulation, but some patients certainly do ovulate, and Stokhuyzen reported a case with normal regular cycles and a seceretory endometrium at menstruation. In one of the author's patients a fresh corpus luteum was found at laparotomy, and the endometrium obtained at the same time showed a normal secretory pattern.

Other Signs and Symptoms

Hirsutism is a very common, though again not invariable, component of the syndrome. In a few cases it has been of a very severe degree and even accompanied by the other signs of virilism, such as enlargement of the clitoris, voice changes, acne, and a muscular physique. These, however, are extreme examples. In some the hirsutism may be so mild as to give rise to no complaint.

Sterility is one of the commoner complaints, though of course would be expressed only by those patients who are married. Obesity occurs in some patients, but many are of normal weight, and some individuals with the syndrome may be markedly underweight. It seems probable in fact that any significant variations from the normal in weight are more likely to be due to psychological causes than to underlying endocrine changes.

Hormone Studies

Very little has been published about hormone studies in these patients, but certain points have been established. In the first place, the 17-ketosteroid output is almost invariably within the normal limits, and attempts to demonstrate the excretion of excessive amounts of androgen in the urine do not appear to have met with success. Occasionally pregnanediol may be found in possibly significant amounts in the urine, but it is certainly not in excess in other cases. Oestrogen excretion studies have not been reported, but on clinical grounds it may be concluded that, although in some patients the oestrogen level is normal or even high, in others it is relatively low. The output of gonadotrophins is uncertain in these cases; in the author's patients no excessive secretion of urinary gonadotrophin has been revealed by techniques which, though in current use, are known to be of limited sensitivity.

Although there has been a good deal of theorizing about the precise nature of the disorder and its hormonal implications, it is fair to say that all this has been purely speculative and that we really do not know the true nature of the condition or how the signs or symptoms are brought about. It may be that in some cases there is an abnormally high output of progesterone or some related hormonal substance with mildly androgenic properties, but this could scarcely hold true for all. It has been suggested that over-production of luteinizing hormone by the pituitary might be the cause of the ovarian changes, but again this fails to account for those cases in which there is no luteinization in the ovaries. The remarkable response to treatment does not help in any way to explain the genesis of the condition, and the conclusion seems inescapable that we really are still very ignorant about the precise nature of this syndrome.

Treatment

Whatever may be doubted about the cause and nature of the *Stein-Leventhal syndrome*, the value of bilateral wedge resection in treatment is undoubted, though the manner in which this procedure produces the beneficial effects is just as mysterious as the cause of the syndrome itself. In point of fact, Stein did his first wedge resection solely for diagnostic purposes, and was very agreeably surprised to find that normal menstruation was restored following the operation. Such restoration of normal ovular menstrual cycles can be expected in about 80 per cent. of cases, and conception is common in those patients who are complaining of sterility. The effects on the hirsutism, however, are a good deal less spectacular. Nearly always there is some reduction in the rate of hair growth, but it is rare for the excessive hair to disappear and the results cannot be compared with those which follow removal of a virilizing adrenal tumour.

The precise duration of the benefits of bilateral wedge resection is uncertain, but it would seem that in general there is little likelihood of relapse, and it may well be that most patients after treatment remain normal until their natural menopause.

In a recent paper Stein reports that in the past twenty five years he has done wedge resections on 88 carefully selected patients, in 95 per cent of whom menstrual function was restored. Fifty-four became pregnant with a total of 118 pregnancies, and there were no recurrences of bilateral polycystic ovaries.

INDEX

H

I

J

K

L

M

N

O

P